BASEBALL IN NORTHWEST IOWA

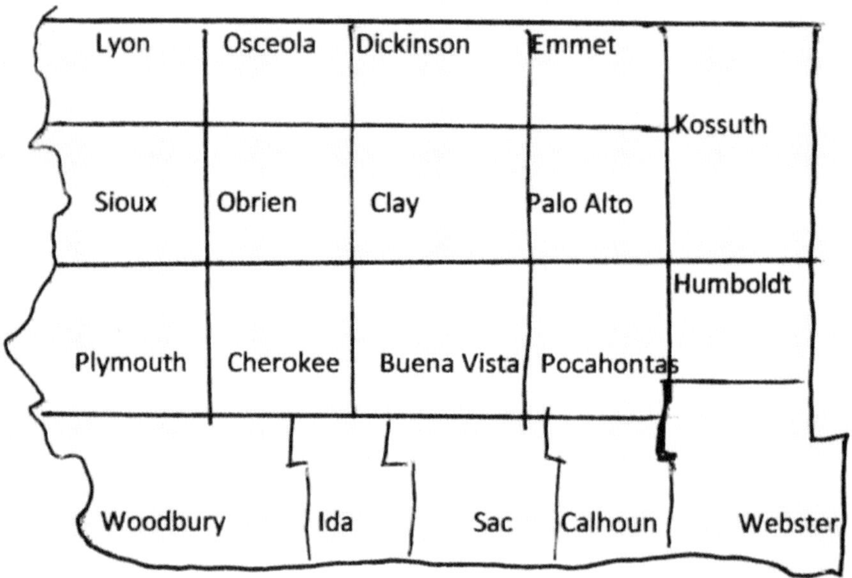

Map of Northwest Iowa. This simple map details the locations of the 19 Northwest Iowa counties covered in this book. As there are varying opinions on what comprises that section of the state, a final chapter touches on bordering counties. (Author's collection.)

Front Cover: Sioux Rapids Team Members of 1912. In 1913, the Sioux Rapids club played some of the best semipro teams in Northwest Iowa and surrounding areas, winning 33 out of 50 games. Because the club objected to playing baseball on Sunday, it declined to join the Northwest Iowa League that year. (Courtesy of State Historical Society of Iowa, Des Moines; photograph by G.L. Horner, Sioux Rapids.)

Cover Background: Baseball Game Crowd in Early, Iowa. This exceptional shot of baseball fans at an Early, Iowa, game exemplifies baseball's community draw in rural towns. Men, women, and children of all ages enjoyed the social gathering as much as the game. Shedding work clothes, they came attired in their Sunday best. A large share of the town's population of 500 likely attended this event. (Courtesy of State Historical Society of Iowa, Des Moines.)

Back Cover: Remsen Team of 1908. From left to right are (first row) Joe Lotz and Dr. S.W. Kuster; (second row) Henry Hey, Dr. A.H. Jastram (umpire), F.E. Wentz (committeeman), and Leo Heyman; (third row) Nick Faber, Mike Strohbeen, Peter Homan, Martin Hatz (manager), E.F. Kieffer, Ralph Creglow, and Mathew Heyman. (Courtesy of the Homan family.)

BASEBALL IN NORTHWEST IOWA

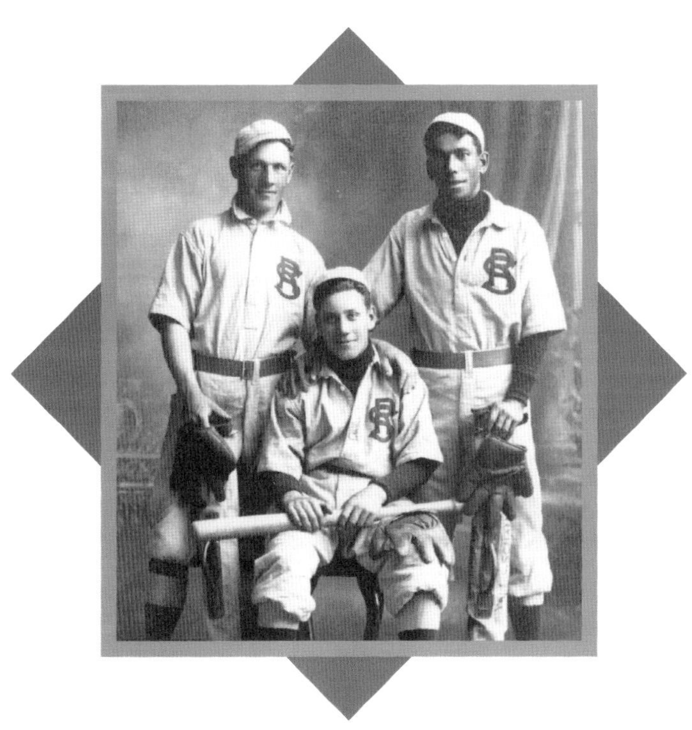

Joan Wendl Thomas

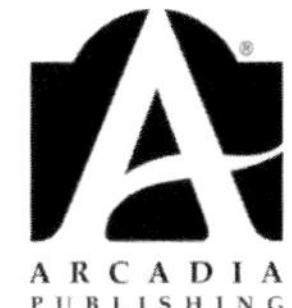

ISBN 978-1-4671-2514-7

Published by Arcadia Publishing
Charleston, South Carolina

Printed in the United States of America

Library of Congress Control Number: 2016951822

For all general information, please contact Arcadia Publishing:
Telephone 843-853-2070
Fax 843-853-0044
E-mail sales@arcadiapublishing.com
For customer service and orders:
Toll-Free 1-888-313-2665

Visit us on the Internet at www.arcadiapublishing.com

*To those resilient Iowa settlers who forged an enduring kinship
with the area's rich land and garnered camaraderie
through the sport of "base ball"*

CONTENTS

ACKNOWLEDGMENTS

Images not credited in this book are from the author's personal collection. Many historical details for the text were gleaned from newspaper archives, public records, and www.baseballreference.com. Additionally, invaluable research materials were contributed by the following individuals and organizations:

Mildred Bryan, President, Emmet County Historical Society, Estherville, Iowa
Barb, Cherokee Area Archives volunteer, Cherokee Public Library, Cherokee, Iowa
Don Curry, Le Mars, Iowa
Bill Dudding, Bancroft, Iowa
Janet Frisbie, Lake View Historical Society, Lake View, Iowa
Pete Gorton, the Donaldson Network
Brenda Groon, Secretary, Akron Historical Society, Akron, Iowa
Karen Harrington, Co-Vice President, Northwest Iowa Genealogical Society
Cheryl Hoekstra, Director, Alton Public Library, Alton, Iowa
Iris Hemmingson, President, Northwest Iowa Genealogical Society
Mary Holub, Registrar, Plymouth County Historical Museum, Le Mars, Iowa
Rose Homan, Remsen Historical Committee, Remsen, Iowa
Jane Hunstein, United Methodist Church of Le Mars, Le Mars, Iowa
Janeene Klein, Director, Remsen Public Library, Remsen, Iowa
Lisa Kunkel, Bancroft Historical Museum, Bancroft, Iowa
Sue Lieske, volunteer, Webster County Genealogical Society, Fort Dodge, Iowa
Thomas Munson, Archival Clerk, Sioux City Public Museum, Sioux City, Iowa
Tom Murray, Bancroft Memorial Park Historian, Bancroft, Iowa
Delores Newbrough, Depot Museum, Lone Rock, Iowa
Northwest Iowa Genealogical Society, Le Mars, Iowa
William Reuter, Le Mars, Iowa
Society for American Baseball Research (SABR)
Wilma J. Vande Berg, Researcher and Archivist, Greater Sioux County Genealogical Society
Lenka Wanzer
Linda Ewin Ziemann, Plymouth County, Iowa, Historian

INTRODUCTION

Iowa became the 29th state in the union in 1846, and with the advent of the railroads, intrepid pioneers cultivated its virgin soil. Soon, 19 counties evolved in what came to be called Northwest Iowa. The growing agricultural economy stimulated construction of towns along the railroads' paths. Founded in 1854, Woodbury County's Sioux City grew to become one of the largest cities in the state. Of the state's 99 counties, the area's Kossuth County consumed the most square miles at 973. Nonetheless, that county's population tallied at less than a fifth of that of Sioux City. Most of the acreage stretching between town centers remained rural and sparsely populated. Raising livestock and tilling the land, settlers survived prairie fires, blizzards, tornadoes, and locust swarms. Combating the isolation inherent with farm life, they found respite through leisure activities that brought them together. The most popular such diversion was the American game then called "base ball."

Following the Civil War, which contributed to the spread of the sport, each town, no matter its size, formed a baseball team. Supporters found any available real estate to lay out a diamond. Often, farmers like Carl Wilde, of Sioux County's Maurice, would allow use of their pastures for that purpose. Before long, ball fields were placed within city limits. As early as 1874, a Sioux City contingent faced a Le Mars team in town. Le Mars, the Plymouth County seat, hosted the game, its club sharing supper with the opponents before seeing them off on the 5:30 St. Paul train. Two years later, the citizens of Le Mars held baseball games at the Plymouth County fair, offering prize money in a contest for the championship of Northwest Iowa. Reflecting the rural character of the area, a team called the Plow Boys won second place.

In the 1880s, polo drew interest in some communities, and the matches were often played after the baseball games. This was primarily due to the influence of the English Close Brothers, who recruited second sons of the British aristocracy to learn farming in northern Iowa. Sibley, in Osceola County, was one of the towns that had a polo club. At one match between Sibley and Le Mars, a farmer's horse suffered a broken leg and had to be shot. Eventually, interest in that sport waned, while baseball grew in popularity.

In 1888, the newly formed Western League Sioux City Corn Huskers became the first professional club in Northwest Iowa. When the Iowa–South Dakota League organized in 1902, the Huskers joined it along with three other teams from that part of Iowa. In addition to the Le Mars Blackbirds, Lyon County's Rock Rapids Browns and O'Brien County's Sheldon club turned professional to compete in the league, which lasted one more year. Then, in 1904, Webster County's Fort Dodge Gypsum Eaters joined the Class D Iowa League of Professional Baseball Clubs. The only team representing the northwest in that league through 1907, it was joined by Estherville and Emmetsburg when the organization resurfaced in 1912. In Emmet and Palo Alto Counties respectively, those towns also fielded professional teams. Though the Iowa League dispersed the following year, the area's passion for baseball persisted. Before long, teams from every conceivable group lured baseball enthusiasts to witness their contests.

During the first half of the 20th century, a multitude of semipro and amateur ball clubs formed. Area businesses, schools, churches, and organizations like the Junior Legion and American Legion organized teams. There was even a Farmers League. Furthermore, the local citizenry flocked to town to see the various barnstorming teams of the times. Some were major-league clubs traveling postseason, but others were strictly designed for travel. Two of the most popular were the All Nations and the House of David traveling teams. The first, which derived its name from the various nationalities of its players—and even one woman—would arrive in a Pullman car. The other, whose members all wore beards, was named for the Israelite House of David, a religious group. Another barnstorming club, the Bloomer Girls, stirred up controversy but always drew big crowds. These clubs faced teams representing the towns where they played, all of which were fierce competitors. Places like Arnolds Park in Dickinson County and Humboldt County's Humboldt drew throngs of spectators to see their clubs face the barnstormers. Remarkably, two Kossuth County towns sponsored African American clubs.

Chip's All Stars, a talented all-black team based in little Lone Rock, traveled in a bus. Algona supported an independent, interracial baseball team called the Algona Brownies in 1902 and 1903 and an all-black club of the same name in the late 1930s. Additionally, many small towns brought in outside Negro Leagues clubs for exhibition games. In 1939, Calhoun County's Pomeroy featured a match between the Odessa Black Oilers and the San Antonio Black Giants. In 1929, the Spencer Cubs split a two-game series with the Cuban Stars. That same year, the team from Clay County's Spencer faced Gilkerson's Union Giants, an independent African American semipro team. Such contests brought in revenue needed to support local enterprises. But there was one restraint on the sport then, the question of Sunday ball.

In the early days, some Iowa communities banned Sunday baseball games. In 1913, the Sioux Rapids team from Buena Vista County declined membership in the Northwest Iowa League for that reason. In 1917, a judge in Des Moines, the state capital, dismissed a case against a local club owner for violation of Sunday blue laws. He declared that "baseball cannot be classed or termed as 'labor.' " Nonetheless, there were some individual players whose religious convictions prevented them from participating in the sport on the Lord's Day. But as time passed, attending a baseball game after Sunday services became a treasured tradition in many families.

Well into the mid-20th century, baseball leagues and teams continued to sprout in Northwest Iowa. Often, lasting rivalries between towns resulted. But the widespread interest in the sport did not stop with the local teams. Rail excursions allowed big-league fans an opportunity to see major-league games in person long before the advantage of television viewing. In 1931, one such round-trip to Chicago from Sac County's Sac City cost $17.06, a considerable sum at the time. Often, travelers went to see hometown boys play in those games. All of the area's counties, including Cherokee, Ida, and Pocahontas, contributed a good supply of talent to the big leagues. That tradition continues into the 21st century. Despite the current interest in other games like football and basketball, baseball remains ingrained in the region's culture. The sport now thrives, with local high school, college, and Little League teams. Plus, Sioux City still fields a professional club, the American Association Explorers. And modern fans are just as ardent.

Buena Vista, Calhoun, and Cherokee Counties

Sharing its name with the 3,200-acre natural glacial lake that hugs its edge, the city of Storm Lake is the seat of Buena Vista County. A relatively large town, its continual population growth is a tribute to its water's-edge setting and the rich farmland that spreads beyond its city limits. Early on, hearty settlers throughout the county instituted baseball as a preferred leisure activity. As implied by the cover photograph, the original county seat, Sioux Rapids, took pride in its baseball club of 1912. A Marathon team represented Northwest Iowa in the state amateur tournament in 1936. In 1950, the semipro Storm Lake White Caps joined the Iowa State Baseball League. Decades later, the town of Linn Grove produced Rick Grapenthin, who pitched for the Montreal Expos from 1983 to 1985.

In 1937, Calhoun County's little Pomeroy hosted the first game of an amateur league that it helped form that year. Two years later, the town's American Legion post sponsored a home game between the local club and the Negro League Odessa Black Oilers. The following day, the Oilers played the San Antonio Black Giants at the same venue. That event attracted throngs of spectators from far-reaching communities. The sport's allure continued into 1940, when retired baseball great Babe Ruth put on a batting exhibition prior to a local ball game at Rockwell City, the county seat. Some 2,500 enthusiastic fans amassed at the local ballpark on June 30 would forever treasure memories of the occasion.

In 1861, officials chose the town of Cherokee to serve as seat of the county of the same name. When it was selected as the site for a new mental health hospital in 1894, baseball was already growing in interest there. As early as 1896, the local media mentions the town's strong baseball rivalry with Le Mars. The players on a Cherokee team of 1922 developed the reputation of being among the fastest in the area. In 2016, Cherokee High graduates Cody Ege and Matt Koch started playing in the major leagues, both as pitchers. Lefty Ege was with Miami Marlins and the Los Angeles Angels, and Koch got his first start with the Arizona Diamondbacks late in September. The tradition continues.

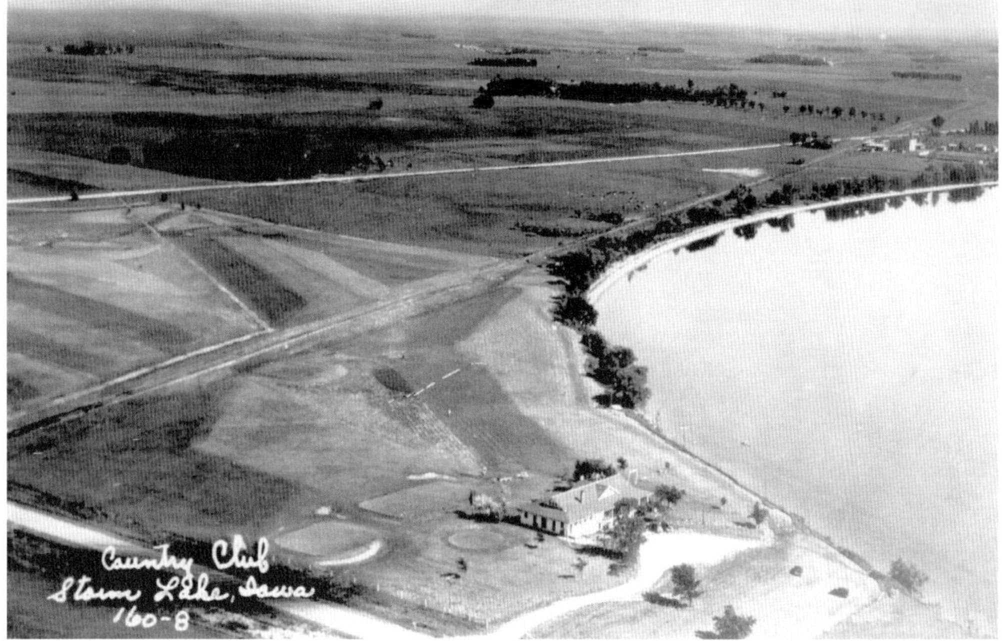

STORM LAKE SCENE. This vintage panoramic view of a country club along Storm Lake's shore captures the essence of the town and the area farmland. The lake provided a place for hard-earned recreation. In addition to water sports, baseball was included in the activities. Notice the outline of a ball diamond at bottom left.

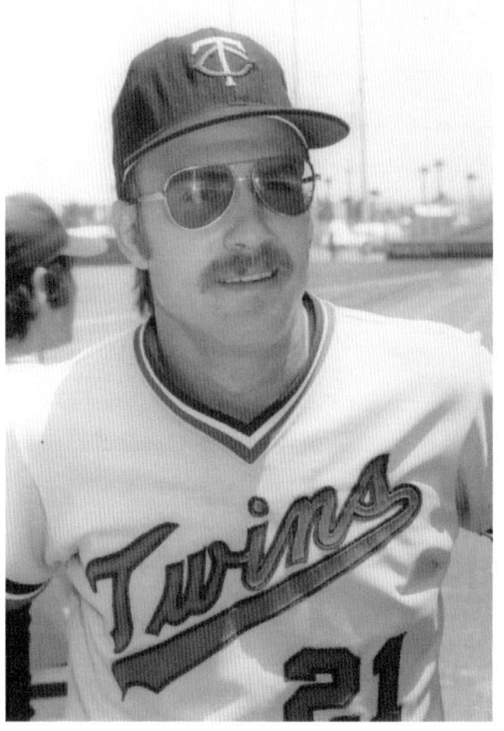

GEORGE HENRY "JOE" DECKER (1947–2003). Born in Storm Lake, Joe Decker attended high school in Petaluma, California. He was drafted by the Chicago Cubs in 1969 and pitched for that club until 1973, when he went on to play for the Minnesota Twins through 1976. He then ended his professional career with the Seattle Mariners in 1979. He put in his best work with the Twins in 1974, with a win-loss record of 16-14. He is now buried in the land of his birth at Buena Vista Memorial Cemetery in Storm Lake.

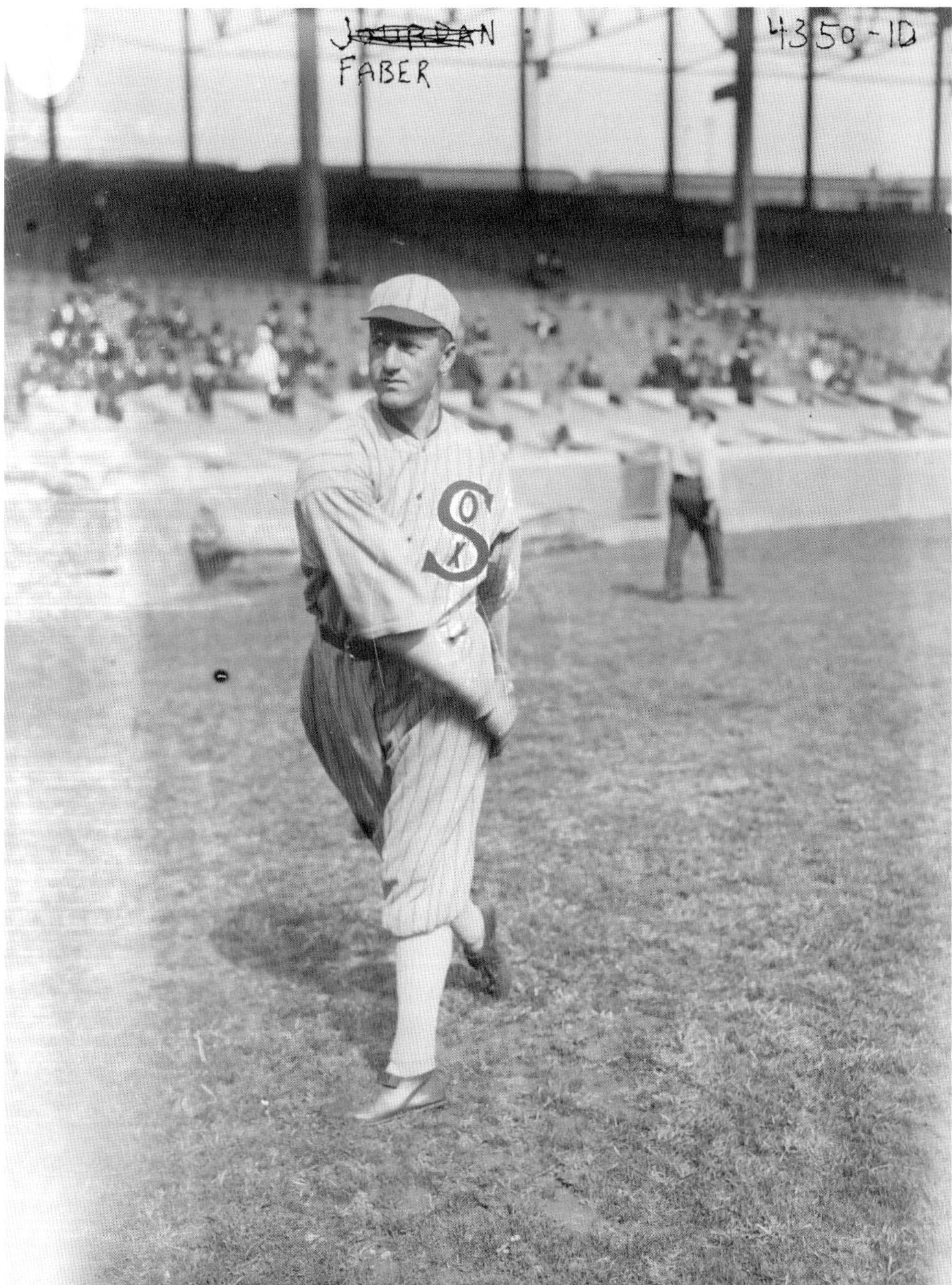

URBAN CLARENCE "RED" FABER (1888–1976). Born in Cascade in eastern Iowa, Red Faber was inducted into the National Baseball Hall of Fame in 1964. The gifted right-handed pitcher played his entire 20-year major-league career with the Chicago White Sox. Although not from Northwest Iowa, he had relatives there. The surname Faber often surfaces while scanning news archives from that part of the state. (See page 17.) (Courtesy of Library of Congress, Bain Collection.)

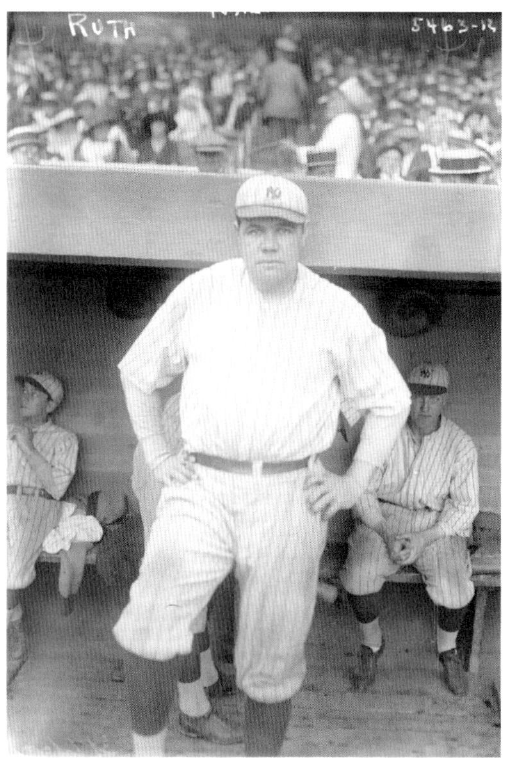

George Herman "Babe" Ruth (1895–1948). Baseball's most recognized name and face, Babe Ruth put on a show for Rockwell City admirers five years after retiring. When fans shouted for a shot over a barn at the edge of the ball field, he responded, "How big do you think the major-league parks are?" (Courtesy of Library of Congress, Bain Collection.)

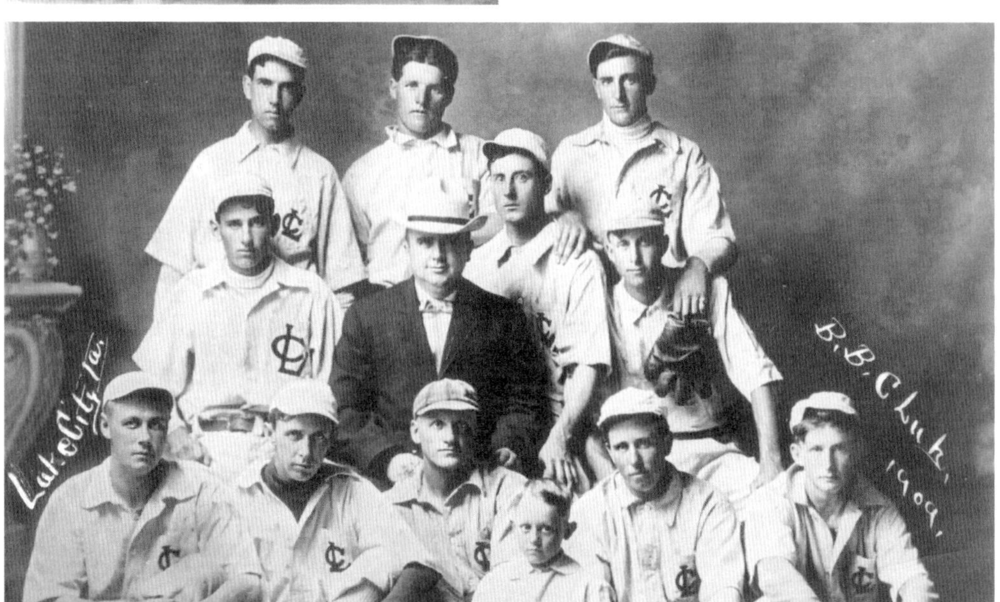

Lake City Baseball Club, 1909. Calhoun County's Lake City fielded this semipro team, managed by Harry Dodge. Purportedly the highest paid club in the state outside the leagues, it proved too expensive for Lake City. Late in July 1910, it was sold to Frank Gotch, a professional wrestler from Humboldt. It then went on to represent that town for the remainder of the season. (Courtesy of Rob Podlasek.)

FREDERICK BLAIR "CHICKEN" STANLEY (1947–). Born in Farnhamville, a small town in both Calhoun and Webster Counties, infielder Fred Stanley spent 14 years in the big leagues. Beginning with Seattle in 1969, he went on to Milwaukee, Cleveland, San Diego, the New York Yankees, and finally Oakland. Then, after filling non-player positions with the Brewers, he was appointed director of player development for the Giants.

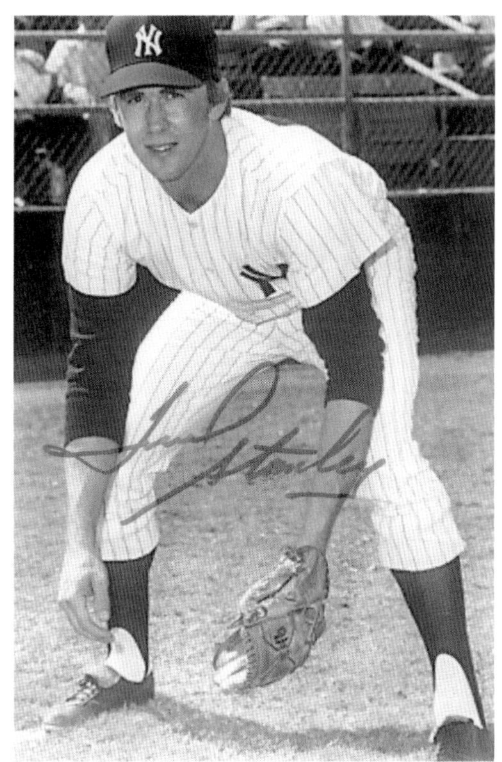

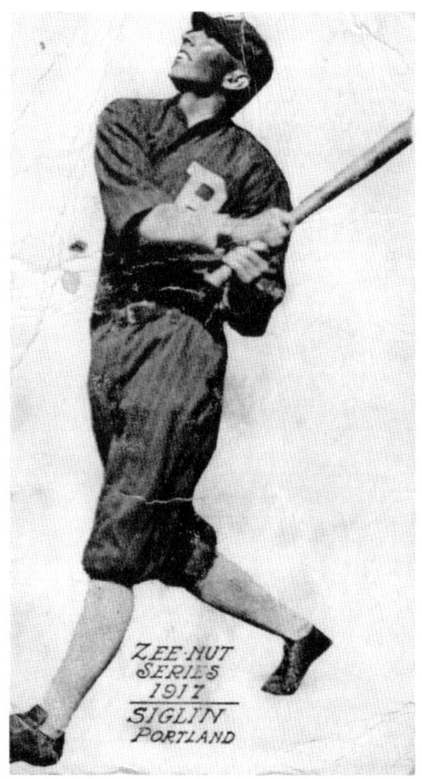

WESELY PETER "PADDY" SIGLIN (1891–1956). Aurelia's contribution to baseball, second baseman Paddy Siglin began his professional career with the Waterloo Jays in 1913 and most of 1914, going to Pittsburgh late that season. With the Pirates off and on for the next two years, he then played for minor-league teams through 1926. Located in Cherokee County, Aurelia now supports nonprofit youth summer baseball and softball programs.

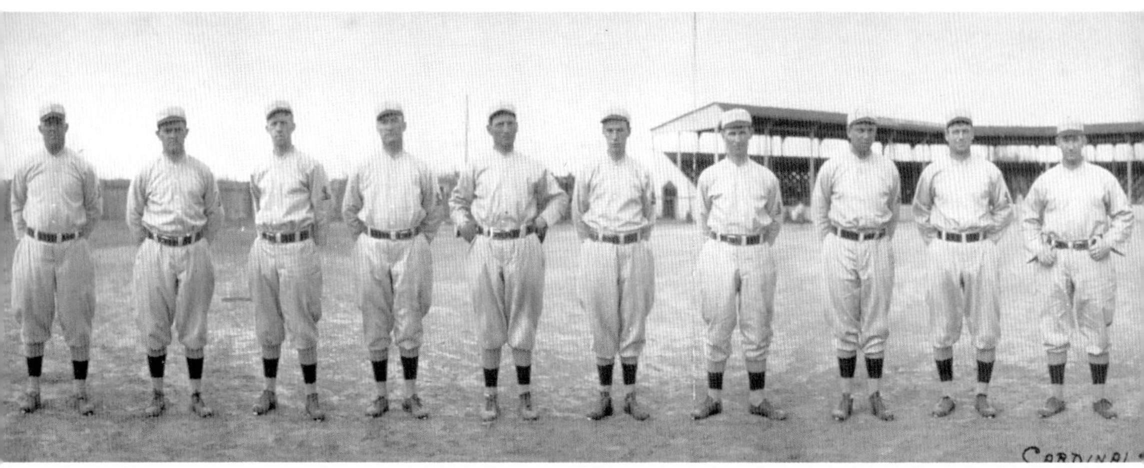

St. Louis Cardinals, 1909. Stephen Blasius Melter (1886–1962), a pitcher from Cherokee, began his professional career in 1909 with Northwest Iowa's Sioux City Packers. He debuted with the St. Louis Cardinals in June that year and appeared in 23 games for them. That comprised his big-league career. He then went on to play for minor-league teams in 1910 and from 1913 through

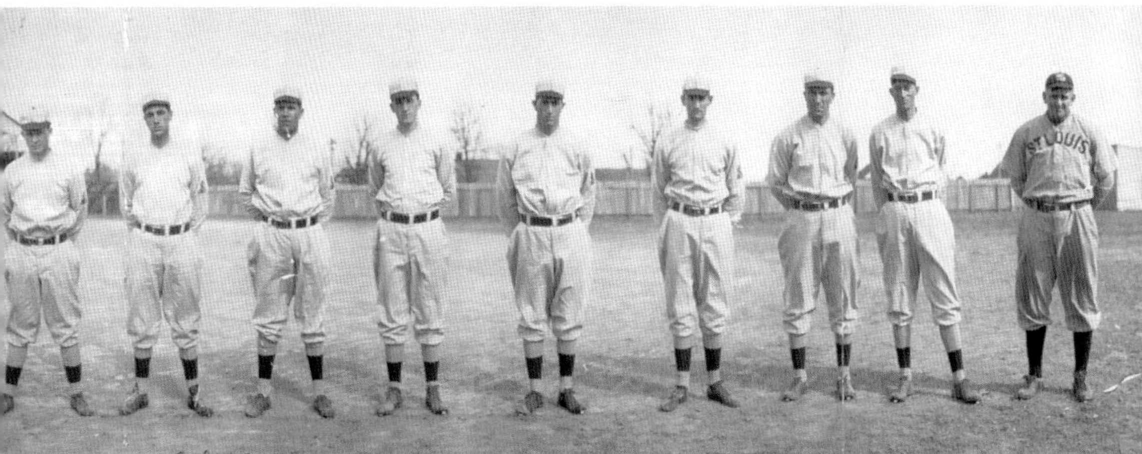

1917. He pitched well wherever he went, recording a win-loss record of 17-10 at Grand Rapids in 1916. Though his major-league career was brief, he stayed in St. Louis long enough to be included in this panoramic team photograph taken at Robison Field, the Cardinals' home field at the time. Steve Melter stands ninth from the left.

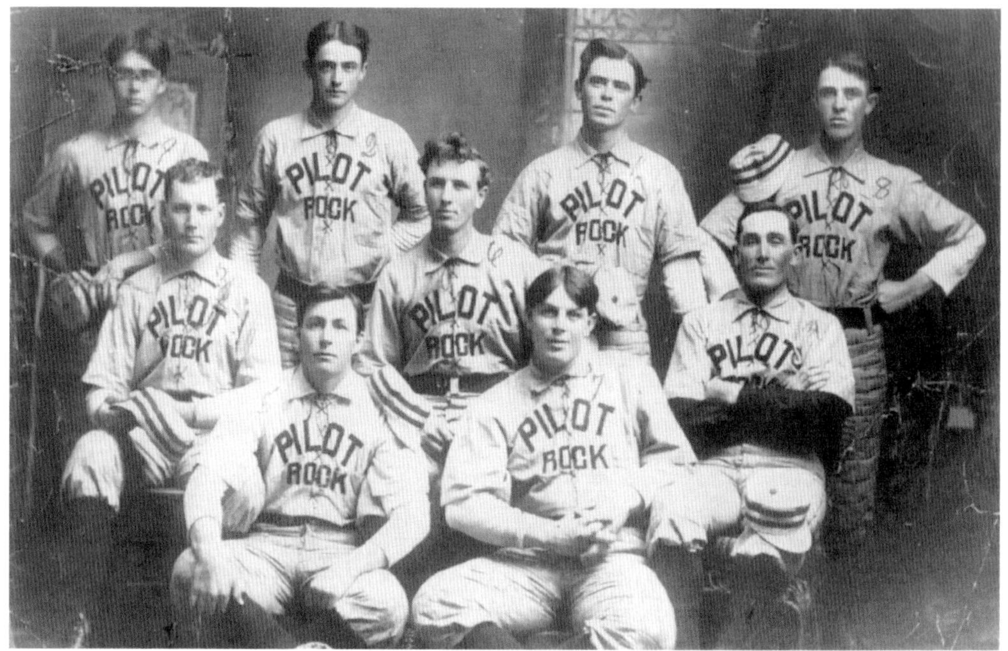

CHEROKEE'S PILOT ROCK TEAM, 1905. Named for an enormous glacial boulder overlooking the Little Sioux River south of Cherokee, this club includes, from left to right, (first row) Ed Melter (brother of Steve) and Tom Fairweather; (second row) Jerome Clow, Fred Ritchie, and Perry Boughton; (third row) Chick Liffring, Tom Patterson, John Patterson, and Frank Ritchie. Fairweather later served as president of the Three-I League. (Courtesy of Cherokee Area Archives.)

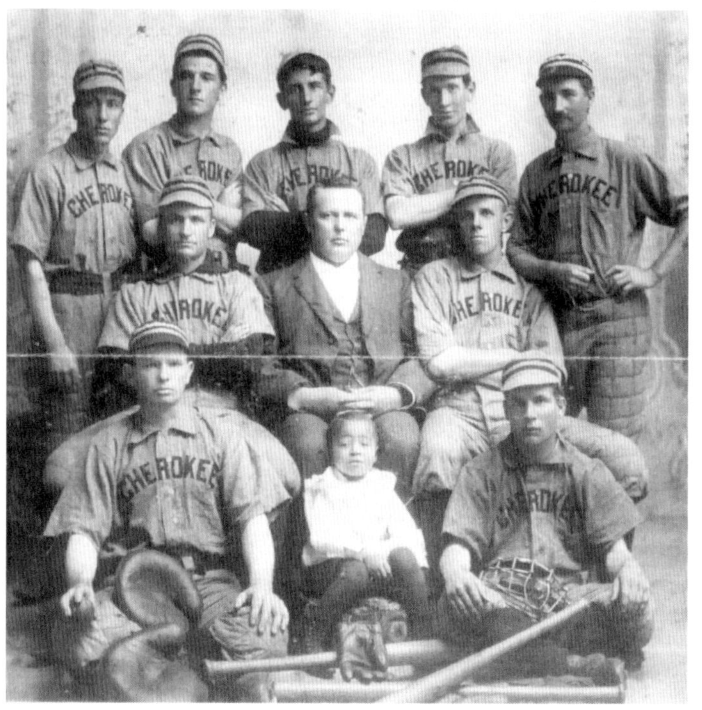

CHEROKEE BASEBALL TEAM, 1911. The players in this 1911 Cherokee team photograph have yet to be positively identified. However, the two men at left in the middle row appear to be the Melter brothers, Steve and Ed. Ed was likely the manager. Local news archives of the times indicate that Steve pitched for local semipro and amateur clubs that year. (Courtesy of Cherokee Area Archives.)

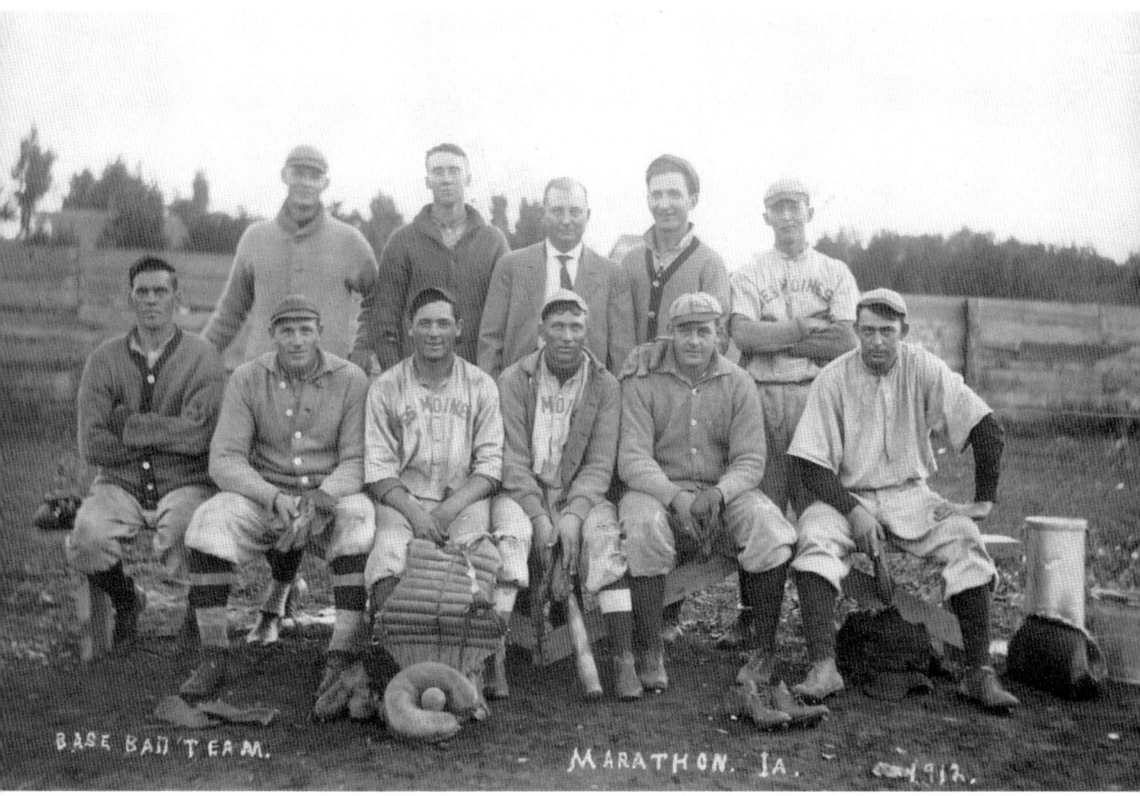

BASEBALL TEAM AT MARATHON, IOWA. The printing on this period postcard suggests that it pictures a Marathon, Iowa, club. However, the name Des Moines on the jerseys denotes otherwise. Tournaments were held in Buena Vista County's Marathon, and this photograph was likely shot there. Notice the player fifth from left in the first row. It is clearly Red Faber, who pitched for the Western League Des Moines Boosters in 1912.

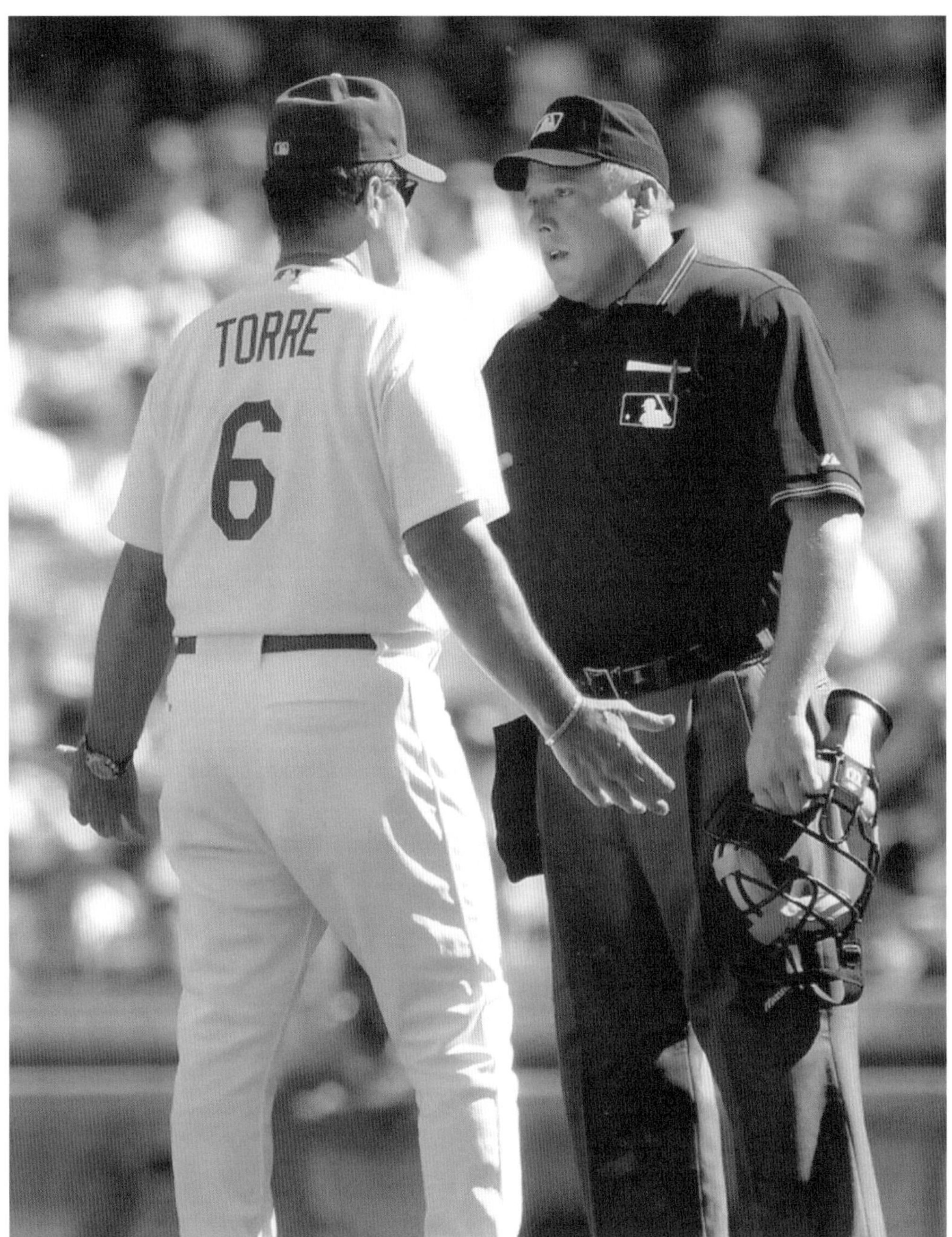

Bruce Dreckman (1970–). Born in Le Mars, Bruce Dreckman makes his home in Marcus, Cherokee County. He rose to the position of major-league umpire in 1997. A few of his many credits include working the 2009 and 2013 National League Championship Series and the 2010 All-Star Game in Anaheim. He is seen here discussing a play with Yankee manager Joe Torre.

Clay, Dickinson, and Emmet Counties

Spencer, the seat of Clay County, is its largest city by far. During the late 1920s, the Spencer Cubs competed against area teams like the Cherokee Cardinals and barnstorming teams popular then. In 1930, when night baseball was a rarity, local fans witnessed the first such event at a newly lighted Leach Athletic Park there. Piloted by former big-leaguer Art Ewoldt, the Spencer Cubs took on Estherville. In 1949, the semipro Spencer Cardinals became charter members of the Iowa State League. Between 1924 and 1952, two Clay County–born men joined the majors—Wattie Holm and Vern Fear. As of 2016, the sprawling Pederson Park east of Spencer offered venues for softball as well as baseball.

Home to Iowa's Great Lakes, Dickinson County is widely considered a vacation destination. But in addition to its fishing and water recreation, it hosted baseball games as early as 1873. That year, the county seat of Spirit Lake held an Independence Day celebration game between its club, the Rustics, and the Estherville Blizzards. In 1929, the Spencer Cubs and Gilkerson's Union Giants drew a crowd of some 2,200 to see a doubleheader at Arnolds Park, one of Dickinson County's bigger towns. The following year, the Junior League district championship game between the Iowa Great Lakes team and Cherokee was held at Peck's ballpark in Arnolds Park. Today, youngsters ages four to 18 can join the Spirit Lake Baseball League.

Estherville, the population center and seat of Emmet County, fielded a team called the Westerns before 1870. Before long, the Northern Blizzards—so named because the word *blizzard* was purportedly coined in Estherville—were organized. In 1911, the town called its team the World Beaters. The following year, it joined the Class D Iowa League of Professional Baseball Clubs. In 1930, a semipro team called the Estherville Eagles was organized. The Eagles won the league championship that year and were so overpowering that other teams soon dropped out of the league. Jumping forward to 1950, another semipro team, the Estherville Red Sox, joined the Iowa State League. Currently, a youth program satisfies the town's hunger for baseball.

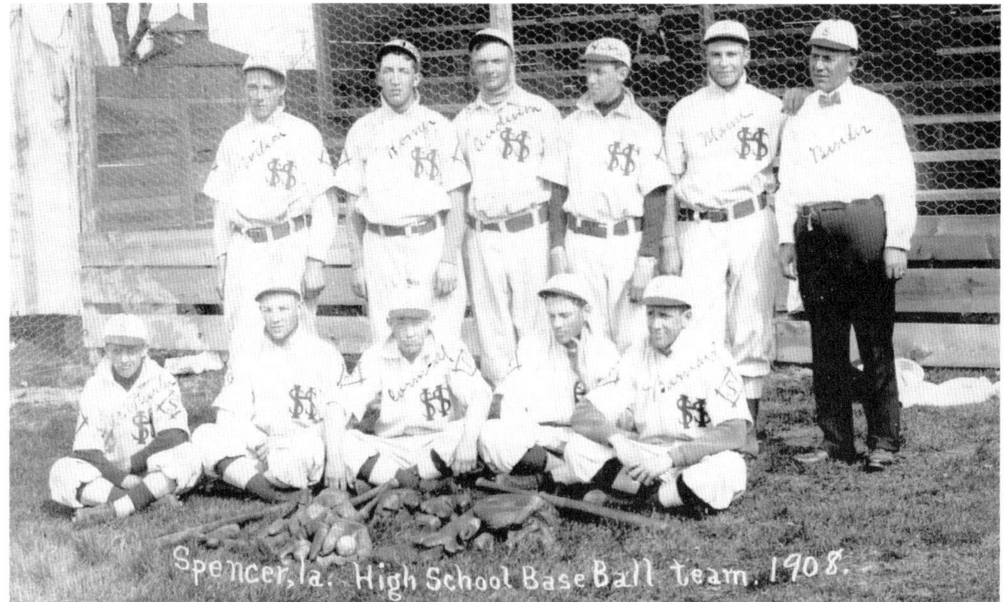

SPENCER HIGH SCHOOL BASEBALL TEAM, 1908. Spencer and other Clay County towns have demonstrated an affinity for baseball all along. A local group presented a comedy titled *My Partner* at the town's opera house on March 11, 1908. Proceeds from the benefit went to support the team pictured in this vintage postcard.

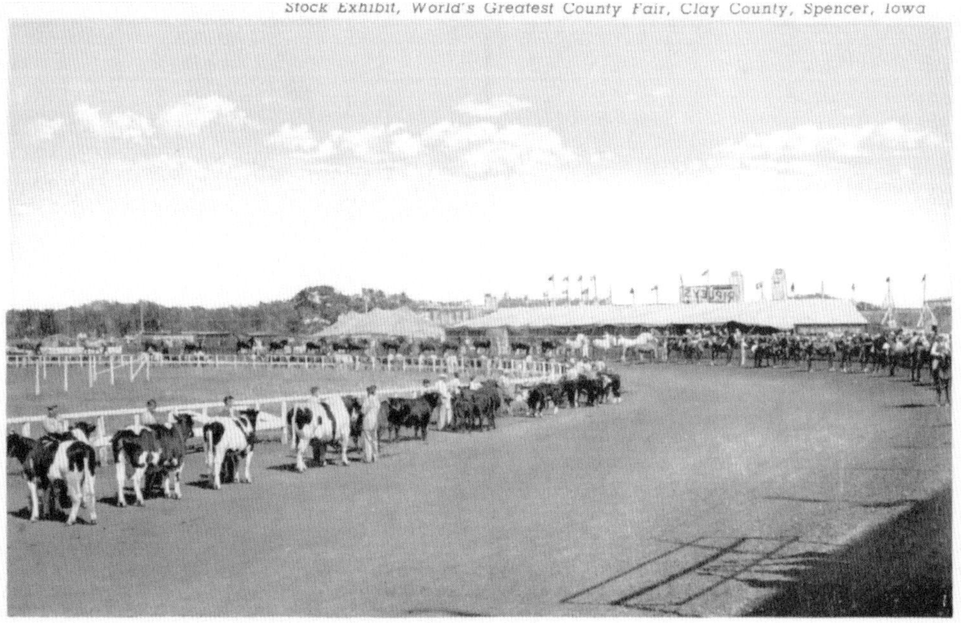

CLAY COUNTY FAIR AT SPENCER. Dubbed "The World's Greatest County Fair" since 1917, the Clay County Fair brings over 300,000 people to Spencer's fairgrounds each September. Iowa's agricultural society makes the county fair one of the state's most popular attractions. Patrons of the event pictured here found baseball just as stimulating.

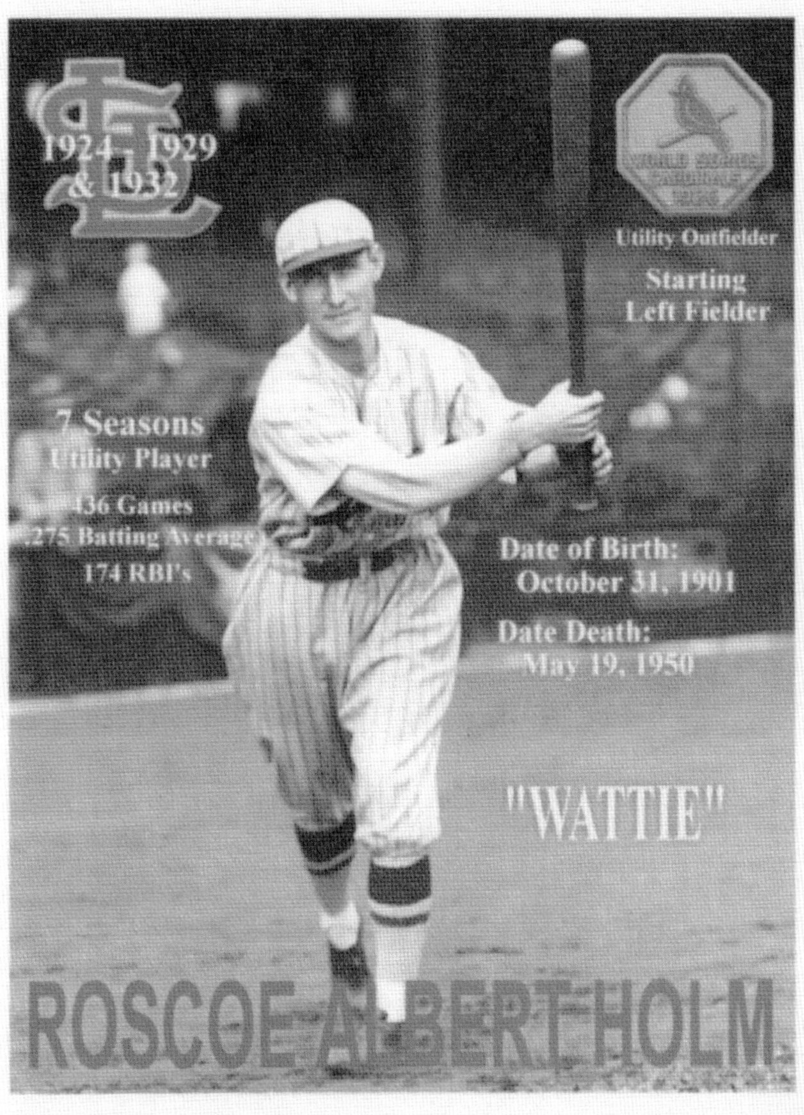

ROSCOE ALBERT "WATTIE" HOLM (1901–1950). Born in Clay County's Peterson, Wattie Holm moved with his family to Alton, Iowa, when he was in grade school. There, he acquired the enduring moniker "Wattie." His father, Bob, who managed an Alton team, undoubtedly aided him in developing his baseball skills. When he was 15, both Wattie and his father were listed on the Alton lineup. After playing for the Fairbury Jeffersons of the Nebraska State League, the outfielder and third baseman was acquired by the International League Syracuse Stars of New York in 1923. The following year, he joined the St. Louis Cardinals, playing for that club for seven seasons and participating in World Series games in 1926 and 1928. This keepsake image pays homage to his impressive career.

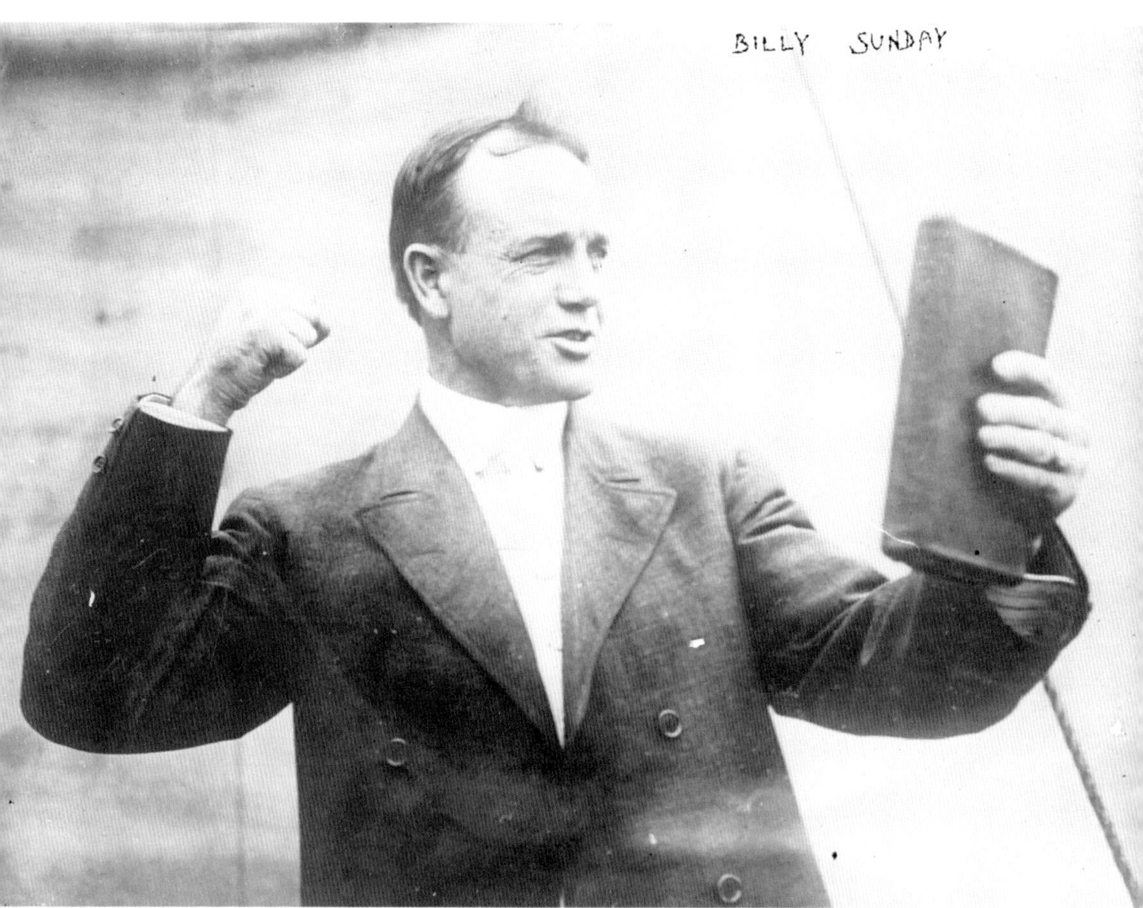

WILLIAM ASHLEY "BILLY" SUNDAY (1862–1935). Born in Ames, in Central Iowa, Billy Sunday was a professional baseball player who gained more fame as an evangelist. A left-handed batter who played for three National League clubs from 1883 to 1890, he was sometimes called "Parson" even then. Quitting baseball, he took up preaching as an evangelist favoring prohibition in 1896. His lengthy career as a fire-and-brimstone speaker began with meetings in little Garner, Hancock County, just east of Kossuth County. In 1930, after touring the country, he was still making news and appearing in Iowa towns. On June 26 of that year, he was featured at the Spencer Chautauqua, delivering a sermon titled "Corkscrews and Bootleggers—They Shall Not Pass." (Courtesy of Library of Congress.)

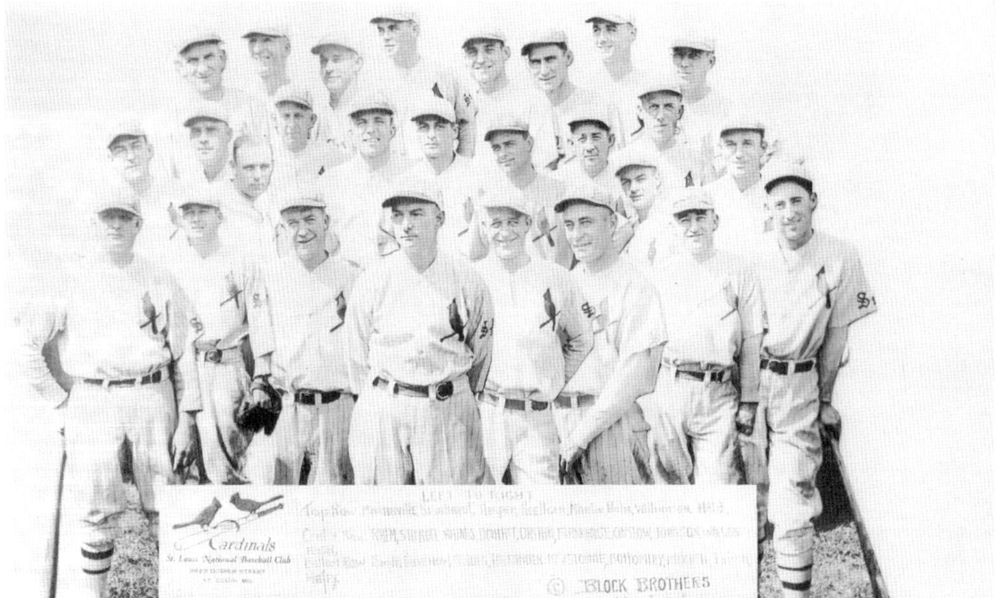

1928 St. Louis Cardinals. Wattie Holm (top row, third from right, in this 1928 team photograph) played third base for the Cardinals that year. The team captured the National League pennant with a win-loss record of 95-59. However, the Cardinals lost the World Series to the New York Yankees in four straight games. Wattie played in three of those games, tallying one hit in six at bats.

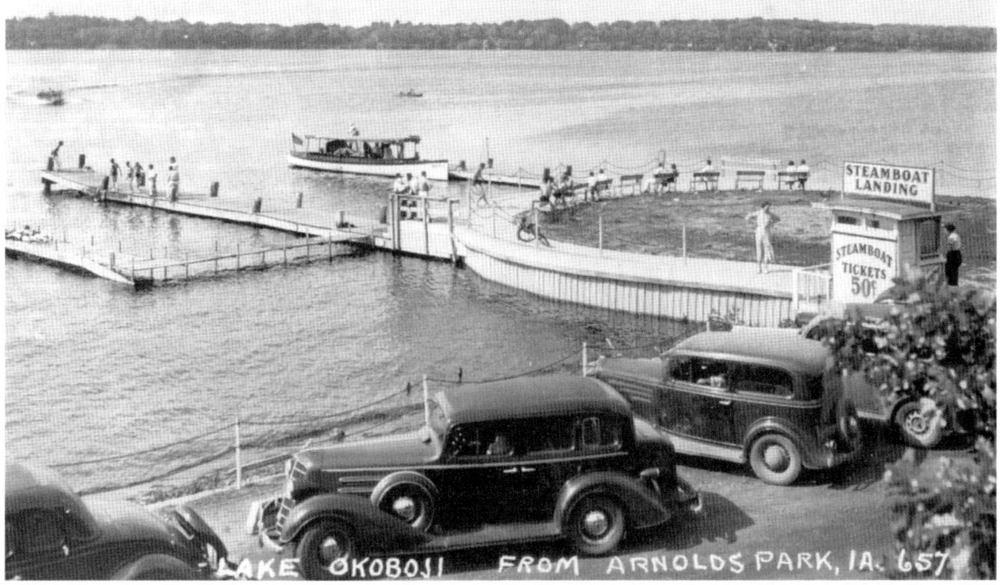

Lake Okoboji at Arnolds Park. Arnolds Park is a town on the shore of Lake Okoboji in Dickinson County. The waterfront has always attracted boating enthusiasts, and the town's amusement park is legendary. Generations of Iowans remember riding its wooden roller coaster, which first carried thrill-seekers in 1927. And the town apparently had an exemplary baseball park then. In 1933, the Spirit Lake club leased it for the season.

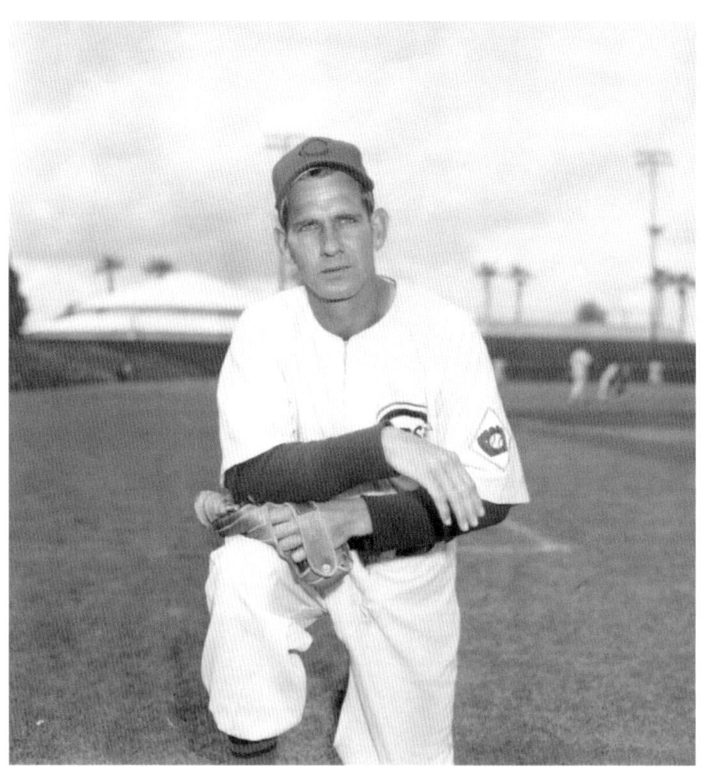

Luvern Carl "Vern" Fear (1924–1976). Born in Clay County's Everly, switch-hitting right-handed pitcher Vern Fear attended Everly High School. His eight-year professional pitching career began in 1947 and ended in 1954. During that time, he played for the Chicago Cubs, debuting on August 3, 1952, and making his last appearance there on September 3 of the same year. His best season was with the 1950 Des Moines Bruins, when he won 15 games. (Courtesy of William N. Jacobellis.)

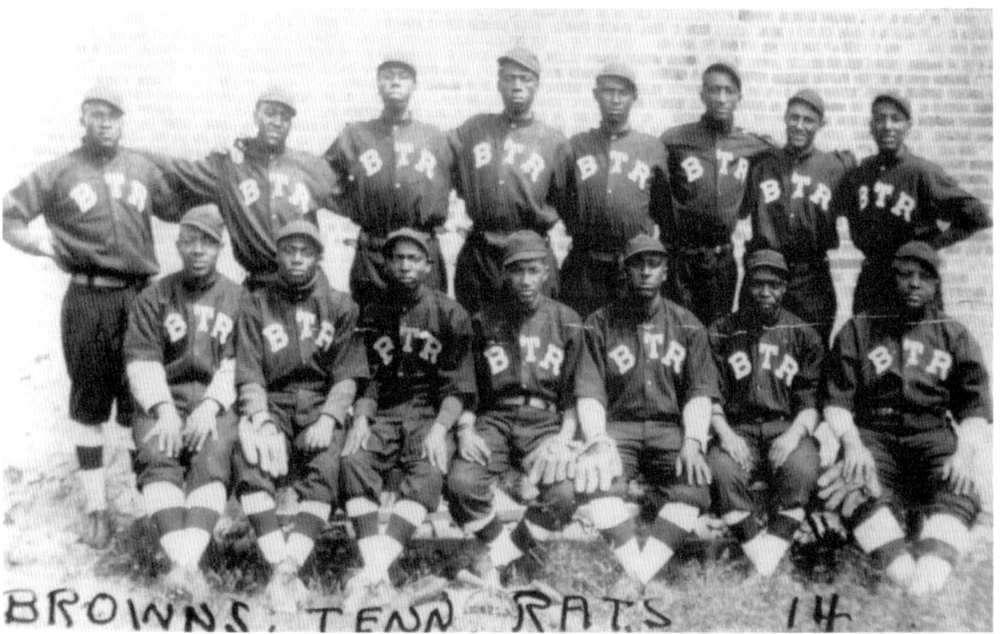

Tennessee Rats Negro League Team. In August 1916, the city of Terril, Dickinson County, held a fair with a band concert and a prominent speaker. There were also dances and a "moving picture" show. The main attraction was a ball game between the Tennessee Rats and the Chicago Union Giants. This was not unusual for a town with a population of less than 500 then.

Iowa Great Lakes. This picture postcard provides an overview of the Iowa Great Lakes. It features Dickinson County's seat, Spirit Lake. The side images emphasize the importance of water sports to the area. When Northwest Iowans planned a holiday outing, they would often say they were going to "the lakes." But records reveal that baseball meant just as much to visitors as well as county residents.

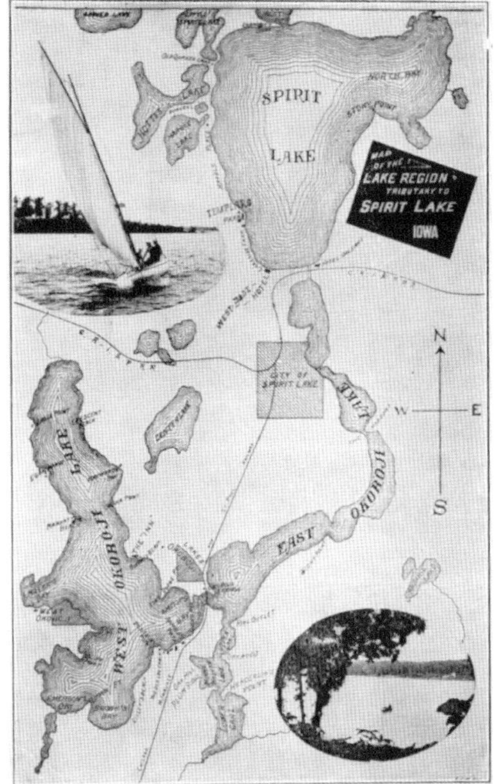

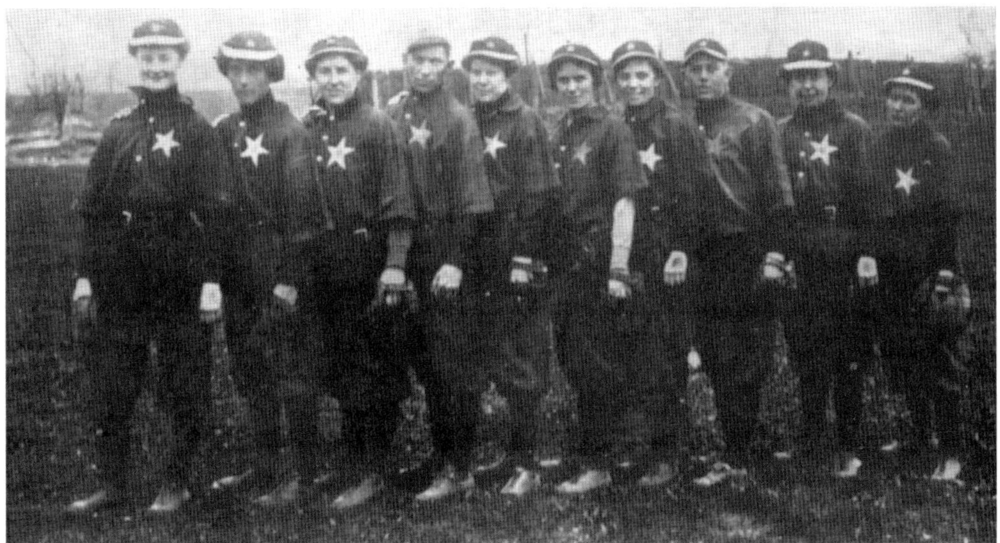

Star Bloomer Girls Baseball Club. Women's baseball clubs were uncommon during the heyday of the sport. Two traveling clubs, the Blondes and the Brunettes, amused fans across the country in 1875. A more serious aggregation, Bloomer Girls teams, surfaced in the late 19th century, lasting into the early 1930s. Some team members were men. This club played Arnolds Park's men's team on its home diamond in 1907.

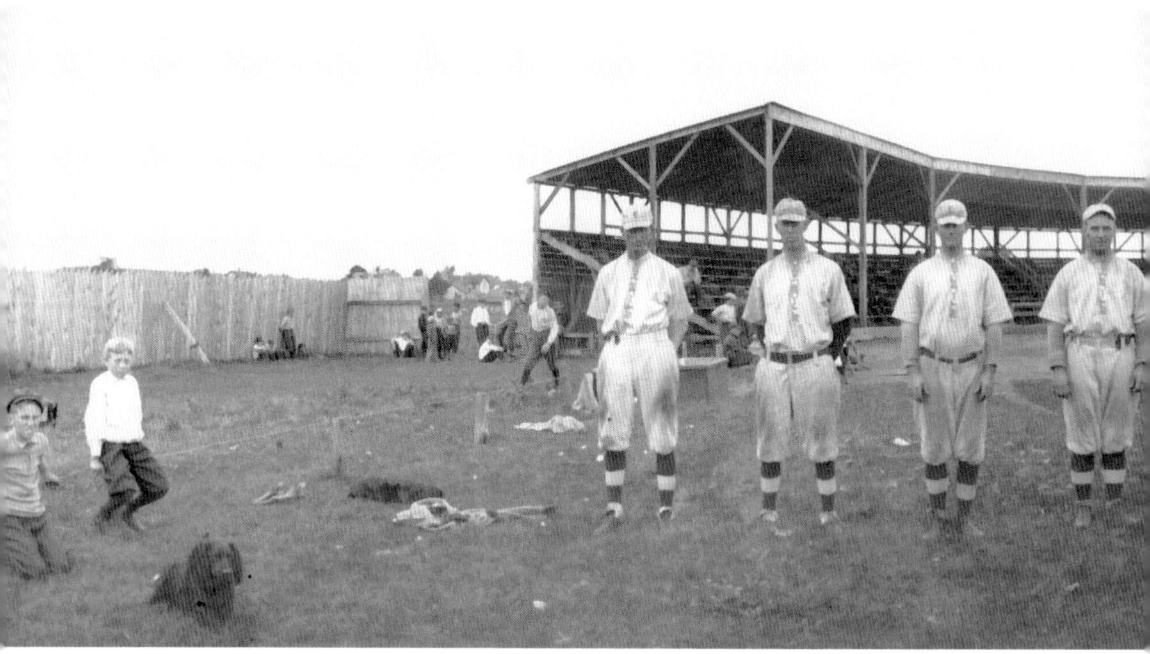

ESTHERVILLE'S PROFESSIONAL BASEBALL CLUB, 1912. The seat of Emmet County, Estherville enlisted its team in the Class D Iowa League of Professional Baseball Clubs in 1912. Its ballpark, Converse Park, was located on grounds where the John Morrell Packing Plant later stood. Two

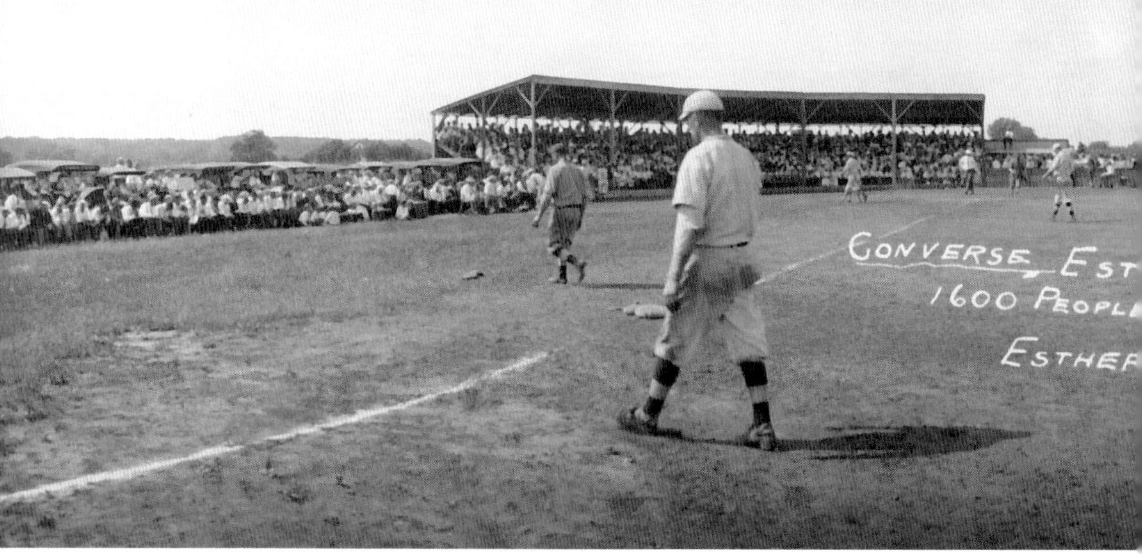

ESTHERVILLE VERSUS EMMETSBURG, 1912. In a tournament held in 1912, Estherville captured the Northern Iowa championship. This panoramic shot of a game with Emmetsburg allows a rare glimpse of a typical ball field of the day. Notice the railroad tracks in the background and the

other Northwest Iowa towns, Emmetsburg and Fort Dodge, entered teams in the league that year. (Courtesy of Emmet County Historical Museum.)

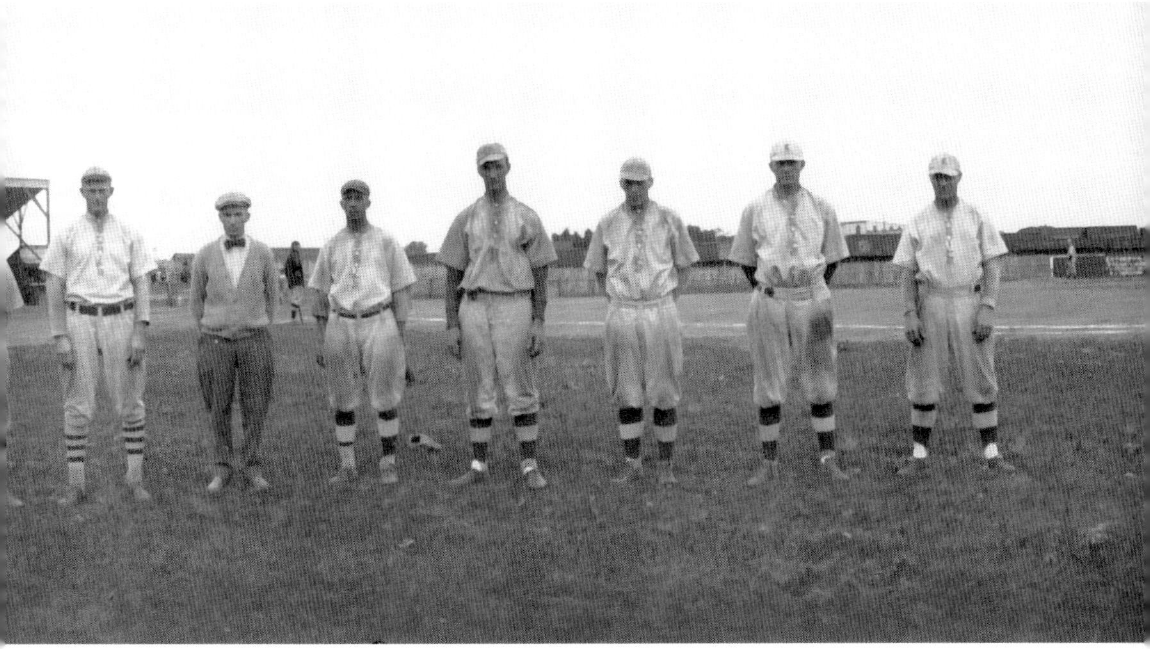

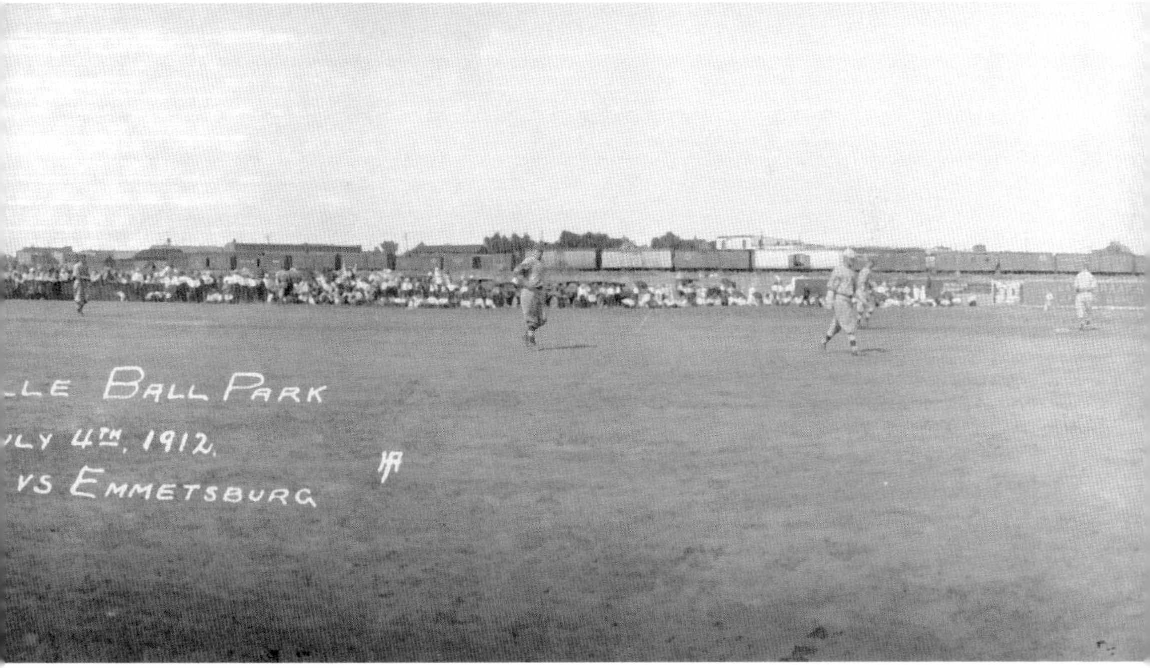

throngs of fans on either side of the grandstand. Many are seated in horseless carriages. (Courtesy of Emmet County Historical Museum.)

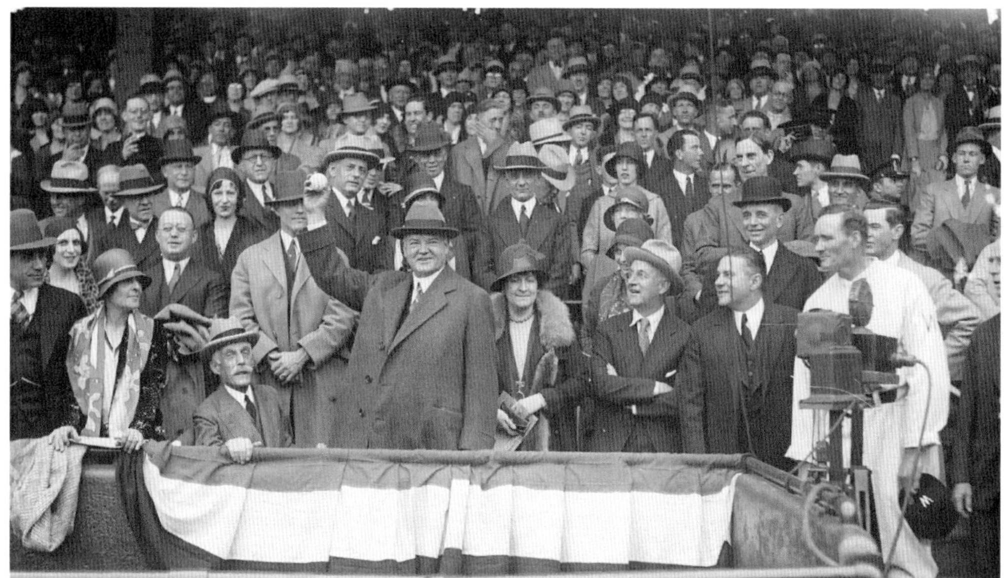

US President Herbert Hoover, 1931. The same year that Pres. Herbert Hoover posed for this shot at a major-league ballpark, he threw out the first pitch at Estherville on July 10. The occasion was a booster game between two picked nines from local talent. By then, Estherville's ballpark was in the southeast part of town. (Courtesy of Library of Congress, Harris and Ewing Collection.)

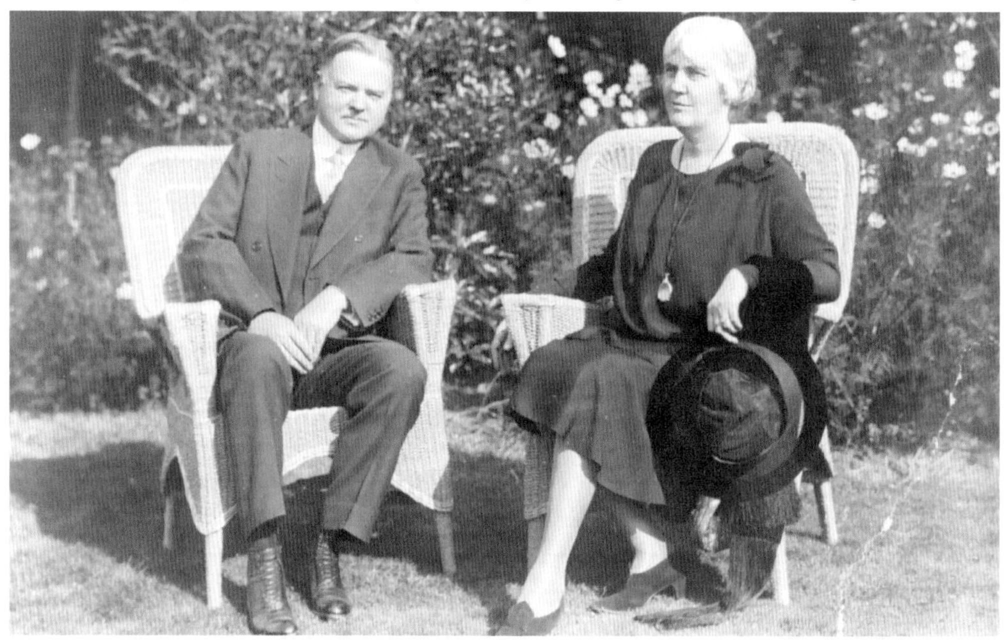

Pres. Herbert Hoover and His Wife, Lou Henry Hoover, 1929. The 31st president of the United States (1929–1933), Herbert Clark Hoover is the only Iowan elected to that position. Born in West Branch in Southeastern Iowa in 1874, he did have ties to Northwest Iowa. At the age of 10, he went to live with his grandmother in Kingsley, Iowa, for several years. (Courtesy of Library of Congress.)

Humboldt, Ida, and Kossuth Counties

Humboldt is Humboldt County's largest city, but smaller Dakota City, just east of Humboldt, is its seat. Like its neighbors, Humboldt has always maintained baseball clubs. By the time its Fats and Leans teams were competing against each other in 1904, Humboldt's native son Gus Thompson had already pitched for the Pittsburgh Pirates. But the county's smaller towns, such as Bode, fielded teams too. In 1911, little Bode decided that, with its wealth of talent, it must have a baseball club. By 1935, it had an independent team that faced such respected clubs as Bancroft. The following season, the Humboldt Red Caps also competed against other counties' teams, such as Sac County's Lake View club. Today, baseball still prospers in area parks, including Humboldt's historic Taft Park.

Ida County primarily consists of five small towns, and its two largest have contributed significant talent to the major leagues. Pitcher George Pipgras, who played for 13 years with American League teams, was born in Ida Grove, the county seat. As an indication of the sport's importance to that town's culture, in 1925, an indoor baseball tournament was held on the afternoon of a local convention. Holstein, smaller than Ida Grove, produced two big-league hurlers: Foster Edwards and Biggs Wehde. Before a record-breaking crowd in Holstein in 1925, Wehde struck out 10 batters in a 4-3 victory against Anthon. He went on to pitch for the Chicago White Sox in 1930 and 1931. A new Ida Grove Baseball Complex was built in 2015, stimulating the preservation of the county's love of the game.

Kossuth County is steeped in baseball history. Since 1902, six of its native sons have played in the big leagues. The first, pitcher William Ansil "Solly" Salisbury, was born in Algona, the county seat, in 1876. Although his career was brief, that of those who followed was mostly remarkable. As well as Algona, Bancroft and Wesley also cultivated talent for the majors. But it is the county's chronicle of winning teams that reveals it as a breeder of baseball talent. Bancroft's list of championship teams at the American Legion, state amateur, and high school levels spans decades.

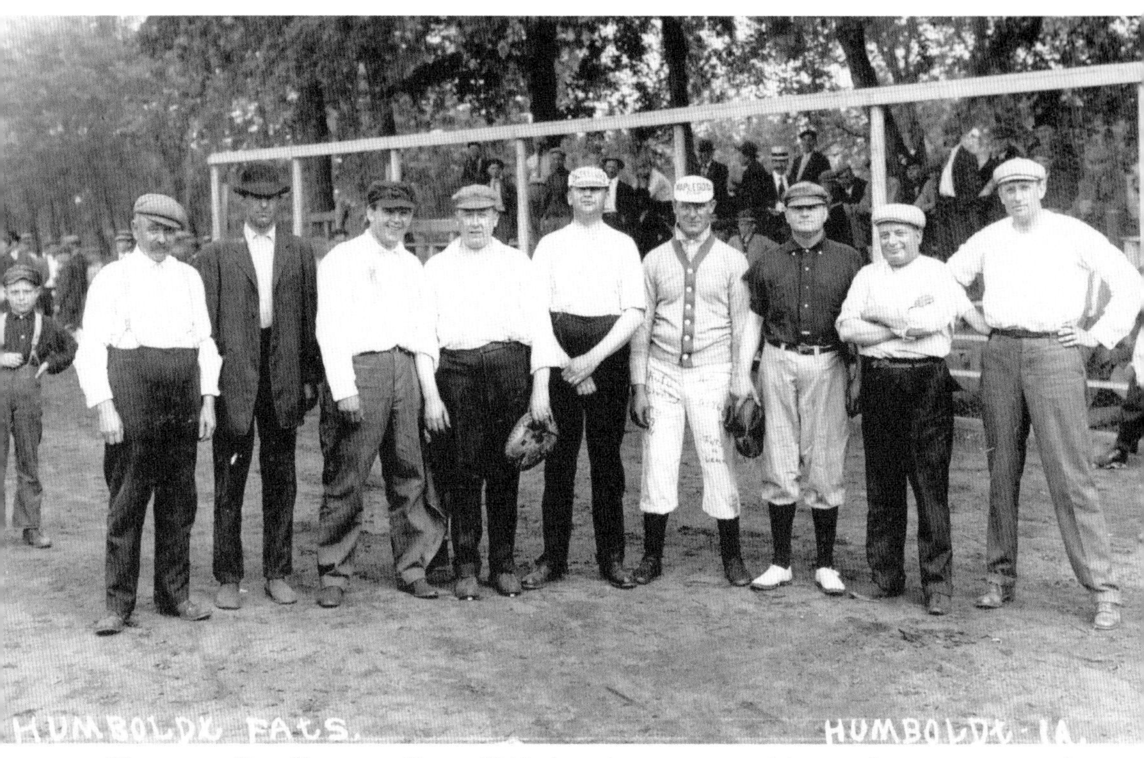

HUMBOLDT FATS BASEBALL TEAM, 1910. Amusing spectators, this group lost a game to another local club by a score of 45-5 in April 1910. The event took place at Humboldt's Taft Park. The *Humboldt Independent* coverage of the game lists the Humboldt Fats' lineup as Duncan, Gotch, B. White, Myles, Saul, McGee, Halgrines, Parker, and Strong. It is unknown which individuals in this photograph match the names. The newspaper story does reveal that manager Pete Saul pitched in that game against the Humboldt Leans. The name Gotch suggests that the famous wrestler Frank Gotch of Humboldt played for the Fats. If so, he would likely be the taller man on the far right. Fats clubs were popular throughout the country in those times, and apparently they were not always seriously competitive. (Courtesy of State Historical Society of Iowa, Des Moines.)

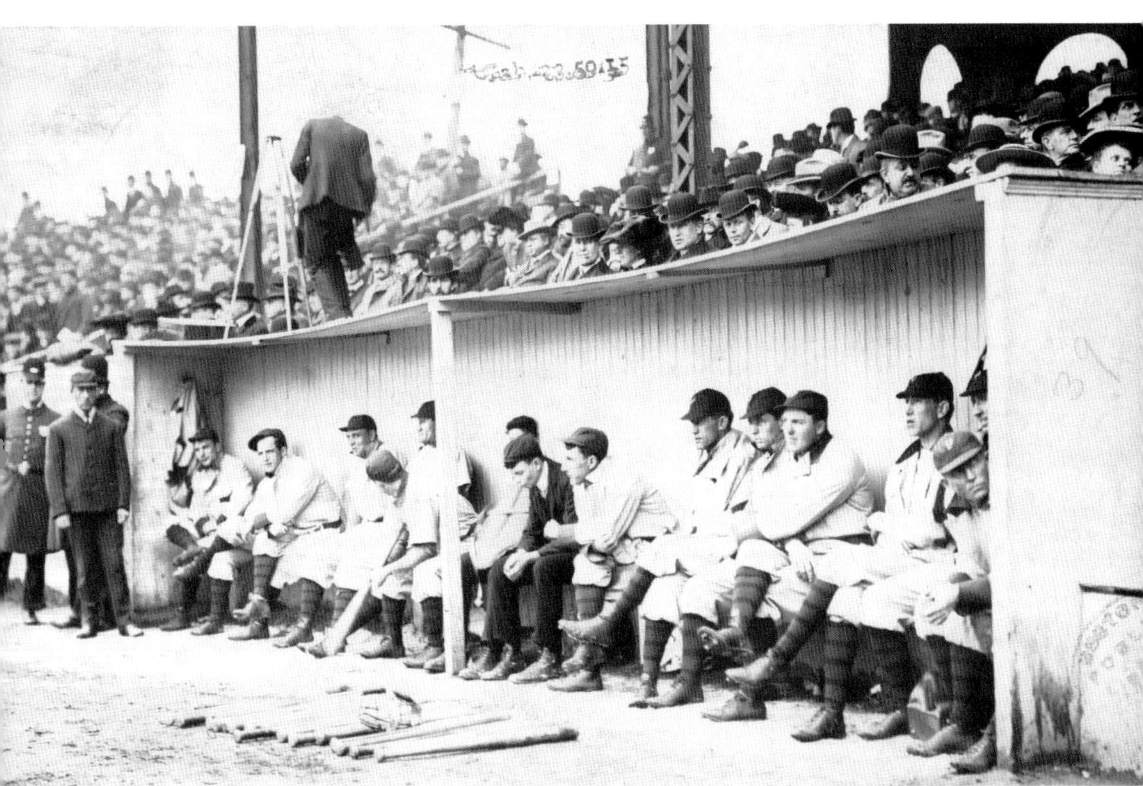

1903 World Series with Humboldt's Gus Thompson. Seen in this photograph taken in the dugout of Boston's Huntington Avenue Baseball Grounds during the 1903 World Series are, from left to right, Pittsburgh Pirates utility player Joe Marshall, infielder Otto Krueger, outfielder Jimmy Sebring, shortstop Honus Wagner, unidentified, catcher Eddie Phelps, the batboy, pitcher Gus Thompson, pitcher Deacon Phillippe, first baseman Kit Bransfield, outfielder Ginger Beaumont, pitcher Sam Leever, second baseman Claude Ritchey, and pitcher Brickyard Kennedy. Boston, with its premier hurler Cy Young, took the series in five of eight games. Following an illustrious career, Young was inducted into the National Baseball Hall of Fame in 1937. The Pirates' Thompson made an appearance in the 1903 series, pitching for two innings. Born in Humboldt, Iowa, in 1877, John Gustav "Gus" Thompson played for Pittsburgh in 1903 and the St. Louis Cardinals in 1906. (Courtesy of Boston Public Library, McGreevey Collection.)

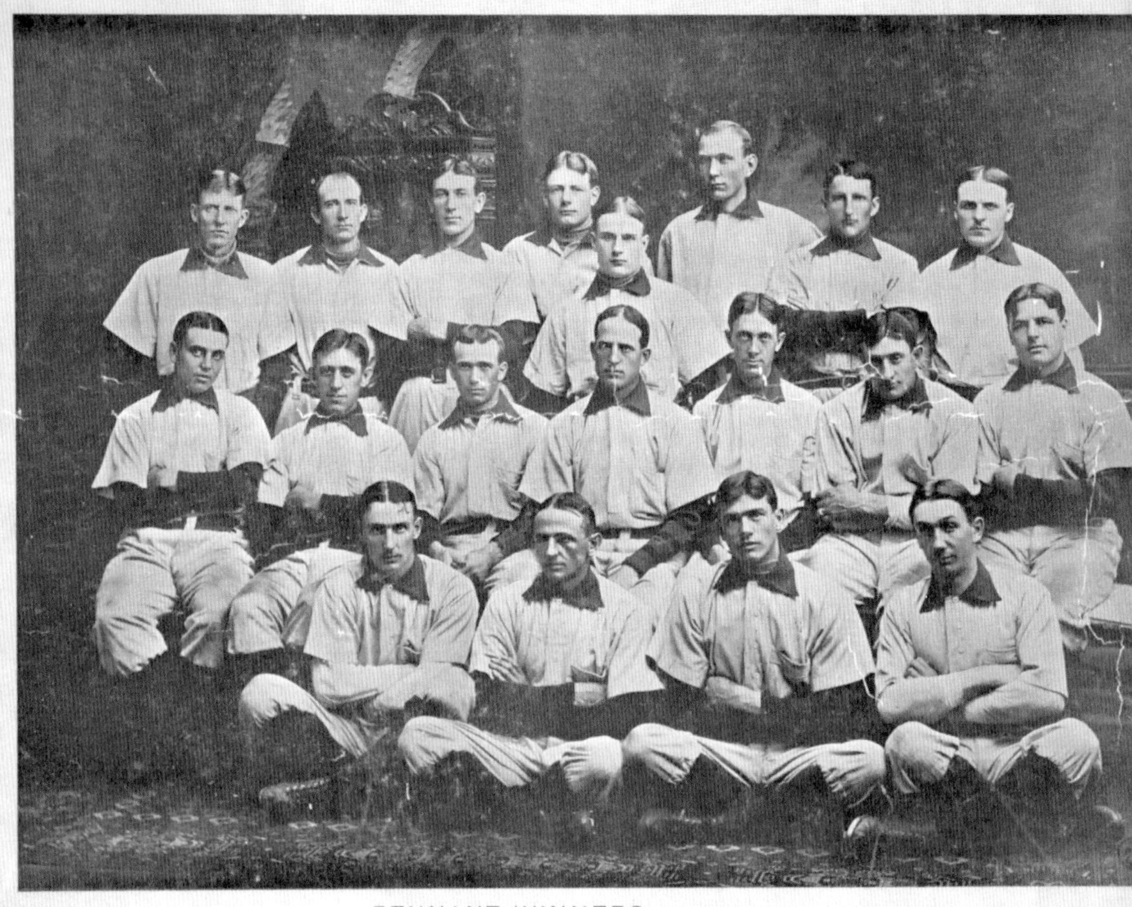

PITTSBURGH BASEBALL CLUB WITH GUS THOMPSON. This team photograph of the Pittsburgh Pirates, National League champions for three years running from 1901 to 1903, was obviously taken in 1903, owing to Gus Thompson's presence. The Humboldt-born pitcher was with the Pirates for just that season and with the St. Louis Cardinals in 1906. He did have a respectable minor-league career, beginning with Helena, Montana, in the Pacific League in 1902, and after Pittsburgh, he went to Boise in 1904. After St. Louis, he went to Omaha, then Aberdeen, Washington, and finally Seattle in the Northwestern League in 1909 and 1910. His best year was with Aberdeen in the Northwestern League, where he tallied a win-loss record of 21-17 in 1908. At six foot two, Thompson, sixth from the left in the top row, towers over his teammates. Future hall of fame shortstop Honus Wagner is shown sixth from the left in the middle row. (Courtesy of Boston Public Library.)

FRANK GOTCH (1877–1917). Frank Gotch, a widely known professional wrestler from Humboldt, Iowa, purchased the semipro Lake City baseball club in July 1910. Moving it to his hometown, he named it "Gotch's Champions." The team boasted a 31-8 win-loss record at the time. But Gotch never gained fame as a baseball magnate. After his death, he was recognized primarily for his skills in the ring.

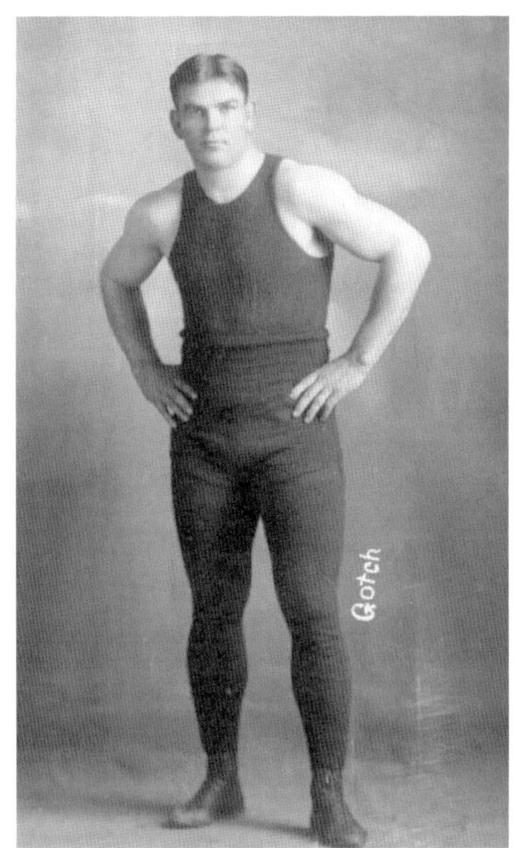

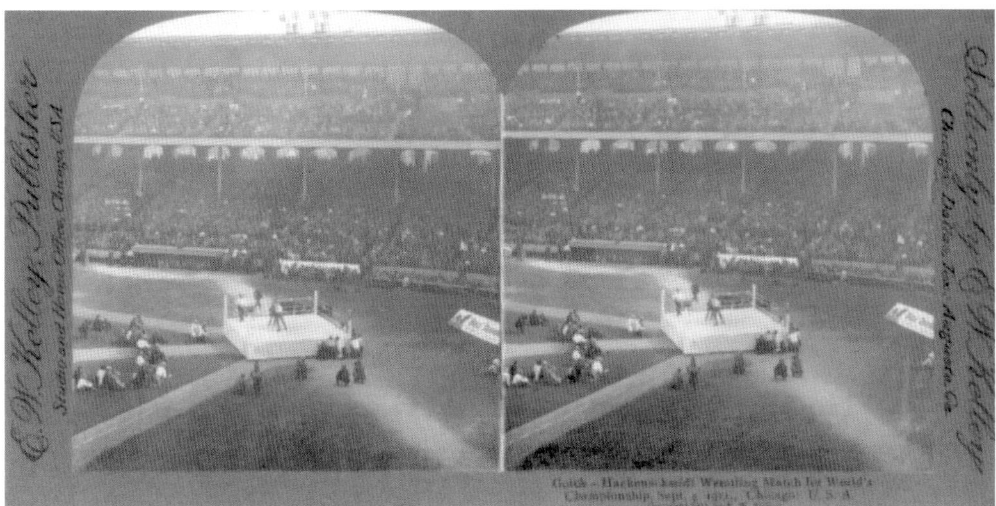

WORLD'S CHAMPIONSHIP WRESTLING MATCH, 1911. This stereoscopic image shows Humboldt baseball club owner Frank Gotch competing against George Hackenschmidt for the world's wrestling championship. The event took place at Chicago's Comiskey Park on Labor Day, September 4, 1911. The first American professional wrestler to win the heavyweight freestyle championship, Frank Alvin Gotch grew up on a farm near Humboldt. (Courtesy of Library of Congress.)

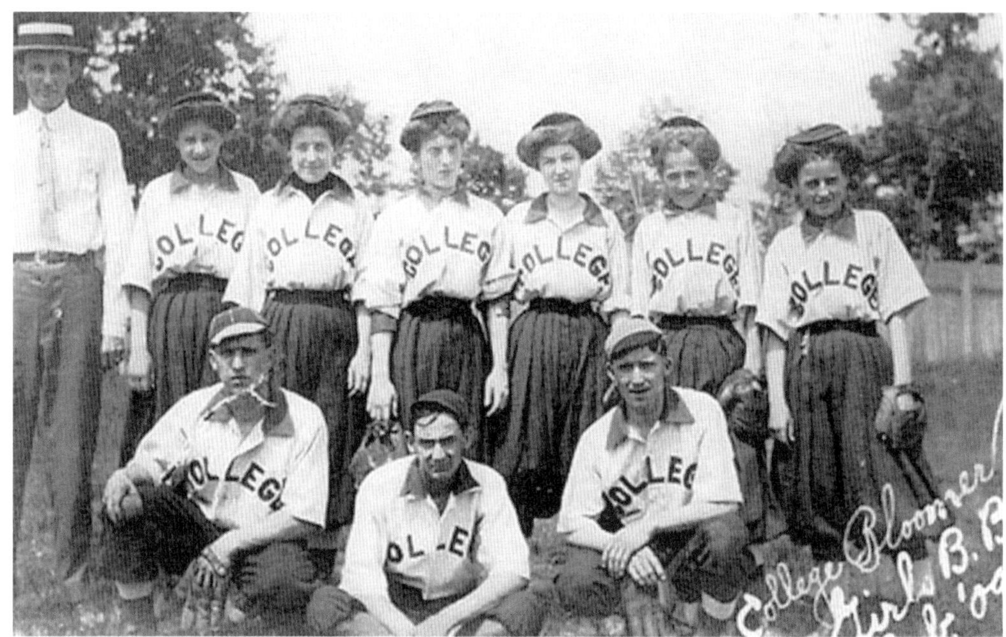

BLOOMER GIRLS. In the early 20th century, barnstorming baseball clubs called Bloomer Girls entertained ball fans across the country. Traveling in a Pullman railroad car, they arrived in Humboldt and played the town's team on July 15, 1907. They brought along a large canvas fence and portable stands to seat 2,000. This College Bloomer Girls picture demonstrates the bloomers worn as well as the male teammates often accompanying such clubs.

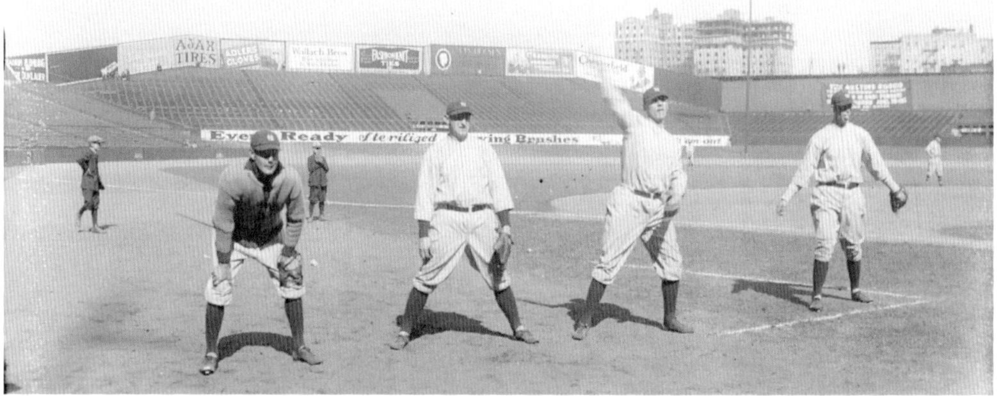

GEORGE PIPGRAS WITH TEAMMATES, APRIL 26, 1923. Ida Grove–born Yankee pitcher George Pipgras (left) is shown warming up with pitcher Carl Mays (second from left), outfielder Harvey Hendrick (third from left), and pitcher Oscar Roettger (right). That first year of Pipgras's major-league career, his team went on to win the World Series 4-2 against the New York Giants. Although Pipgras did not get to pitch in that winning effort, he did play for the Yankees for nine years, with a two-year break in 1925 and 1926. His best season came in 1928, when he recorded a win-loss record of 24-13. That year, the Yankees took the series against the St. Louis Cardinals in four straight. That time, Pipgras got to participate by winning game two, 9-3. He closed out his big-league career with Boston from 1933 to 1935. (Courtesy of Library of Congress, Bain Collection.)

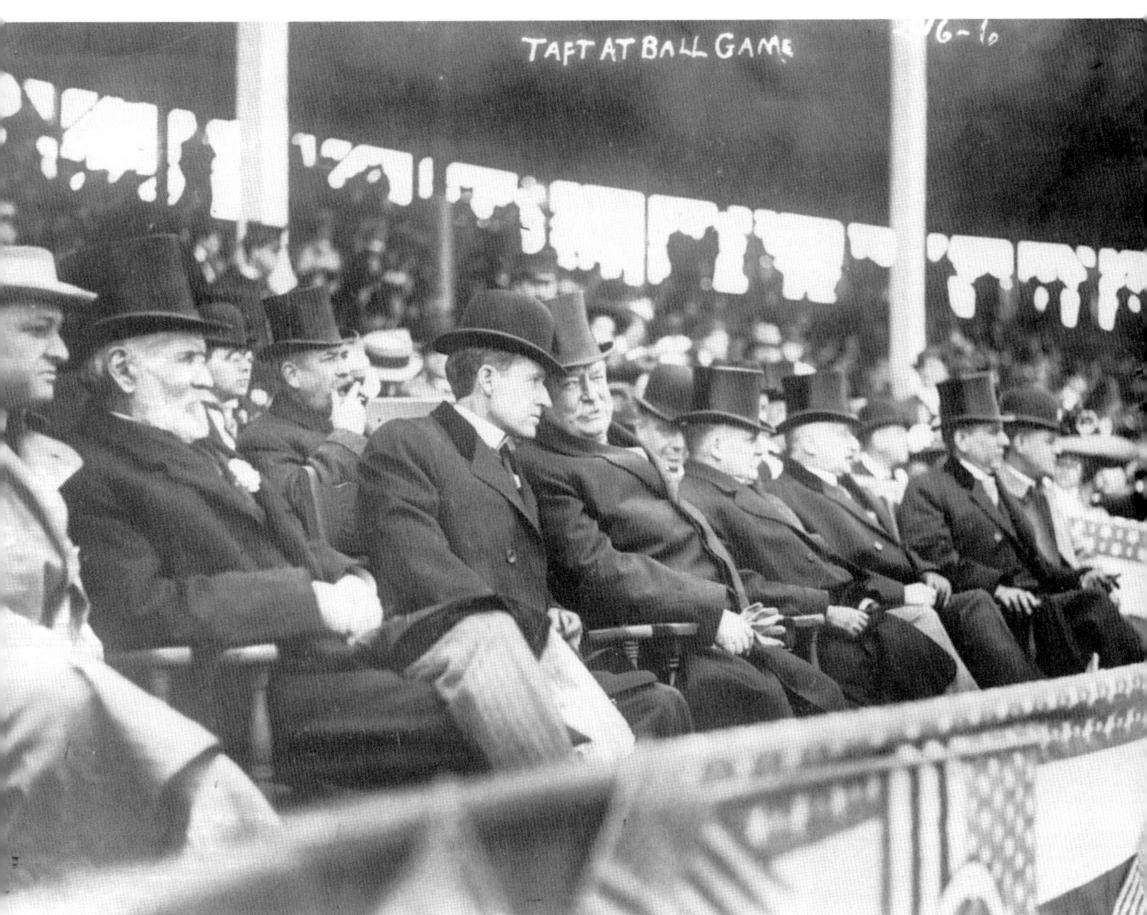

President Taft at the Ball Game, 1910. William Howard Taft, 27th president of the United States, is shown attending a major-league baseball game in 1910. When he served his first term in office in 1909, there was already a Taft Park in Humboldt. Newspaper accounts reveal that splendid ball games would be featured there every day of the Chautauqua being held in July that year. Outsiders may carry the misconception that the park was named for the nation's president. In truth, it was named for the town's founder, Stephen Harris Taft. Some accounts suggest that the two men were distant relatives. Regardless, there is still a Taft Park in Humboldt. There is also a Frank Gotch Park four miles south of town. Both names resonate with the town's history, including that of baseball. (Courtesy of Library of Congress, Bain Collection.)

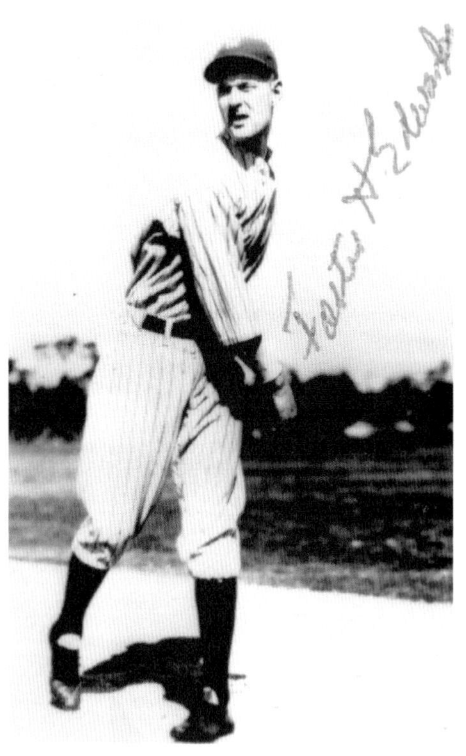

Foster Hamilton "Eddie" Edwards (1903–1980). Born in Holstein, Ida County, pitcher Foster Edwards played professional baseball from 1925 to 1930. He had brief stays with Boston for the next three years, punctuated with minor-league stints. His best performance was with the Eastern League Providence Rubes in 1926, winning 25 games with that club. His last professional appearance was with the New York Yankees in 1930.

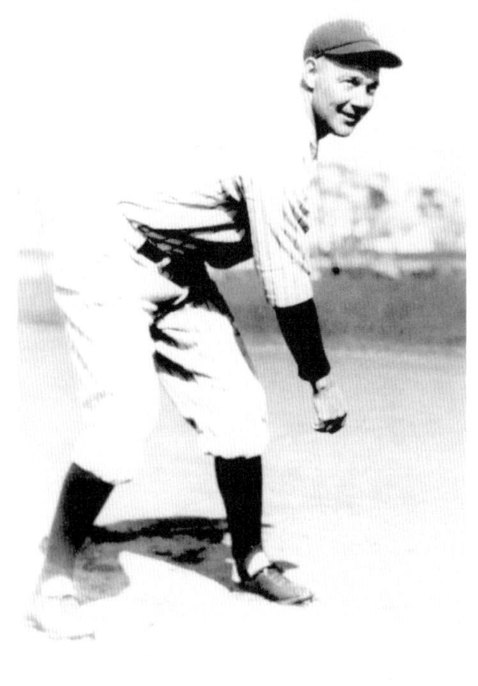

George William Pipgras (1899–1986). Although Yankee pitcher George Pipgras was born in Ida Grove, at some point his family moved to Schleswig, Crawford County, which is just south of Ida County. In Schleswig, George and his brother Herman formed the battery of the local high school team. Another brother, Ed, was born there in 1904. Ed pitched in five games with the Brooklyn Dodgers in 1932.

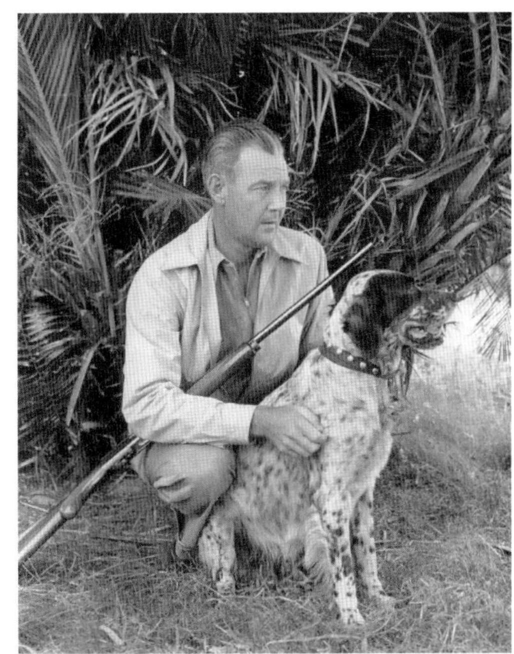

Major-League Umpire and Duck Hunter George Pipgras. Following his playing days, George Pipgras began a new career in baseball as an umpire. He started in 1936, and his proficiency yielded a job with the American League in 1939. Gaining the reputation as one of the best, Pipgras officiated in the 1940 All-Star Game and the 1944 World Series. During his leisure time, he loved fishing and duck hunting.

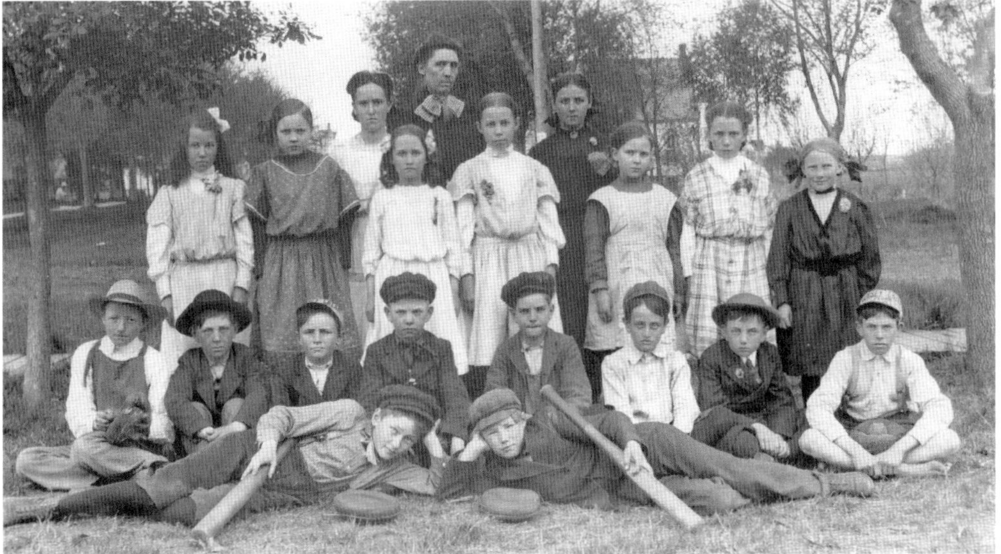

Swea City Class Picture. With a population numbering less than 1,000 since it was platted in 1892, Swea City, Kossuth County, might be the quintessential rural Iowa town. It had a baseball diamond and team in the first decade of the 20th century. Moreover, in 1920, the town's businessmen raised funds to support a semipro baseball team. This photograph of an early school group exemplifies the character of such a place. The stern look cast by the teacher, versus the ornery grins on the impish faces of the two boys in front, pays homage to the stoicism often attributed to Iowans. It is notable that the two reclining lads sport bats and gloves. Although not confirmed, this is most likely a country school class. Country schools served much of rural Iowa in those times. (Courtesy of State Historical Society of Iowa, Des Moines, William Shirley Collection.)

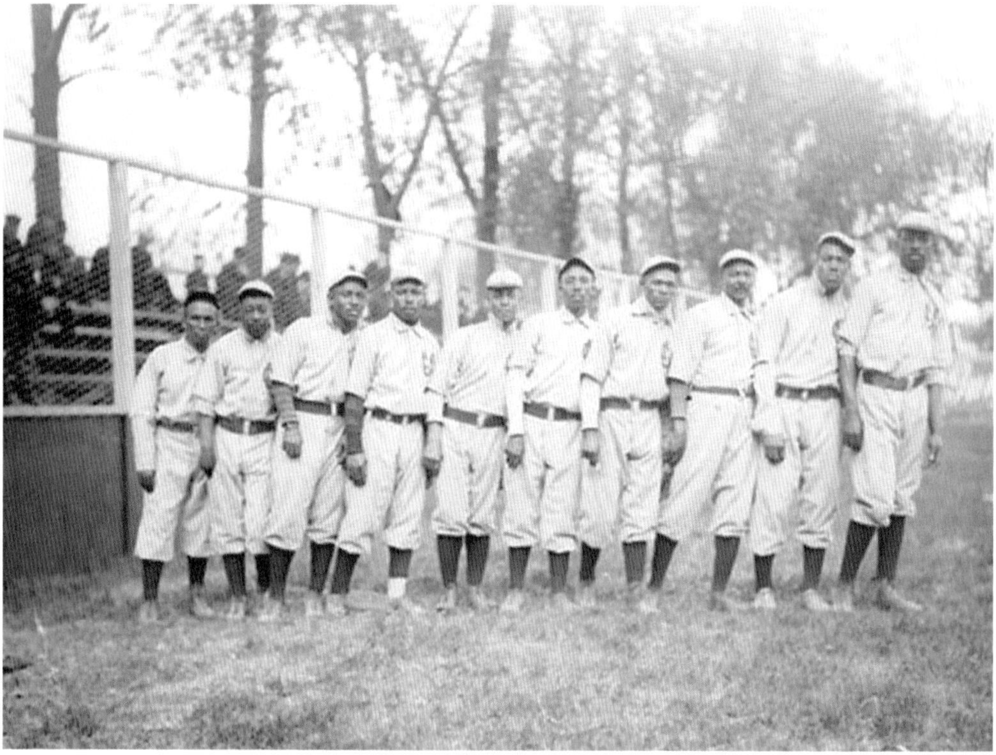

CHICAGO UNION GIANTS 1905. Founded in 1887, the Chicago Union Giants underwent an ownership change around 1917 and went on barnstorming tours of the Midwest. It became one of the best Negro League traveling teams throughout 1930. In 1916, the club was matched against the Bancroft, Iowa, team at a Labor Day celebration in Graettinger, Palo Alto County. (Courtesy of Chicago Historical Society.)

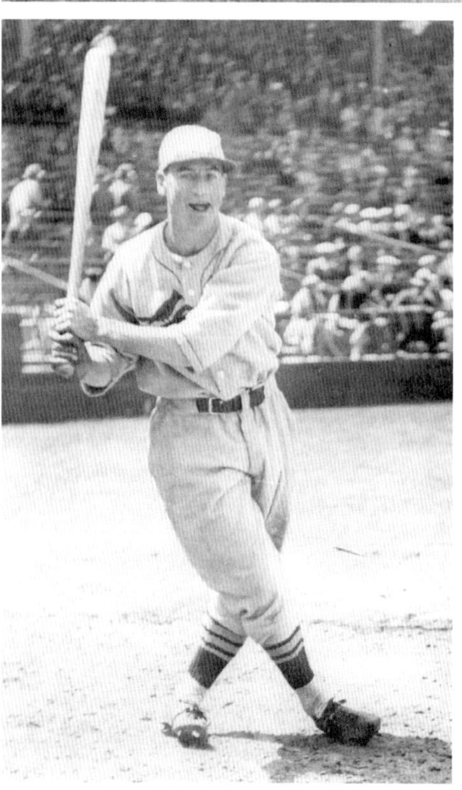

GEORGE ALOYS "SHOWBOAT" FISHER (1899–1994). He was born George Fischer in Kossuth County's Wesley, and his family soon moved to Minnesota. Eventually, he changed the spelling of his last name to "Fisher." Beginning in 1919, his baseball career covered 15 years, two in the majors. With the St. Louis Cardinals in 1930, Fisher earned the handle "Showboat" by batting .374. He went on to play for that city's 1932 American League Browns.

J.L. WILKINSON. Born in 1878, Algona native James Leslie Wilkinson pitched semipro ball as a young man. Following a debilitating wrist injury, he became a baseball entrepreneur. After forming the All Nations team in 1912, he later reorganized the club as the Monarchs. The Kansas City Monarchs became the longest-running franchise in Negro Leagues baseball history. (Courtesy of Larry Lester, Noirtech Research, Inc.)

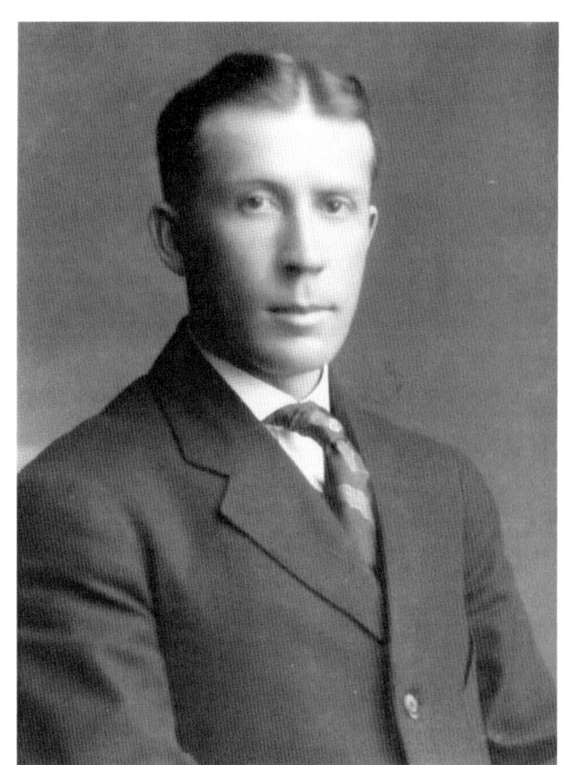

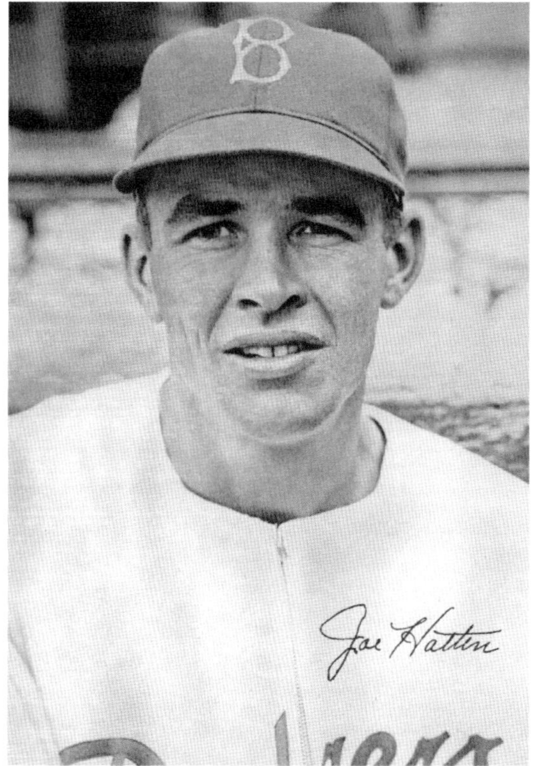

JOSEPH "JOE" HILARIAN HATTEN (1916–1988). Growing up in Bancroft, young left-throwing Joe Hatten first pitched for a farm group, the Country Cubs. By 1939, he began his 19-year professional career. In addition to his minor-league stays, he pitched five prime seasons with the Brooklyn Dodgers starting in 1946 and part of two with the Chicago Cubs. Through 1960, he garnered a lifetime ERA of 3.69.

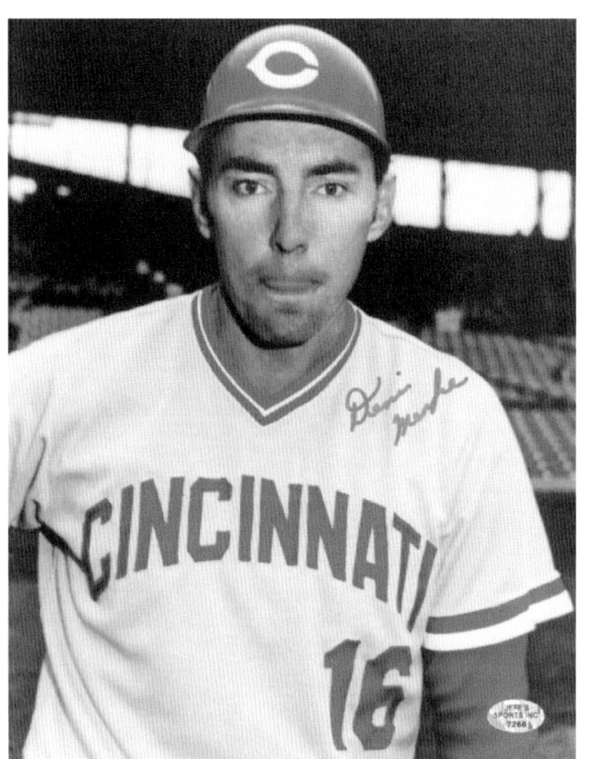

Denis John Menke (1940–). Infielder Denis Menke grew up on a farm near Bancroft, absorbing baseball expertise through his father, Walter, and uncle, John. They both played semipro ball for a number of clubs, including the Bancroft Lions of 1950. Denis began his 13-year major-league career with the Milwaukee Braves in 1962. With Atlanta in 1967 and 1968, he then went to Houston, where he appeared in two All-Star Games, 1969 and 1970. At Cincinnati in 1972 and 1973, he closed out his big-league career back in Houston in 1974.

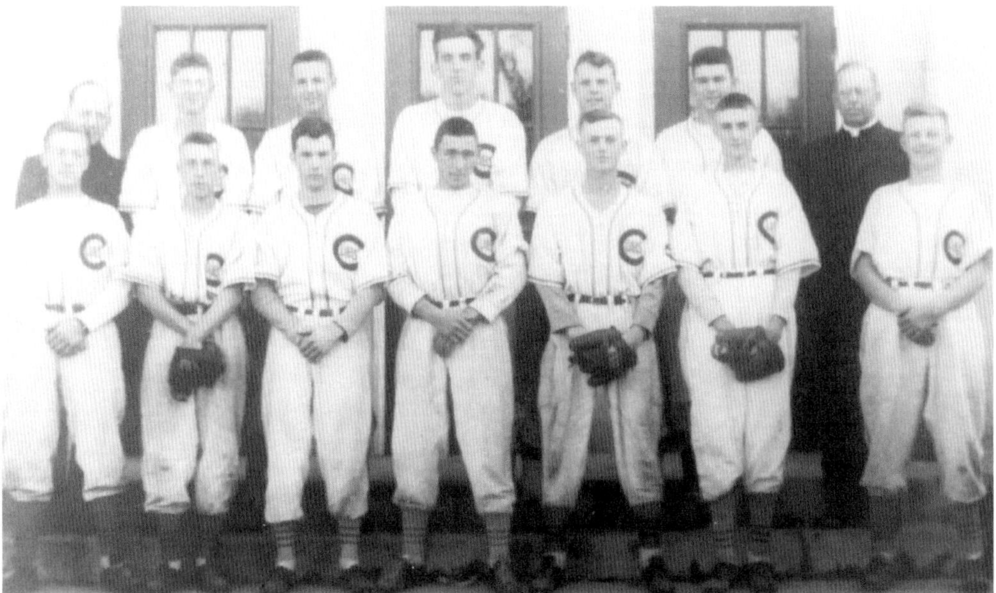

Bancroft's St. John's High School, State Champions, 1943. Sporting Chicago Cubs spring training uniforms purchased from a Humboldt team, Bancroft's St. John's High School team poses after its state championship victory. Pitcher and second baseman Tommy Murray, who was later commemorated by the building of Bancroft Memorial Park, is seen in the first row, sixth from left. His brother John may be second from left in the back row. (Courtesy of Tom Murray.)

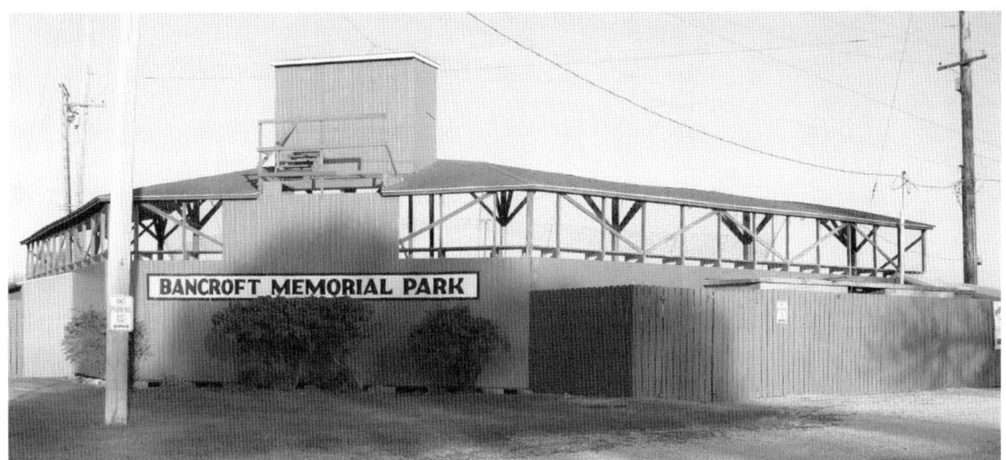

BANCROFT MEMORIAL PARK. Opened in 1948, Bancroft Memorial Park came about as a community effort. The total cost, exceeding $30,000, was financed with proceeds from Joe Hatten Day and contributions from the American Legion, the chamber of commerce, and private individuals. The property for the lighted park was donated by local men, including W.A. Murray, whose son Tommy perished in World War II in 1945. (Courtesy of Lisa Kunkel.)

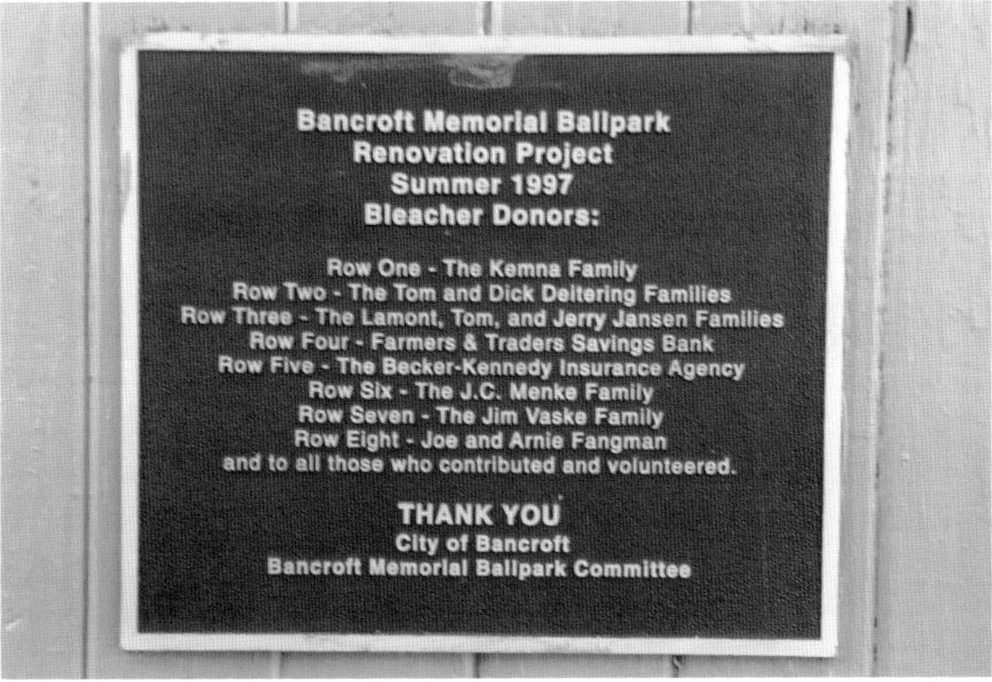

BANCROFT MEMORIAL PARK CELEBRATES 50 YEARS. In 1998, the town that rarely exceeded a population of 1,000 celebrated the 50th anniversary of its beloved baseball park. A campaign to refurbish the stadium yielded both $40,000 in funding and time donated by an untold number of Bancroft residents of all ages. This commemorative plaque recognizes those who helped with the bleachers. Note the surname Menke (relatives of Denis Menke; see page 40). (Courtesy of Lisa Kunkel.)

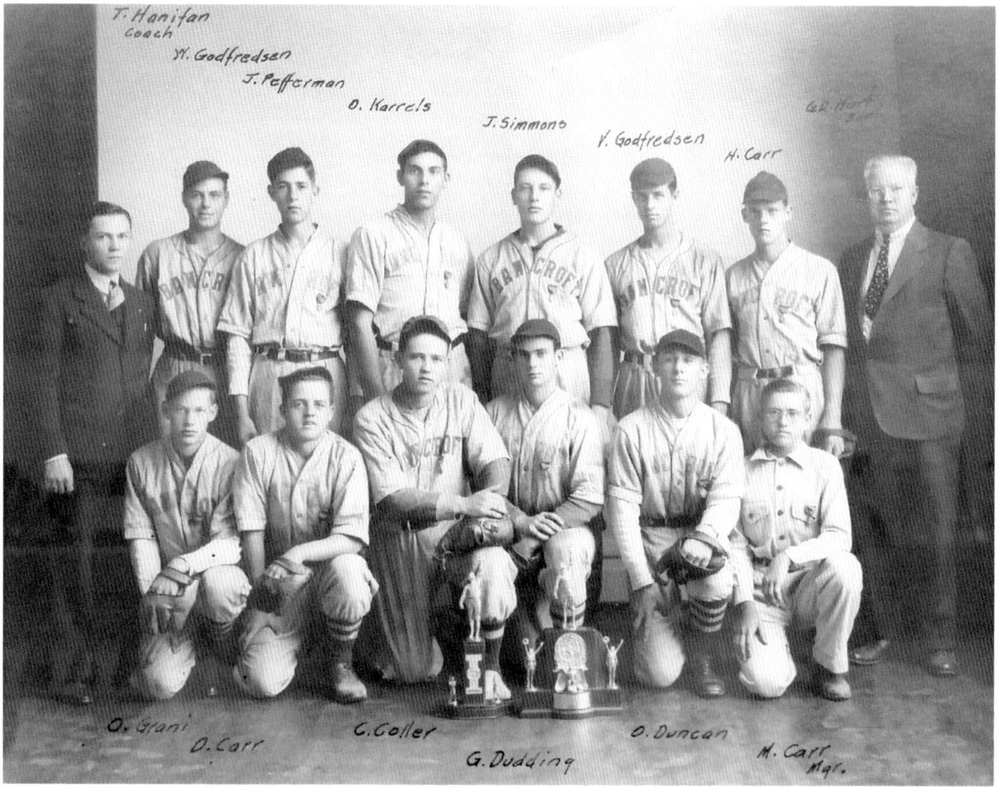

BANCROFT PUBLIC HIGH SCHOOL, STATE CHAMPIONS, 1940. One of Bancroft's abundance of champion baseball teams, the Bancroft Public High School squad of 1940 poses. From left to right are (first row) Oran Grani, Donald Carr, Cecil Collar, Gerald Dudding, Orville Duncan, and Marcus Carr; (second row) Thomas Hanifan, Walt Godfredson, Joe Pefferman, Otto Karels, John Simmons, Vern Godfredson, Hugh Carr, and Guy Hart. (Courtesy of Lisa Kunkel.)

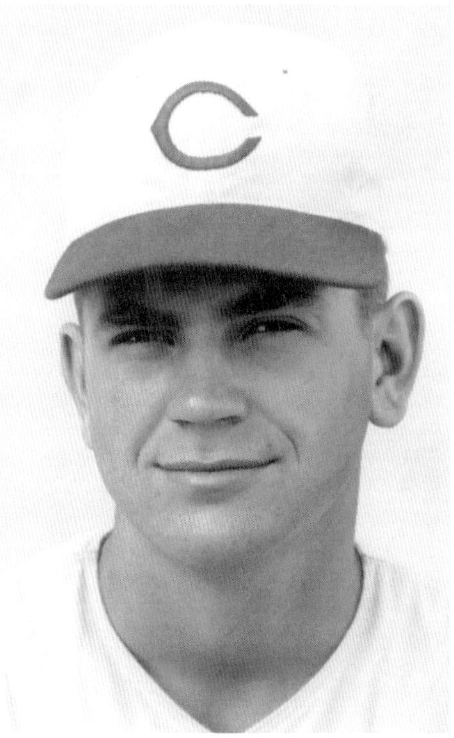

DAVID WENDELL "DAVE" SKAUGSTAD (1940–). Born in Algona and attending high school in Compton, California, left-handed pitcher Dave Skaugstad signed as an amateur free agent with the Cincinnati Reds in 1957. He appeared in two games with that club and spent the remainder of his professional career, from 1958 to 1965, in the minor leagues, interrupted by military service between 1961 and 1963.

BANCROFT'S JOE HATTEN. While with the Brooklyn Dodgers in 1948, Joe Hatten threw 51 pitches in a five-inning complete-game shutout against Cincinnati, the fewest number of pitches for a complete game in major-league history. On May 15, 1983, his hometown of Bancroft dedicated a street named Joe Hatten Drive just west of Bancroft Memorial Park. Shortly after that, the retired major-leaguer arrived for the town's annual Germanfest.

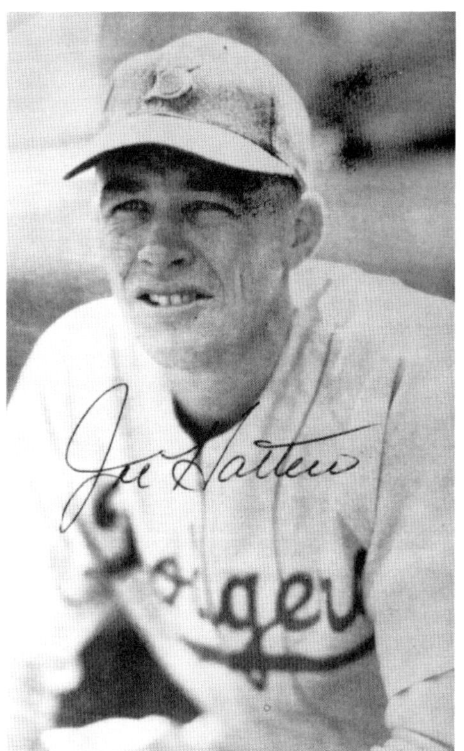

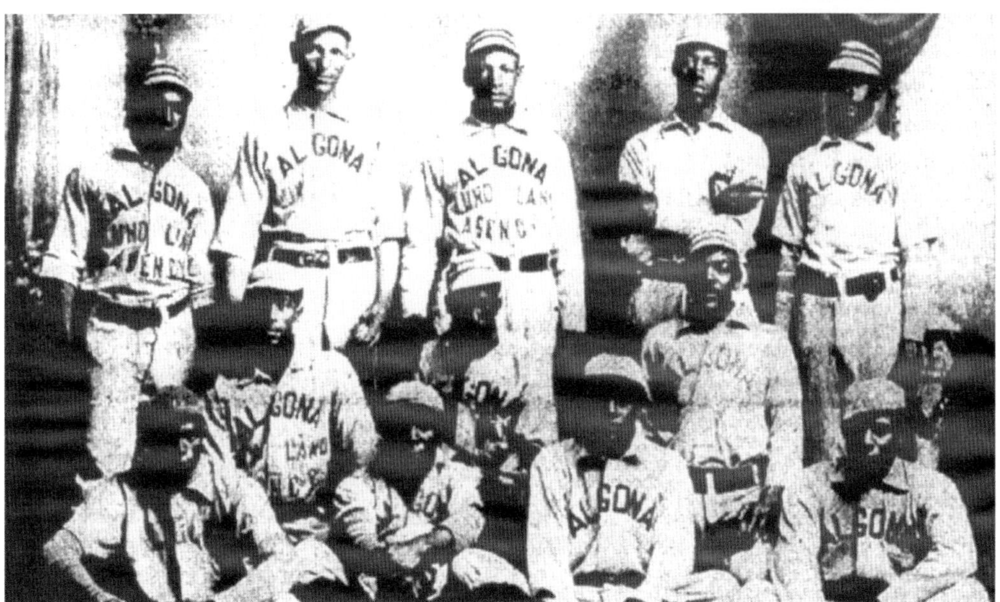

ALGONA BROWNIES. Established in 1902, the Algona-based barnstorming baseball team was at first comprised of both black and white players. It was widely recognized as the fastest team west of the Mississippi. Some of its best talent, including inveterate catcher and first baseman Chappie Johnson, came from Chicago Negro League clubs. In 1903, it was an all-black club. In 1938, the team was revived, recruiting members of the previous year's Brooklyn Giants.

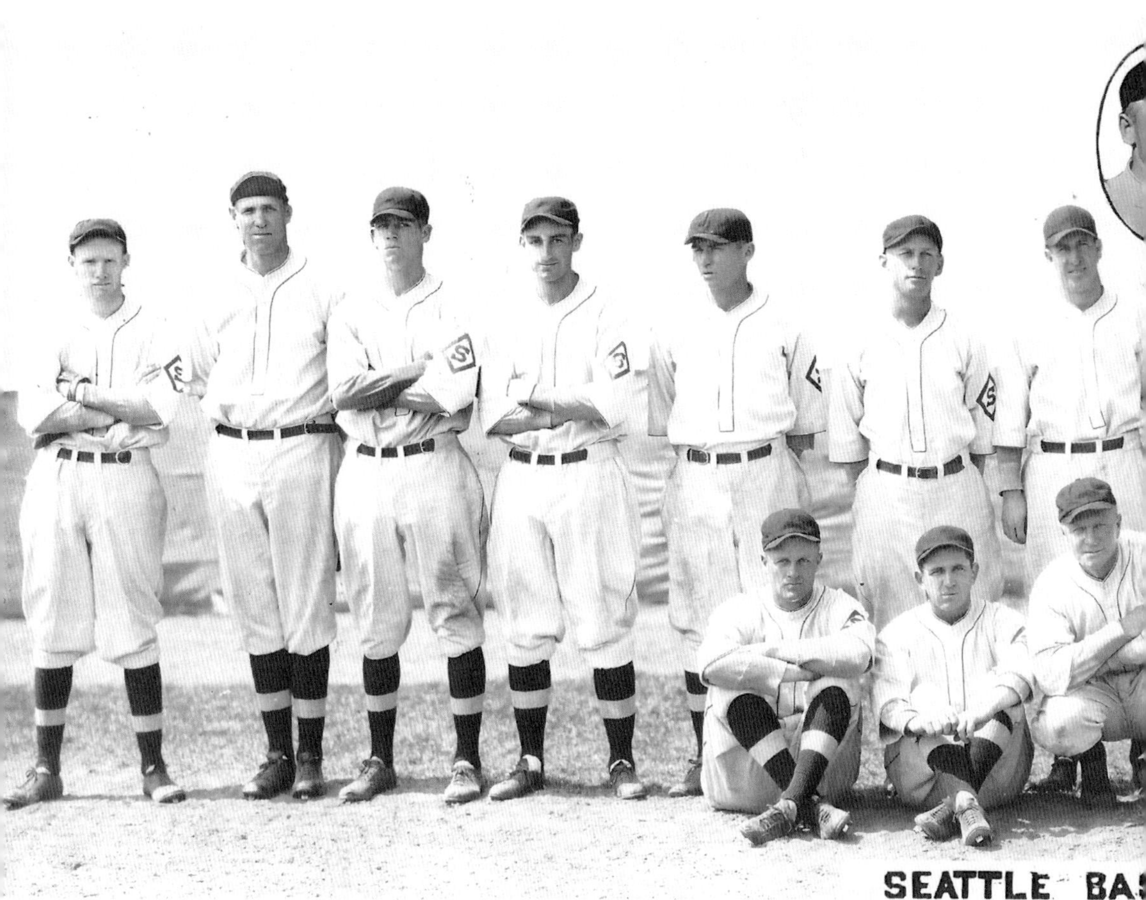

GEORGE ANTON STUELAND (1899–1964). Born in Algona, pitcher George Stueland began his professional baseball career with the Chicago Cubs in 1921. Following three unremarkable years there, he landed with the AA Pacific Coast League Seattle Indians in 1924. That season proved to be his best, as he blossomed into the team's star right-handed hurler. He tallied a win-loss record

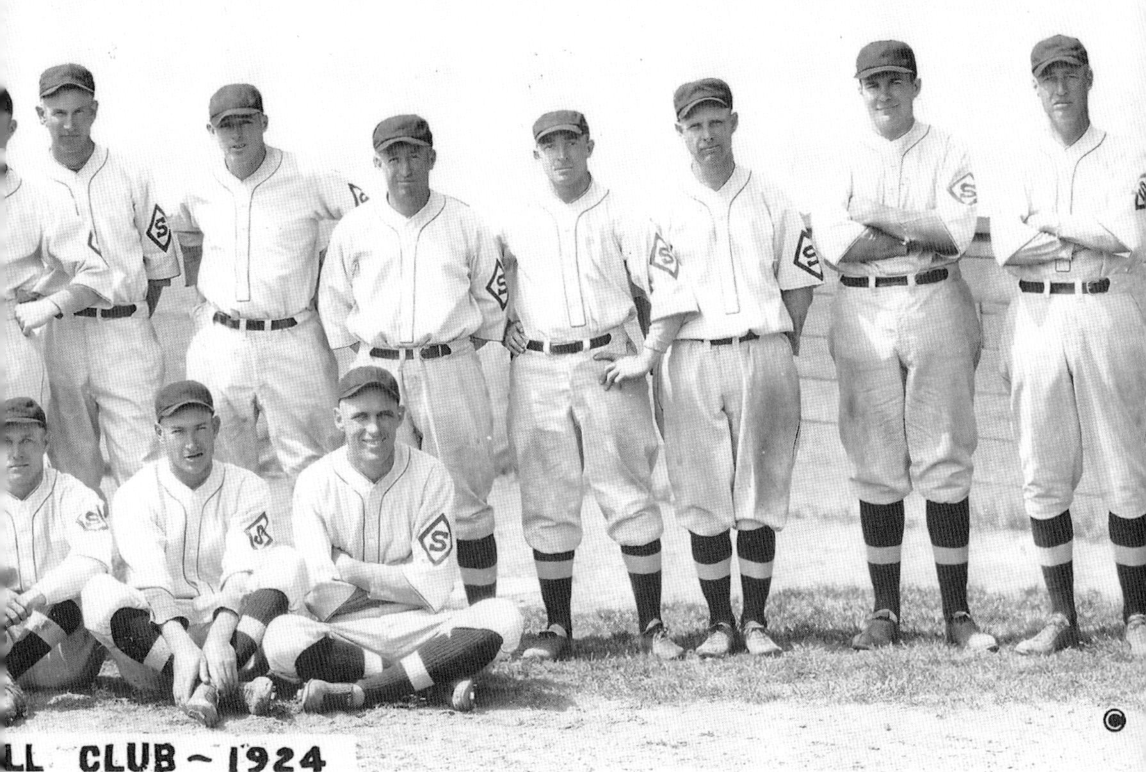

of 18-13, helping the Indians win the league pennant that year. He then had a brief stint with the Cubs in 1925 and played for various minor-league clubs through 1928. In this team photograph of the 1924 Seattle club, Stueland is seen on the far right. (Courtesy of David Eskenazi.)

Ball Games

AT ELDORA

A Big Double Header

SUNDAY, AUGUST 8th

CHIP'S ALL-STARS

of Lone Rock vs. Eldora

These Lone Rock lads are the fastest colored team in the state. Eldora trimmed them once and they beat us once, so this will be a real battle.

Double Header Sunday at 2. Admission 75c

Single Game Mon., Aug. 9

FRIDAY AND SATURDAY

Gilkerson's Union Giants

Single Games called at 3:00 p. m. Admission 50c

CHIP'S ALL-STARS. Owned and managed by local businessman Glen "Chip" Sharp, Chip's All-Stars represented Kossuth County's tiny town of Lone Rock in 1925 and 1926. An all-black aggregation, the men traveled on a bus, drawing huge crowds wherever they played. They competed against professional traveling teams, semipro teams, and any team that would challenge them. This newspaper ad from 1926 provides the flavor of their promotions. (Courtesy of *Hardin County Ledger*.)

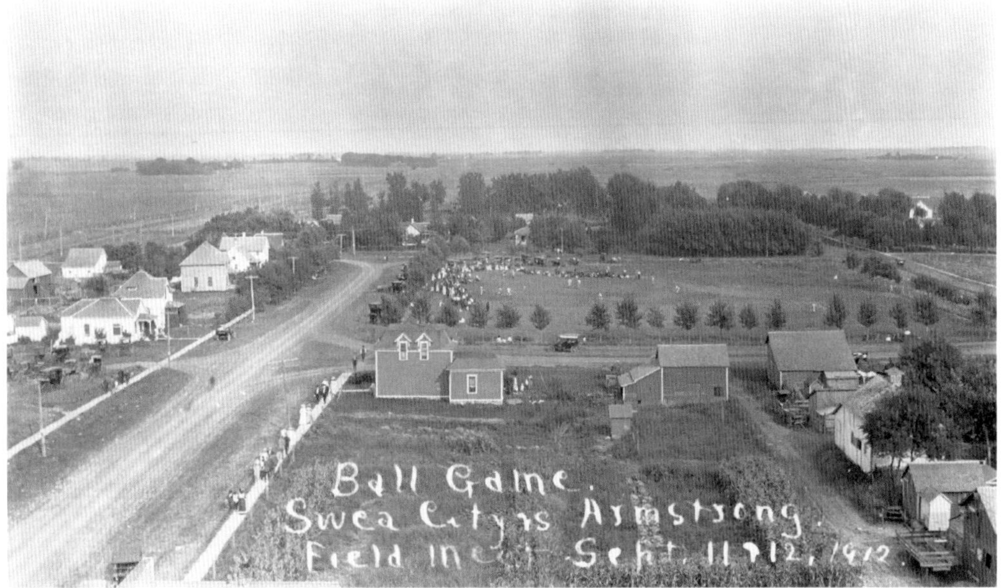

BALL GAME IN SWEA CITY, 1912. Another exceptional image captured at Swea City (see page 37), this aerial view of a ball game in progress reveals much about the times. Notice the many vehicles parked near the playing field. In this rural community, many of its citizens traveled from nearby farms to witness the event. (Courtesy of State Historical Society of Iowa, Des Moines, William Shirley Collection.)

Lyon, O'Brien, Osceola, and Palo Alto Counties

Rock Rapids, the seat of Lyon County, and George are the county's most populous cities. The Rock Rapids Browns played in the Class D Iowa–South Dakota League of 1902. But even little Doon had a baseball team. In 1910, it was charged with disturbing the peace on Sunday. A jury of its peers found in the club's favor. In 1934, the semipro Northwest Iowa League's eight teams included squads from George and tiny Alvord, Lyon County's smallest town.

Primghar is the seat of O'Brien County, but Sheldon is the county's largest city by far. A professional club called the Sheldon-Primghar Hyphens was a member of the Class D Iowa–South Dakota League of 1902–1903. Like O'Brien County's other towns, Paullina always sponsored a baseball team. As early as 1904, its game with Le Mars at the Cherokee County Fair broke up with a row. Spirited town rivalries were quite common at the time.

Of the five towns that comprise Osceola County, the seat of Sibley is the largest, with a population never reaching 3,000. Nonetheless, the town is rife with baseball history. For instance, in July 1906, it hosted a contest between its club and a team made up of Sioux Indians. Feathers and all, the Indians split a doubleheader with Sibley. During the second, evening game, the grounds were illuminated with 40 gasoline arc lights. Ten years later, future major-leaguer Herman Bell pitched for Sibley's high school team.

Emmetsburg, the seat of Palo Alto County, had a team that was a member of the Class D Iowa League of Professional Baseball Clubs of 1912. And there was no dearth of baseball in the county's other towns. Little Ruthven, in 1916, held a match between the Chicago Union Giants and Bancroft's club at its Old Settlers Picnic. Early in the 20th century, the county produced two major-league pitchers, Frank Mulroney and Gil Paulsen. In 1970, former big-league pitcher Gene Ford, who was born in Webster County, died in Emmetsburg after living there for years.

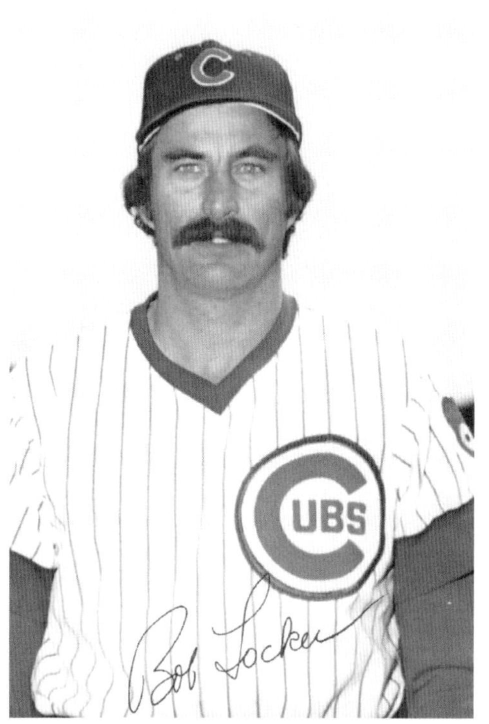

ROBERT AWTRY "BOB" LOCKER (1938–). Graduating from George High School in his hometown and then Iowa State University, right-handed pitcher Bob Locker recorded an impressive major-league career. Following several years in the minors, he landed with the Chicago White Sox in 1965. After developing his sinker ball, he then played for Milwaukee, Oakland, and the Chicago Cubs before retiring after 1976. His telling career ERA is 2.69.

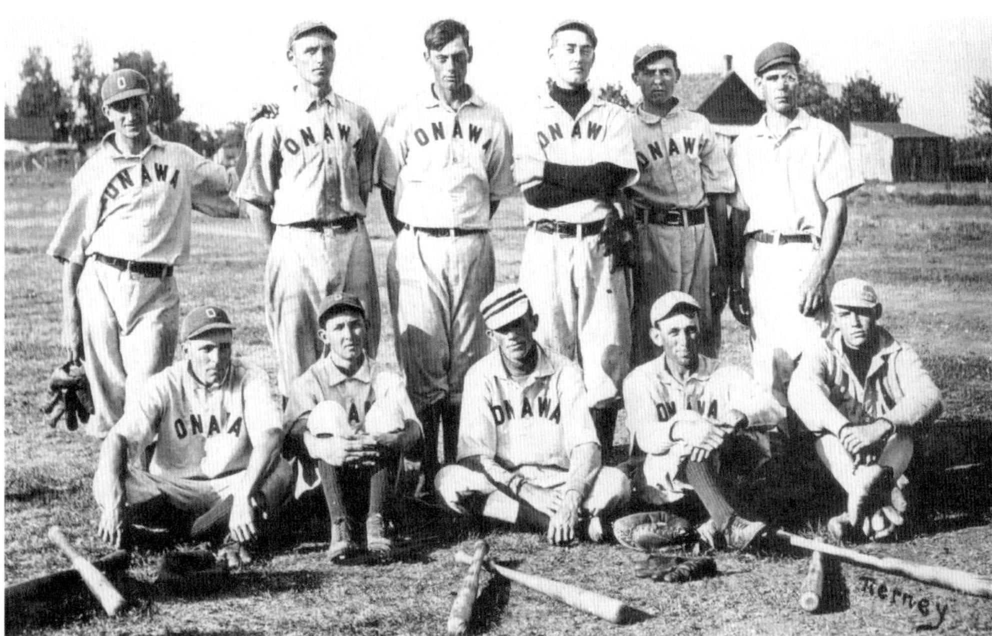

ONAWA BASEBALL CLUB. Although this team was thought to be an Onawa, Iowa, club of 1910, further investigation reveals that it is actually the town's semipro team of 1902. Buster Brown, who later pitched for the Rock Rapids Browns, played for Monona County's Onawa that year. He is seen standing fourth from the left in the back row. Monona County is just south of Northwest Iowa's Woodbury County.

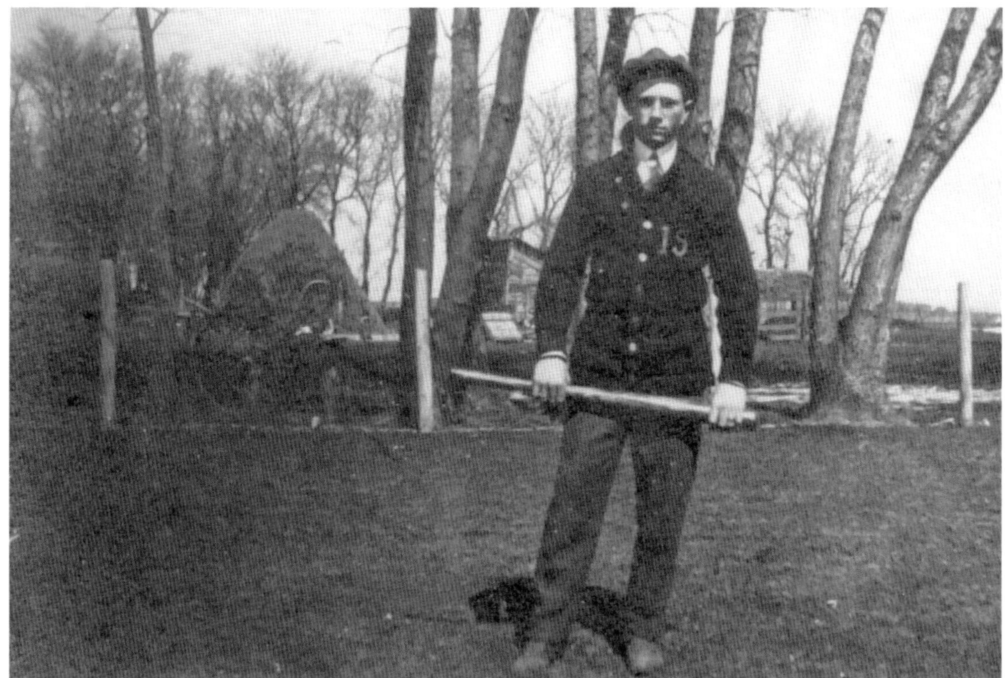

CHARLES EDWARD "BUSTER" BROWN (1881–1914). Born in Boone County, bordering Northwest Iowa's Webster County, pitcher Buster Brown later became captain of Iowa State University's team. In this snapshot, he wears a sweater bearing the school's initials. Brown, also known as "Yank," pitched for Lyon County's Rock Rapids Browns of 1903. His National League career spanned nine years at St. Louis, Philadelphia, and Boston, with an ERA of 3.21.

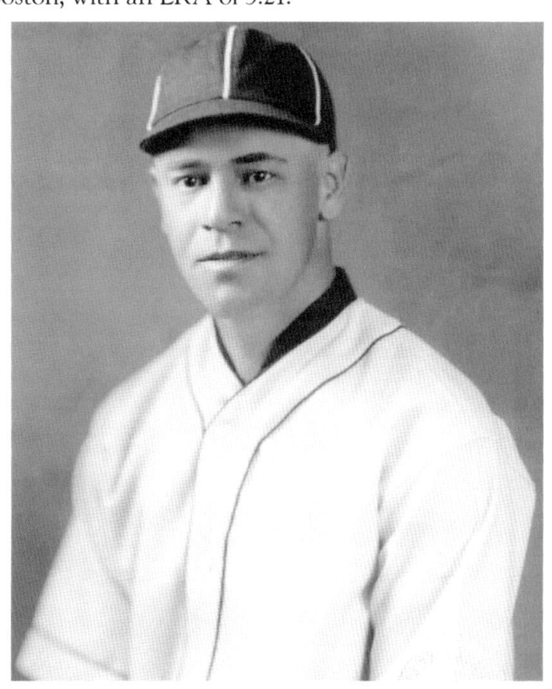

ARTHUR LEE "ART" EWOLDT (1894–1977). Paullina native Art "Sheriff" Ewoldt played semipro ball for Aurelia, Cherokee County, before turning professional. A pitcher at first, he soon switched to the infield. Although his only major-league assignment, with the Philadelphia Athletics in 1919, was brief, he played for numerous clubs from 1913 through 1929. Later, he managed the semipro Spencer Cubs. (Courtesy of T. Scott Brandon.)

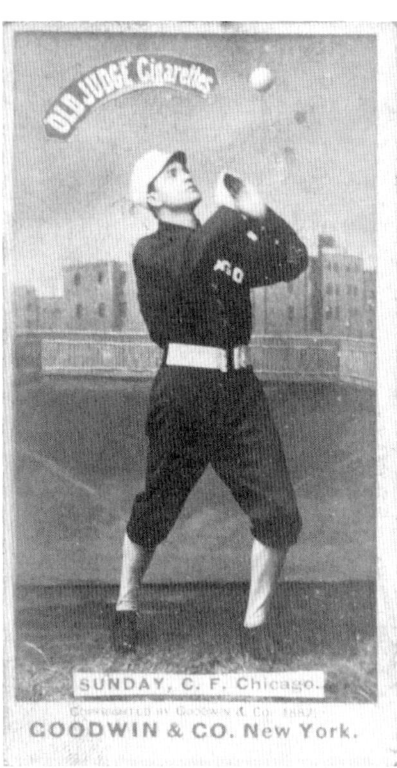

BILLY SUNDAY. During Sunday's preaching heyday, curiosity-seekers from Palo Alto County traveled to Chautauquas and other mass gatherings to witness the baseball player turned dynamic evangelist's oratory. But some local newspaper editors criticized his moneymaking venture. In retort, a former resident of the county's town of West Bend defended Sunday in an editorial, calling him a wonderful man and a great ballplayer.

GUILFORD PAUL HANS "GIL" PAULSEN (1902–1994). Born in Graettinger, Palo Alto County, Gil Paulsen pitched for various minor-league clubs from 1925 to 1932, interrupted by two innings in the majors with the St. Louis Cardinals in 1925. In 1935, he grew a beard and had a successful season with the barnstorming House of David team. This image is of his signed St. Louis Cardinals index card.

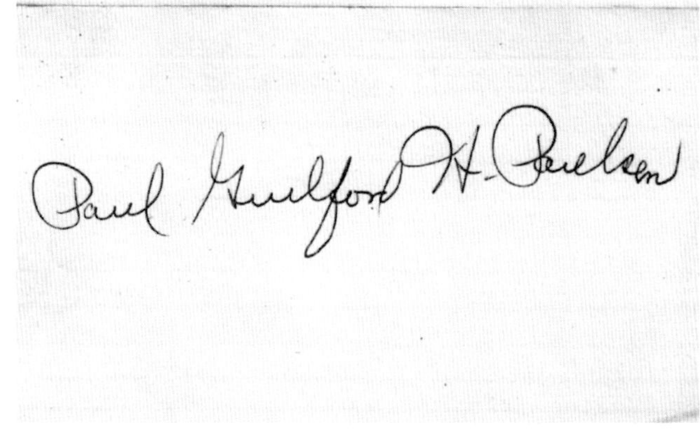

Herman "Hi" Bell (1897–1949). Born in Kentucky, Hi Bell grew up in Sibley, Iowa, where he pitched high school ball. He played for the St. Louis Cardinals and the New York Giants between 1924 and 1934. In 1924, he started and won both games of a doubleheader for St. Louis. He also pitched in three World Series, in 1926 and 1930 with St. Louis and in 1933 with the Giants.

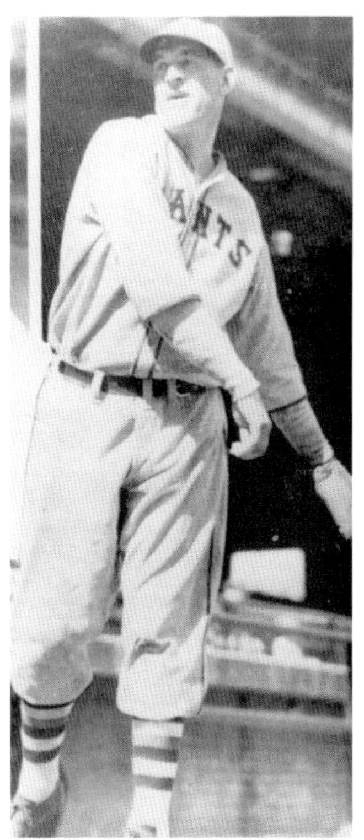

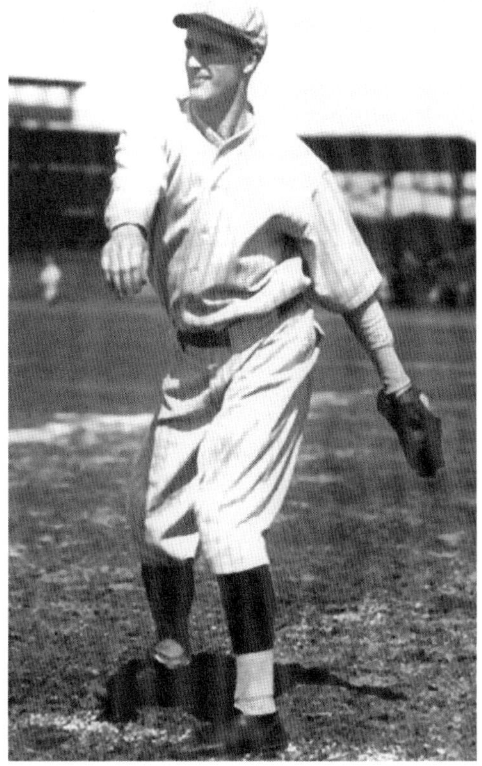

Francis Joseph "Frank" Mulroney (1903–1885). Born in little Mallord, Palo Alto County, Frank Mulroney was a relief pitcher for the Boston Red Sox in 1930. He started his professional baseball career with the Western League Des Moines team in 1928 and wrapped it up with Wichita/Muskogee Oilers in 1933. (Courtesy of Society for American Baseball Research.)

ESTHERVILLE, EMMET COUNTY, IOWA, MAY 15, 1912.

OFFICIAL

Baseball Schedule--Season 1912

IOWA STATE LEAGUE

Read	Estherville at Home	Emmetsburg at Home	Clear Lake at Home	Mason City at Home	Fort Dodge at Home
Estherville	**The Democrat**	July 19-20-21* August 10-11*	June 10-11 June 29-30* August 17-18*	June 19-20 July 1-3 August 19-20	June 15-16* July 17-18 August 8-9
Emmetsburg	May 24-25 July 3-4-4† July 13-14* August 13-14	**For**	June 13-14 July 6-7* July 27-28*	June 1-2* June 26-27 July 24-25	May 30†-31 June 29-30* August 17-18* September 1*-2†
Clear Lake	June 1-2* June 24-25 August 1-2 August 22-23	June 3-4 June 22-23* August 3-4* August 15-16	**Reliable**	May 23-24 July 3-4† July 13-14* Aug. 10-11* -24-25 September 21	May 25-26* June 19-20 July 1-2 August 13-14
Mason City	June 6-7 July 11-12 August 3-4* August 26-27	June 8-9* July 9-10 August 1-2 August 28-29	May 29-30† June 15-16* July 4† 17-18 August 8-9 September 1	**Baseball**	May 21-22 July 6-7* July 19-20-21*
Fort Dodge	June 8-9* July 9-10 August 24-25*	June 10-11 June 24-25 July 11-12 August 26-27	June 6-7 June 26-27 July 24-25 August 19-20 August 28-29	June 13-14 June 22-23* July 27-28* August 22-23	**News**

*Sundays †Holidays

IOWA STATE LEAGUE SCHEDULE, 1912. Also known as the Iowa League of Professional Baseball Players, the Iowa League of 1912 included three Northwest Iowa teams—Estherville, Emmetsburg, and Fort Dodge. This official schedule appeared in local newspapers. When the league was being formed, Emmetsburg organized a stock company, raising $1,500 to back its team.

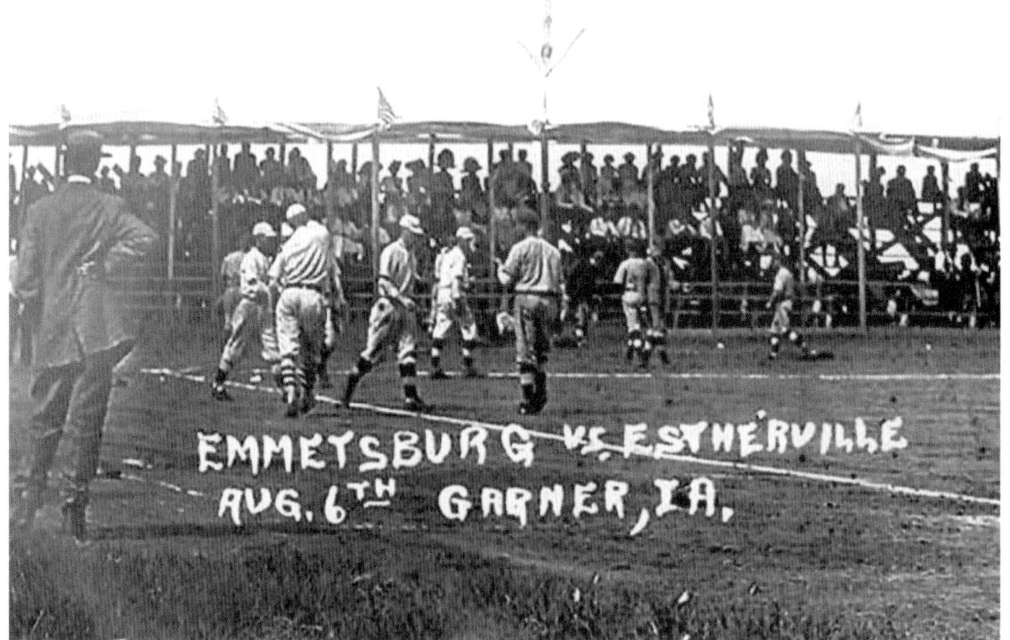

EMMETSBURG VERSUS ESTHERVILLE, 1912. This vintage postcard shows players between innings of a game between Iowa League teams Emmetsburg and Estherville. The match occurred at a tournament held at Garner, Hancock County, which borders Kossuth County. The Fort Dodge and Mason City teams also competed in that series. (Courtesy of Palo Alto US Gen Web Project.)

Plymouth and Pocahontas Counties

Plymouth County towns nurtured their fair share of major-league pitchers prior to the mid-20th century. Le Mars, the county's seat and largest city, is the birthplace of Walt Marbet, who pitched for the St. Louis Cardinals in 1913. After attending high school in Le Mars, Homer Hillebrand pitched for the Pittsburgh Pirates in the early 1900s. Big-league hurlers Joe Lotz and Johnny Niggeling both grew up in Remsen, the county's second-largest town. Harry Gaspar spent his youth and honed his pitching prowess in similar-sized Kingsley prior to his major-league debut. Like-sized Akron's left-handed pitcher Lefty Swift played for the International League Baltimore Orioles in the early 1940s. Other than pitchers, Struble, the county's least populous town, yielded left fielder Art Jahn. He played for three National League clubs in the 1930s. Of course, one must also consider the area's numerous skilled athletes, such as pitchers Clare Bertram and Snakes Trafford, who never made it to the big show. It is important to remember the many semipro and amateur clubs that at one time represented every town in the county. All of the men whose names are mentioned here played for such teams.

Today, Pocahontas County's entire population numbers less than that of the town of Le Mars. Its seat of the same name is comparatively small. Nonetheless, the county's baseball tradition has always been integral to its culture. In 1911, Pocahontas featured matches between two of its clubs, the East Sides and the West Sides. The county's towns faced clubs from a wide area. In 1926, Pocahontas County's Havelock defeated Kossuth County's West Bend. The two factions met at a Farm Union picnic at the John Methe farm near Havelock. Little Rolfe hosted a county high school tournament in 1939. But locals could also witness semipro ball at home as late as 1950. Fonda brought in paid outsiders to field its Fonda Cubs that year, its center fielder coming from Hollywood, Florida. Twenty years later, the town of Pocahontas saw its native son Larry Biittner begin his 14-season major-league career.

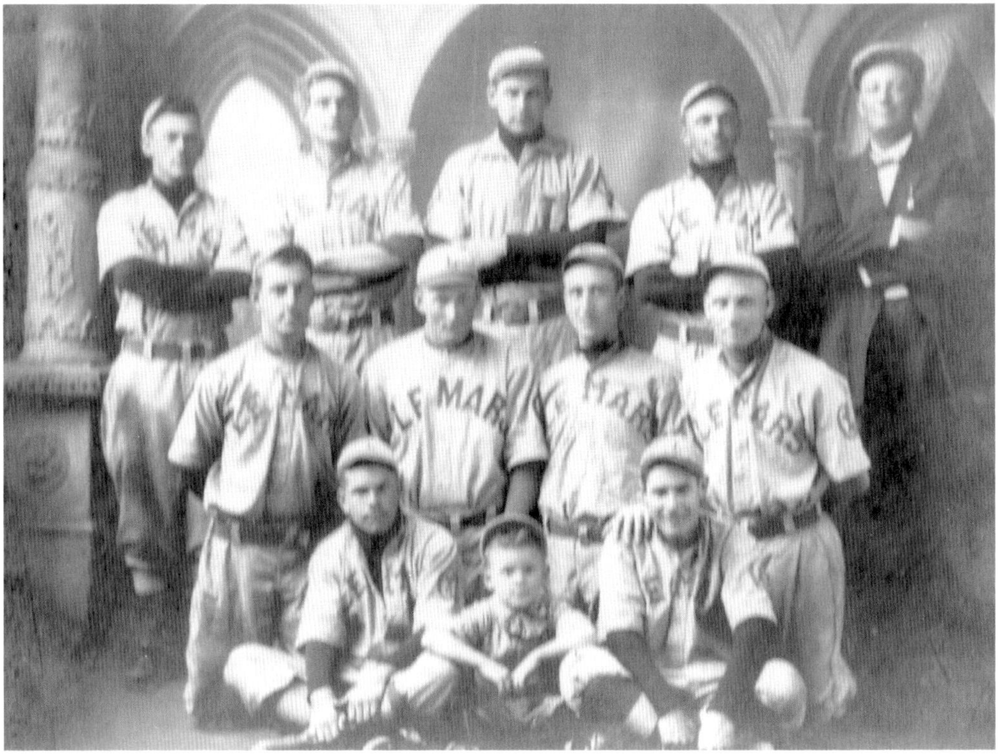

LE MARS BLACKBIRDS, 1903. For years, this photograph of a Le Mars baseball team was undated. Recently, it was determined that it is very likely the Iowa–South Dakota League Blackbirds of 1903. Retired major-league player Bobby Black managed the club, and Branch Rickey caught. The man in the dark suit looks like Black, and the player third from left in the back row looks like Rickey. (Courtesy of Plymouth County Historical Museum.)

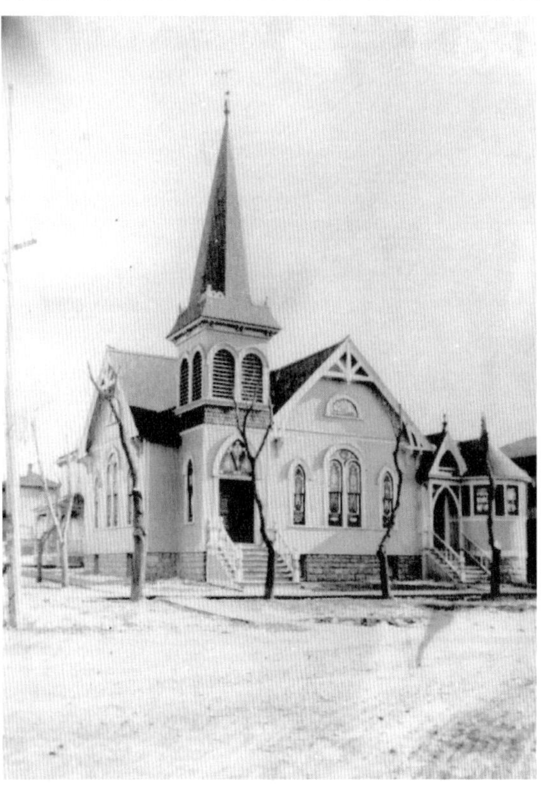

LE MARS GERMAN METHODIST CHURCH, 1910. A Methodist, baseball's renowned Branch Ricky refused to play the game on Sunday, citing his religious convictions. As this was the Methodist church in Le Mars in 1903, it is probable that he attended services here. (Courtesy of United Methodist Church of Le Mars.)

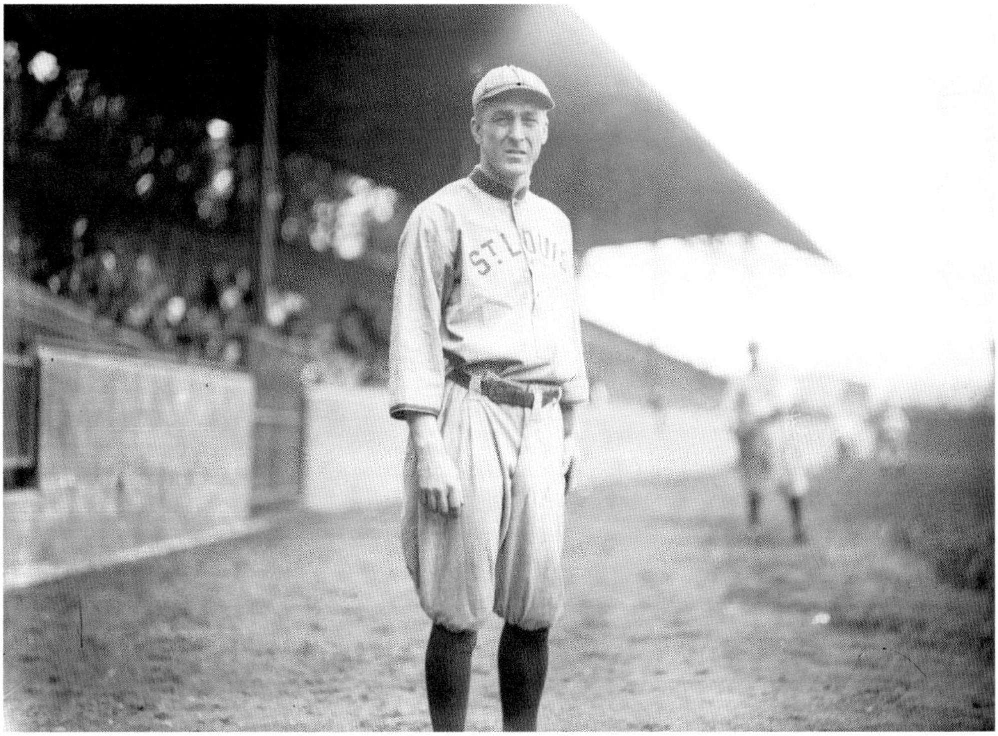

BRANCH RICKEY. In 1903, Branch Rickey came from the Central League Terre Haute Hottentots to catch for the Le Mars Blackbirds. The team captured its league pennant that year with a .607 average. At the conclusion of the season, each player was presented with a gold medal inscribed "I.S.D pennant winners, Le Mars." (Courtesy of Library of Congress.)

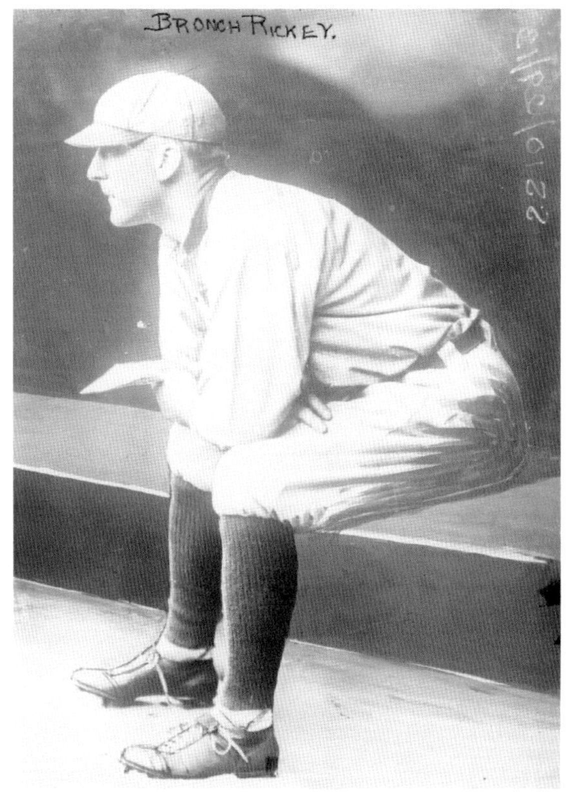

BRANCH RICKEY, 1913. Following his playing career, Branch Rickey managed the St. Louis Browns and the St. Louis Cardinals. Then, as the Cardinals' general manager, he devised the modern farm system. Eventually, as president and general manager of the Brooklyn Dodgers, he signed Jackie Robinson, integrating major-league baseball. (Courtesy of Library of Congress, Bain Collection.)

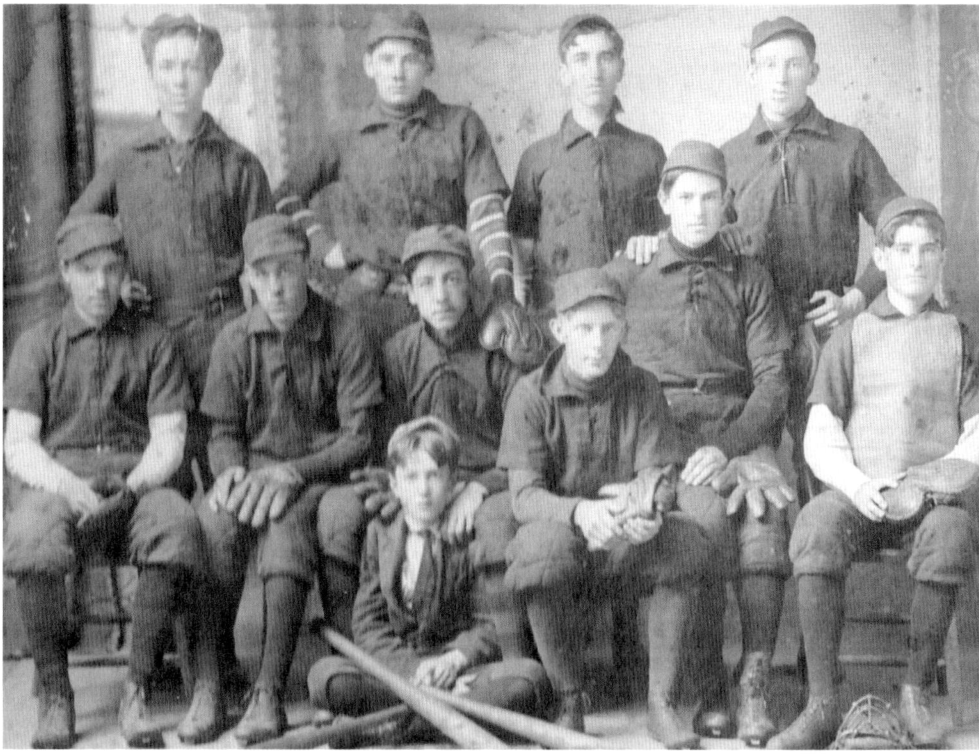

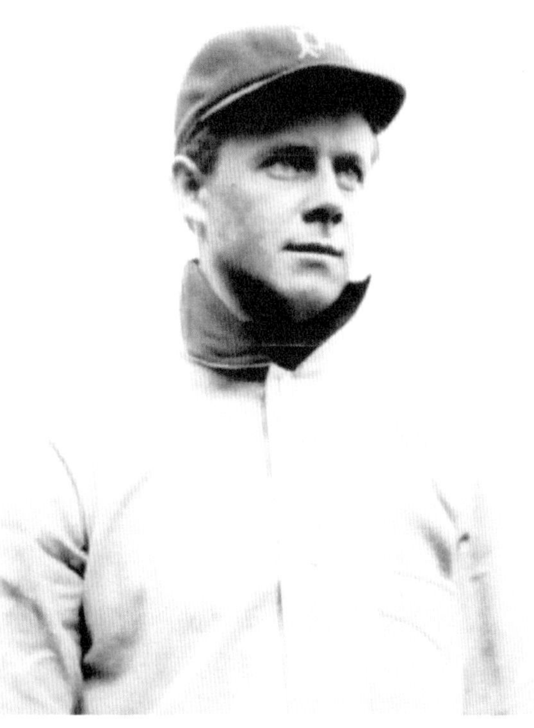

LE MARS HIGH SCHOOL BASEBALL TEAM, 1905. Members of this Le Mars High School team are identified on the back of the photograph. The names are listed as Art Honnold, Pete Haas, Lew Hentges, Clyde Rabey, Ralph Smith, Oz Bartels, An Adler, Wally Wernli, Art Pemberton, Pat Coffey, and Randall Sammis. (Courtesy of Plymouth County Historical Museum.)

HOMER HILLER HENRY HILLEBRAND (1879–1908). Pitcher and center fielder Homer Hillebrand played for the Pittsburgh Pirates in 1905, 1906, and 1908. Born in Illinois, he grew up in Le Mars, where he attended its public high school. He was a member of its 1897 football squad, and his brother Arthur was its coach.

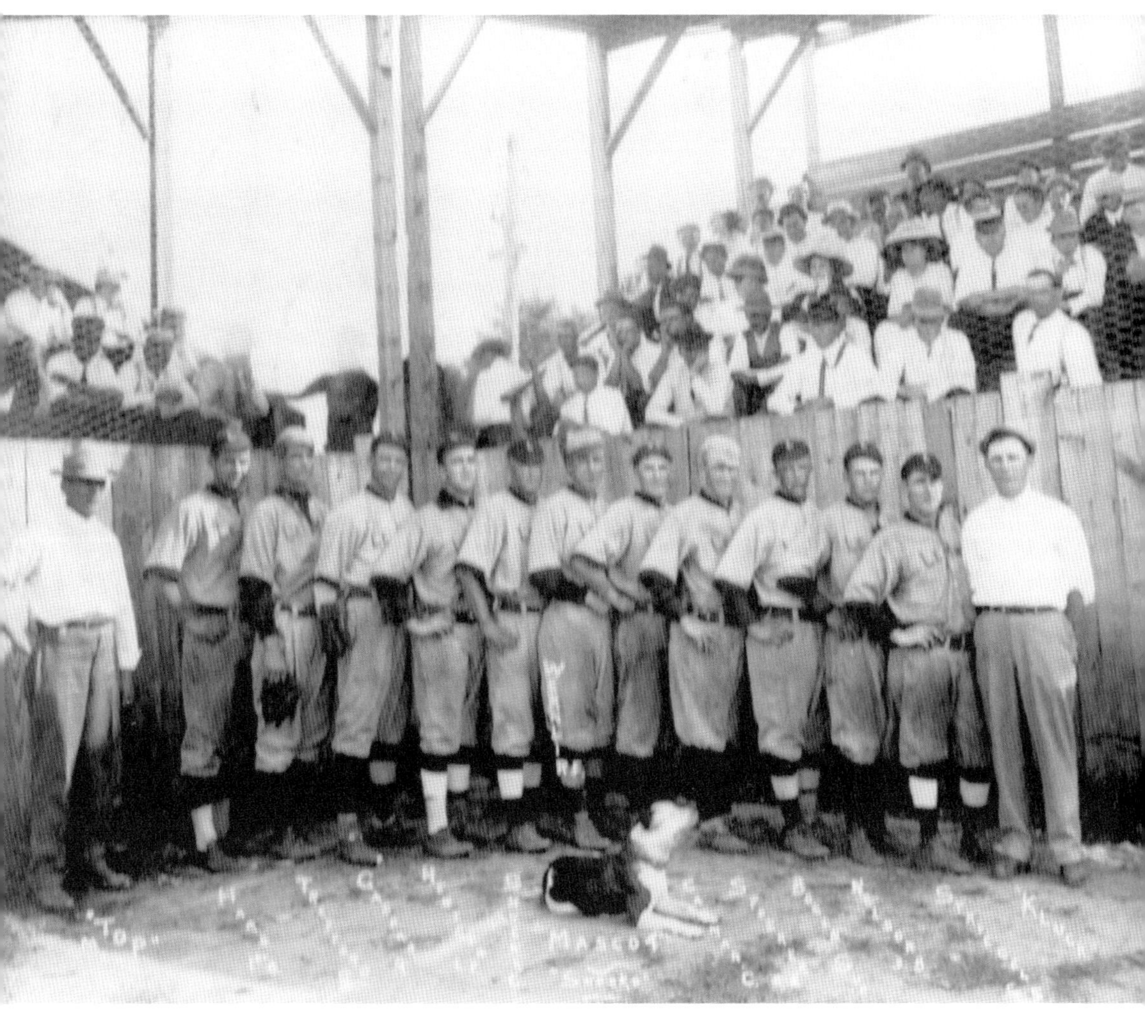

Le Mars Baseball Team, 1913. Because of the presence of pitcher Harry Gaspar and the mascot Snooks, the year of this photograph has been narrowed down to 1913. Gaspar was in the majors from 1909 to 1912 and with Sioux City's club from 1914 to 1916. George Kluckhohn's pet bull terrier, the team's mascot Snooks, died in 1916 at age eight. From left to right are manager Toppings, Haas, Trafford, Gaspar, Hentges, Sheunk, Wernli, Cadman, Spoerer, Bogen, Nelson, Striegel, and Kluckhohn. Of course, Snooks takes center stage. (Courtesy of Plymouth County Historical Museum.)

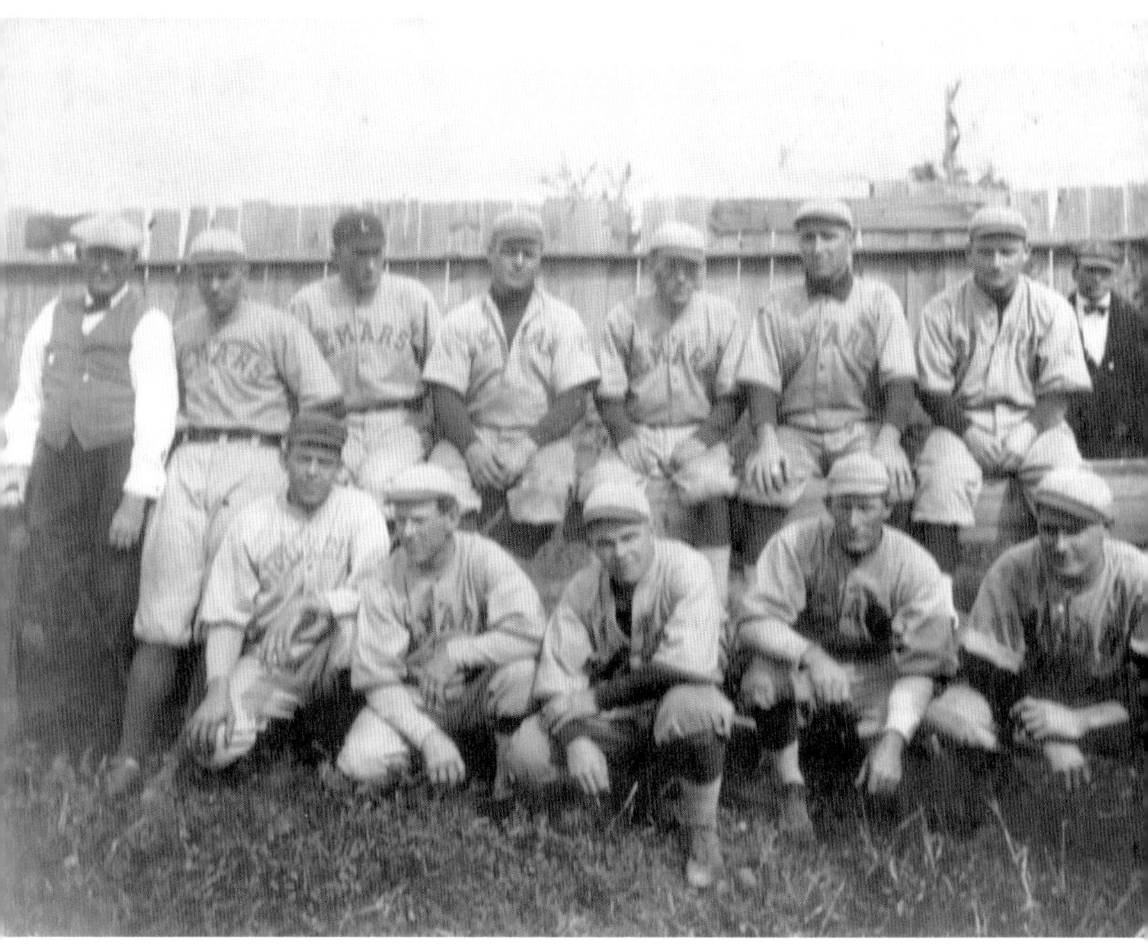

Le Mars Baseball Team, 1914. Seen posing at Athletic Park north of the Le Mars business district on September 4, 1914, the Le Mars team played an exhibition game with the Sioux City Indians that day. Notice the player on the far left in the first row wearing a Sioux City jersey. The Indians' Harry Gaspar pitched for Le Mars that day. By then, he and his wife, Coyla, lived in Le Mars and operated a photography studio there. (Courtesy of Plymouth County Historical Museum.)

HARRY GASPAR'S BASEBALL CARD. Harry Lambert Gaspar was born in Quorn, Iowa, in 1883. His parents soon moved to nearby Kingsley, where he grew up. After several years in the minor leagues, he pitched for the Cincinnati Reds from 1909 to 1912. After that, he played for and managed several minor-league and semipro teams in Iowa until at least 1923. This image of him is the one most commonly seen.

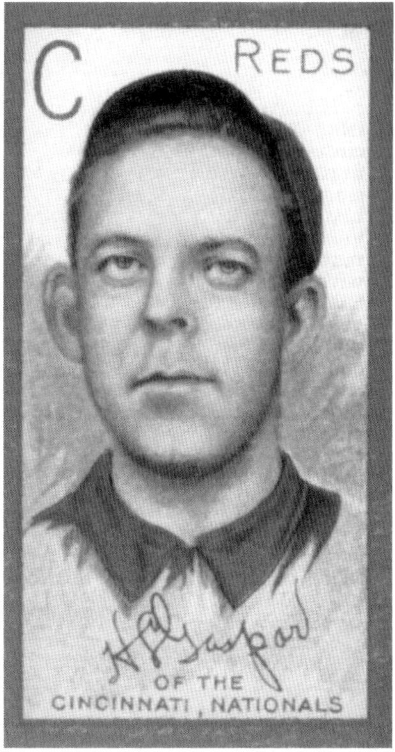

HARRY L. GASPAR

Harry L. Gaspar, the promising young twirler of the Cincinnati National League team, first appeared on the professional diamond in the I. I. I. League, and after pitching for various teams in the minors made a great name for himself with Waterloo, of the Iowa State League, in 1907. That year he won 32 out of 36 completed games, and had such control that during the whole season he only gave 36 passes. Since being drafted by Cincinnati he has become one of their regular staff, and is expected to be of much service in their future games.

2-87-204.523

BASE BALL SERIES 400 DESIGNS
SWEET CAPORAL
CIGARETTES
The Standard for Years
FACTORY Nº 25, 2ᵈ DIST. VA.

REVERSE SIDE OF HARRY GASPAR CARD. This back side of Harry Gaspar's cigarette baseball card gives a brief rundown of his career up to the time he started with Cincinnati. During his four-season tenure in the big leagues, he garnered an impressive ERA of 2.69.

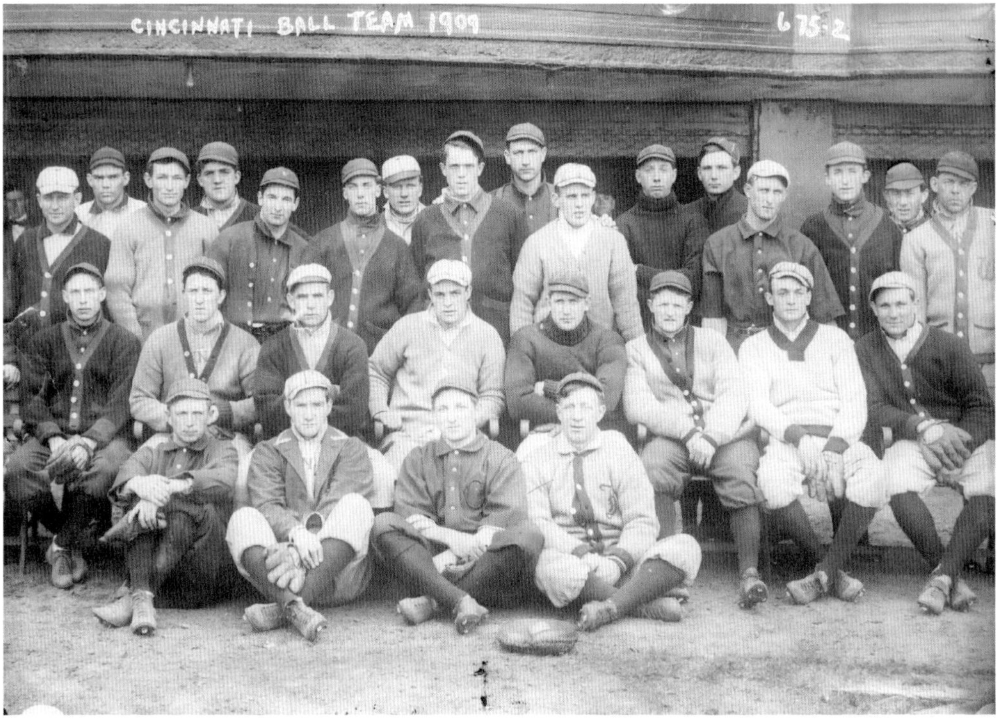

CINCINNATI REDS BASEBALL CLUB, 1909. Plymouth County's Harry Gaspar is seen in this team photograph standing on the far right. His face is easy to identify, considering his protruding ears. The storied Cincinnati club finished fourth in the National League in 1909, Gaspar's first year in the majors. He ended that season with a win-loss record of 19-11 and an ERA of 2.01, making him a fan favorite. (Courtesy of Library of Congress.)

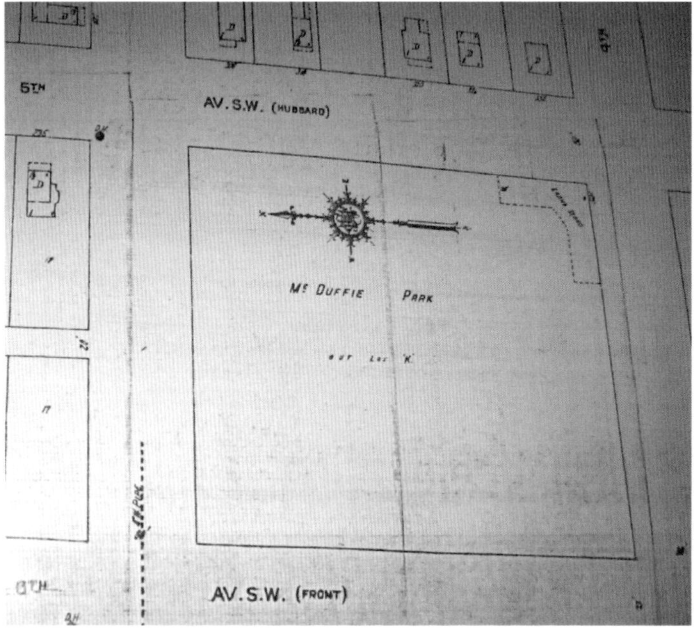

FIRE CODE MAP OF MCDUFFIE PARK. In 1920, the Le Mars school board purchased property three blocks west of the high school and built a baseball park. Named McDuffie Park after longtime board member I.J. McDuffie, it opened in 1921. Used for baseball and other events for years, it was dismantled in 1956. This fire code map marks the location at Fourth Street and Fifth Avenue SW.

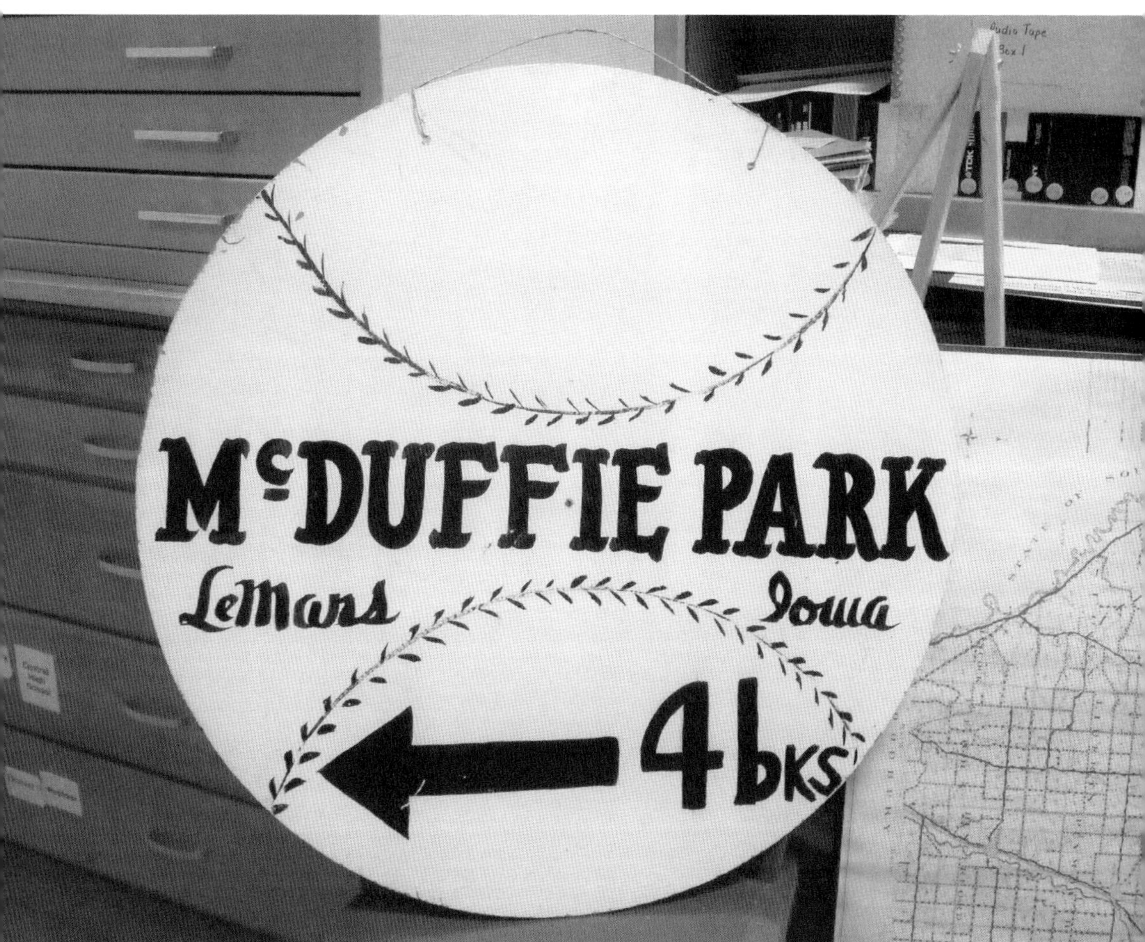

Original Sign Pointing to McDuffie Park. The only known overview image of McDuffie Park is the fire code map seen on the preceding page. During the ballpark's 35-year existence, an untold number of baseball games and other events took place there. This sign, which was posted outside the town's Central High School, now the Plymouth County Historical Museum, directed visitors to the park. Today, the Le Mars Truck Stop occupies the site of McDuffie Park. (Courtesy of Plymouth County Historical Museum.)

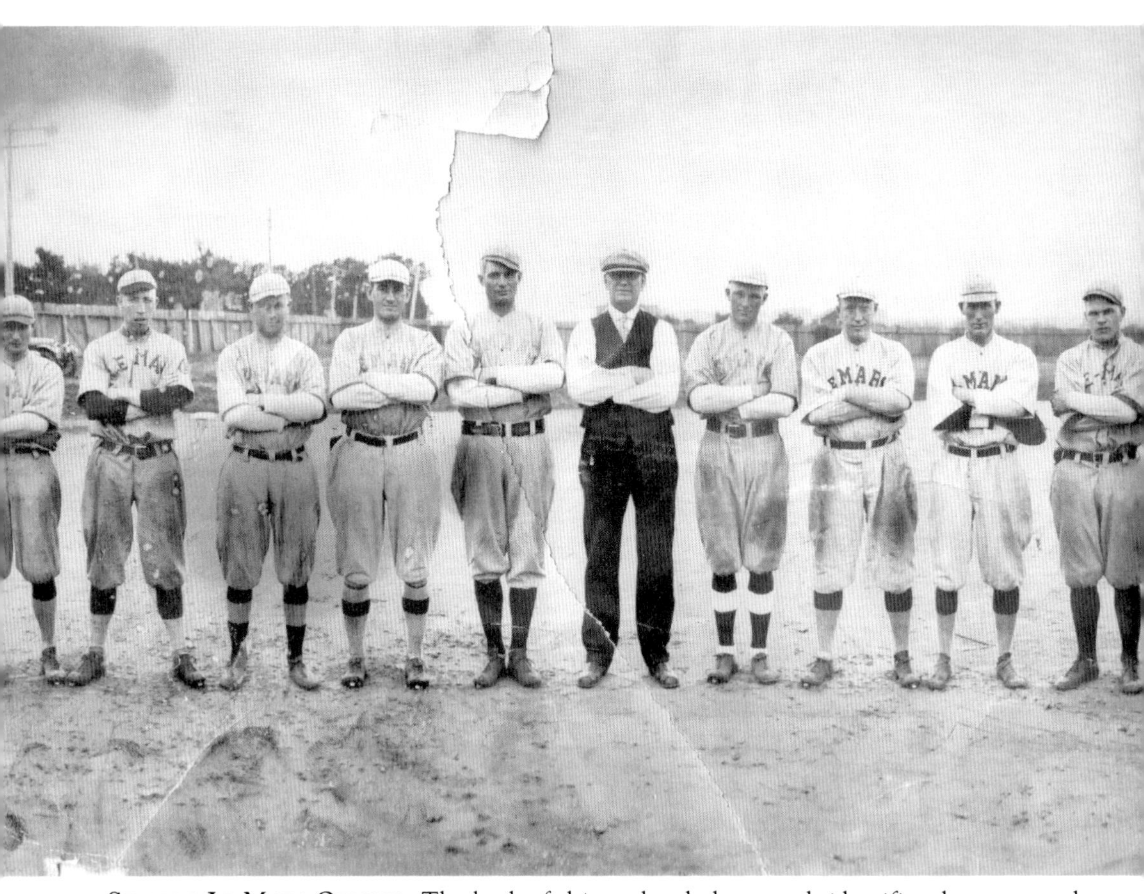

SEMIPRO LE MARS ORIOLES. The back of this undated photograph identifies the team as the semipro Le Mars Orioles. The club existed from 1926 to 1948, with McDuffie as its home park. The players here are unidentified, but it is probable that the man in the center with the dark clothing is either longtime manager Billy Coad or Joe Lotz, the Orioles' manager in 1937. (Courtesy of Plymouth County Historical Museum.)

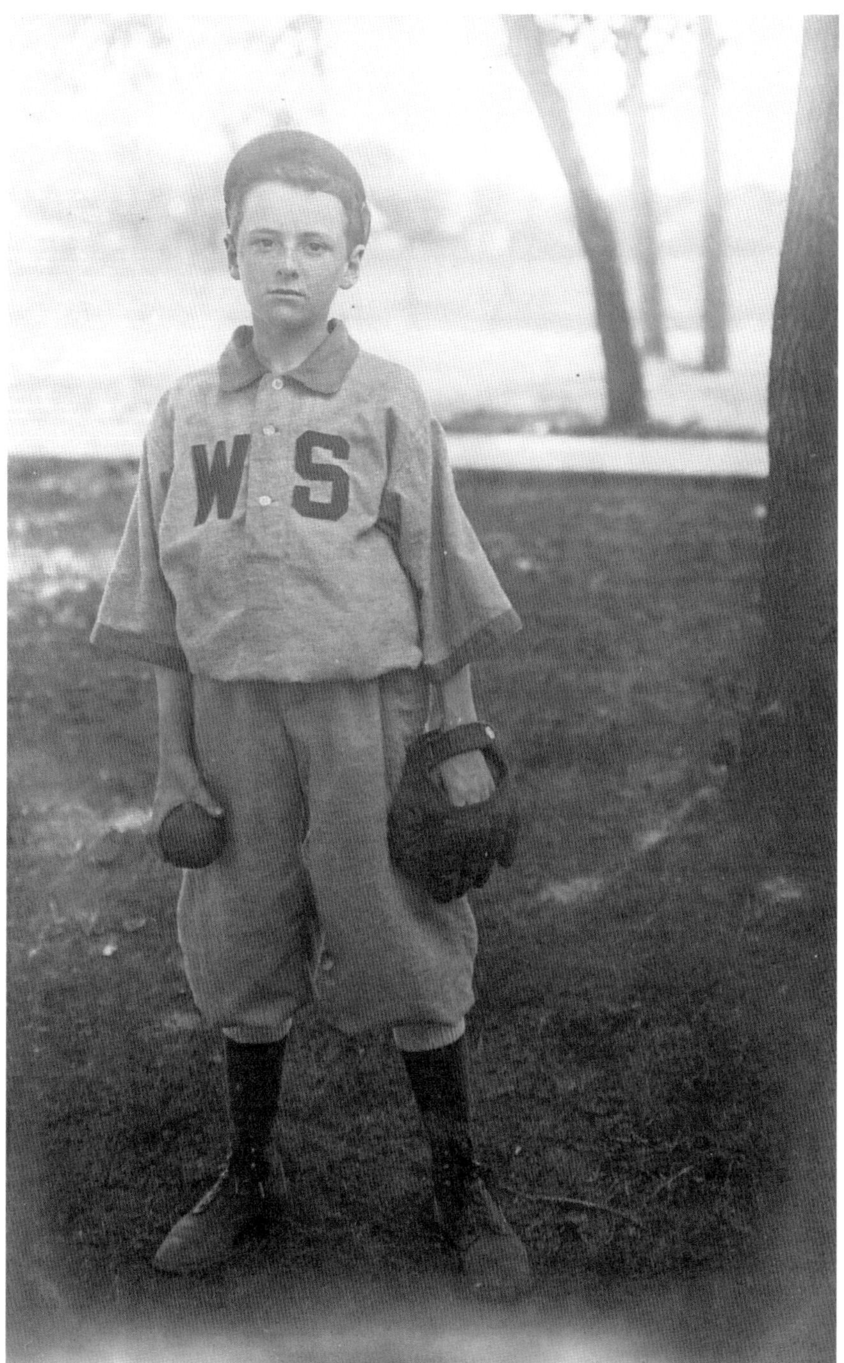

GASPAR POSTCARD PHOTOGRAPH. This postcard photograph of a young baseball player is credited to Gaspar Studio. The initials *WS* very likely stand for Whiskey Slough. A Whiskey Slough baseball club existed as early as 1880. Until around 1930, in an area east of Hinton in Plymouth County, there was a recreational facility located along the Whiskey Creek. Called Whiskey Slough, it had a dance hall, boxing and wrestling rings, horses, and baseball diamonds.

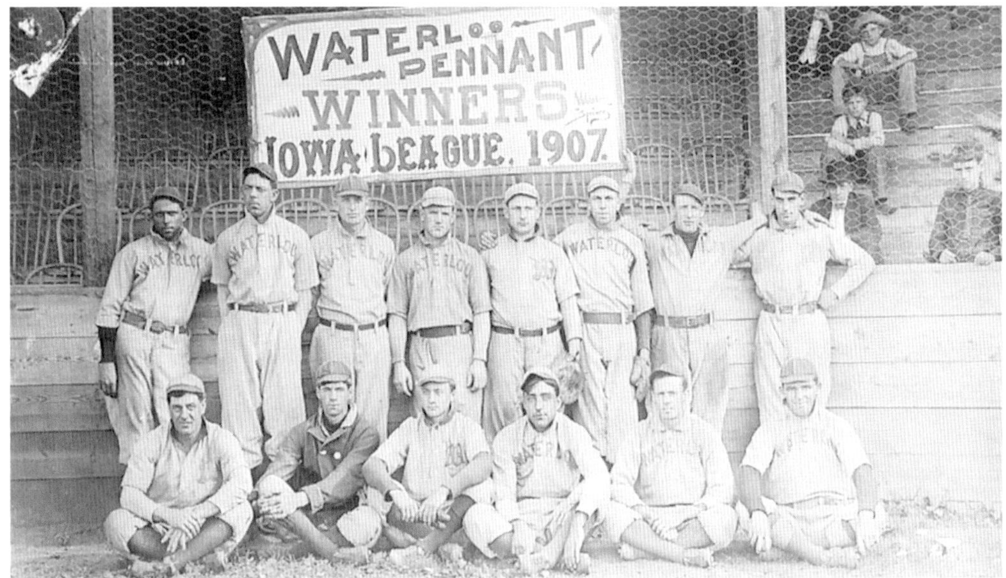

LEAGUE CHAMPION WATERLOO CUBS, 1907. Harry Gaspar, standing second from left, won 18 games for Waterloo in 1907. That included a thrilling 11-inning 1-0 no-hitter against Burlington on September 11. Waterloo went on to win the Iowa League pennant. (Courtesy of *Waterloo-Cedar Falls Courier.*)

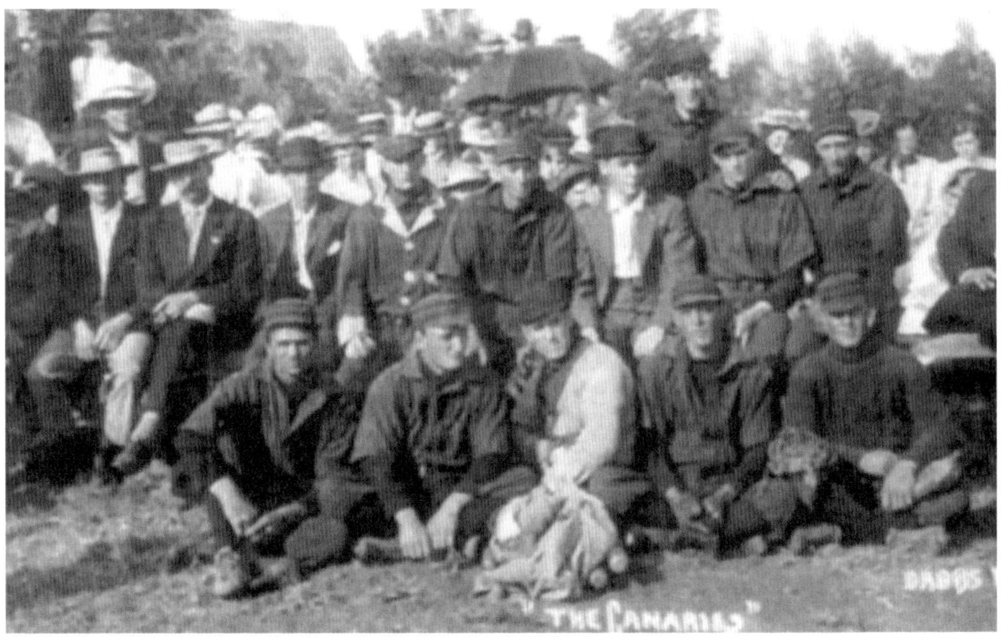

STRUBLE CANARIES. Struble, Plymouth County's smallest town, contributed minor-league pitcher Clare Bertram and big-league left fielder Art Jahn to baseball's annals. Remsen's Johnny Niggeling, who pitched in the major leagues, considered Bertram Plymouth County's best pitcher. In 1937, he tallied two no-hitters for the Class B Pensacola Pilots. This postcard photograph shows one of Struble's early teams. (Courtesy of Plymouth County Historical Museum.)

ARTHUR CHARLES "ART" JAHN (1895–1948). Born and raised in Struble, outfielder and first baseman Art Jahn played professional baseball between 1923 and 1933. His major-league assignments included the Chicago Cubs in 1925 and the New York Giants and Philadelphia Phillies in 1928.

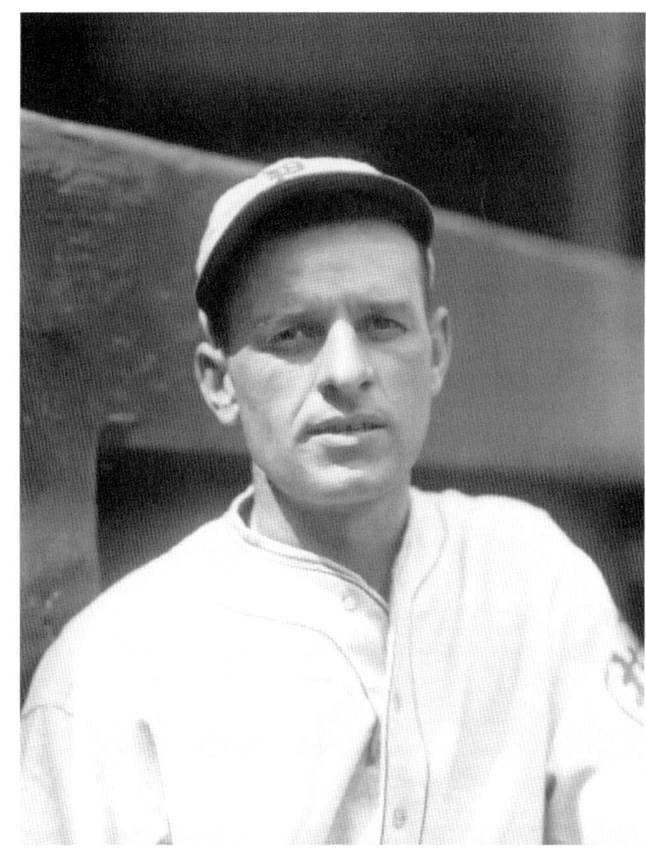

MERRILL BASEBALL CLUB. The group seen in this undated postcard could be the Merrill team that faced the Western Union College club of Le Mars on Saturday, May 21, 1904. Although Merrill lost that day, its team proved a worthy opponent, losing by a score of 1-0. The town of Merrill lies six miles southwest of Le Mars. Like other area towns, it always fielded a baseball team.

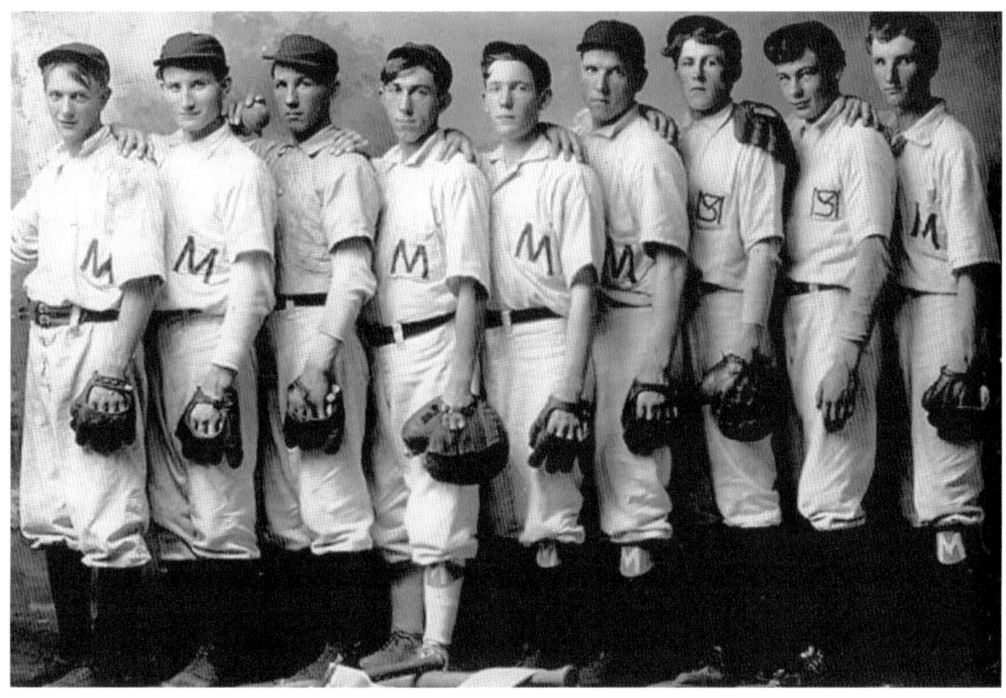

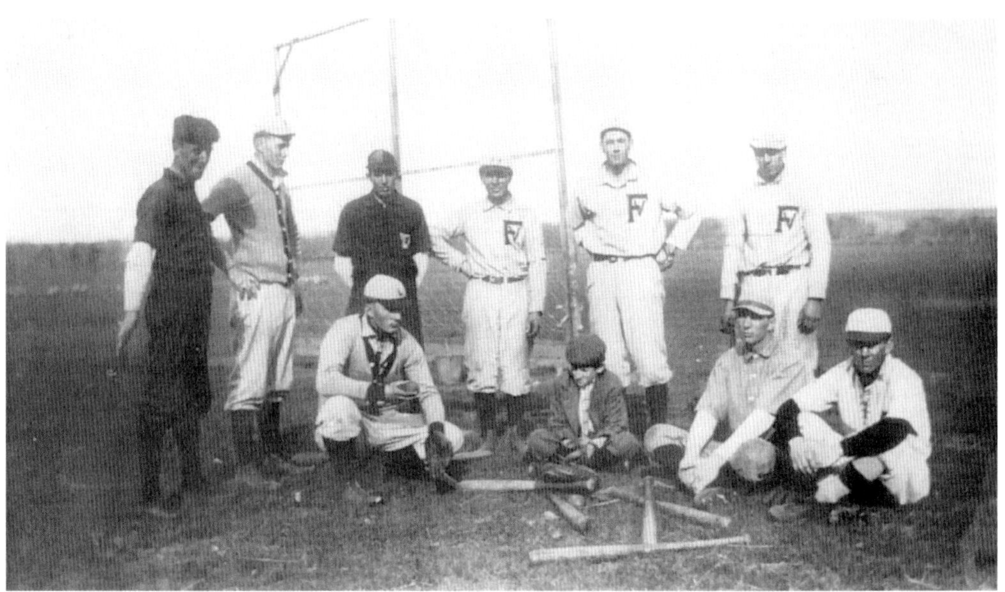

Floyd Valley Baseball Team. This photograph is exemplary of the many amateur baseball clubs throughout rural Iowa in the early 20th century. Individual players in this 1904 photograph of the Floyd Valley team remain unidentified, but members of the club were Jim Nicholson, Tommy Bunt, George Bunt, Les Mann, Hank Braband, Ben Nicholson, Fred Jeffers, and Bill Scheunk. Ben Nicholson owned Nicholson Motors in Le Mars. (Courtesy of Lenka Wanzer.)

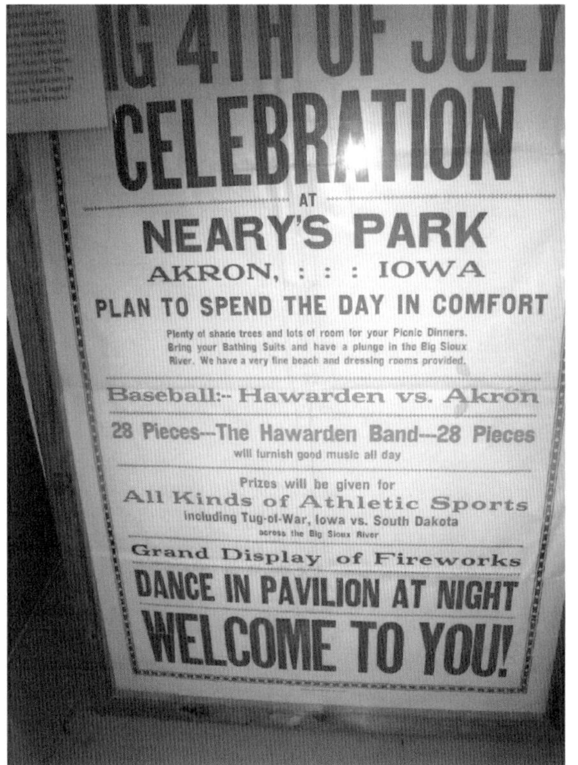

Original Sign for July 4 Event. Baseball was always part of the Independence Day celebration in rural communities like Akron, one of Plymouth County's larger towns. This undated poster is now housed at the Akron Area Museum. Neary's Park, used often in the 1930s, was outside of town near the Big Sioux River.

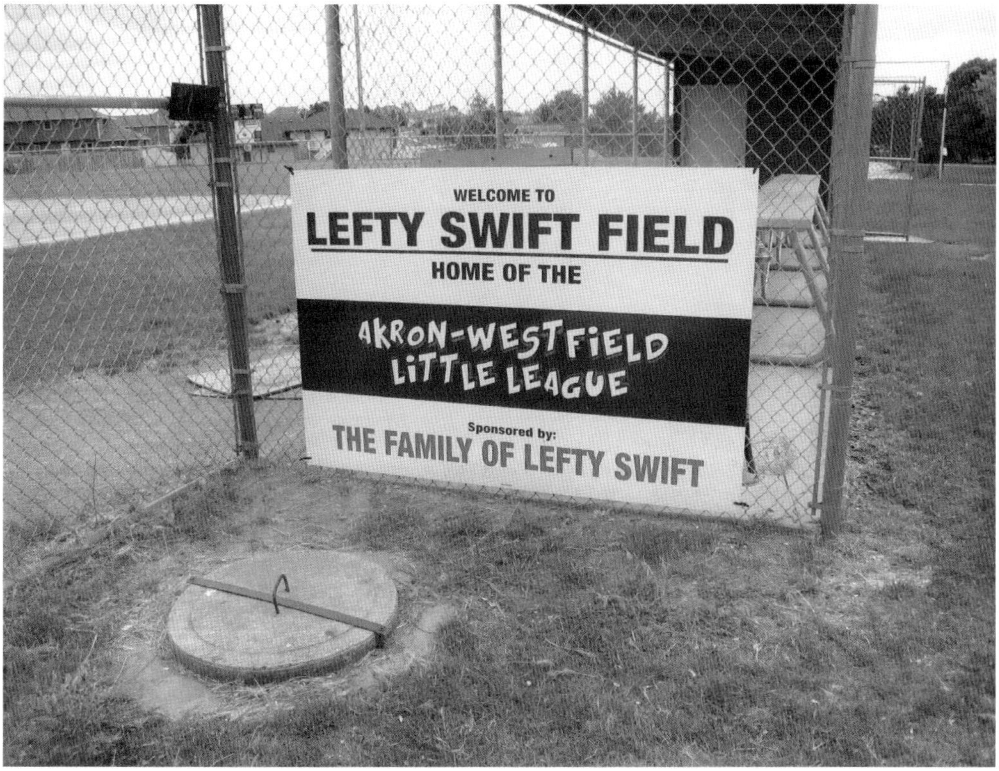

AKRON'S LEFTY SWIFT FIELD. Today, Akron continues to enjoy baseball games. Both high school and Little League teams compete throughout the area. Several ballparks serve Akron as well as the nearby town of Westfield. The family of longtime Akron resident and professional pitcher Lefty Swift sponsored this facility for the Akron-Westfield Little League teams.

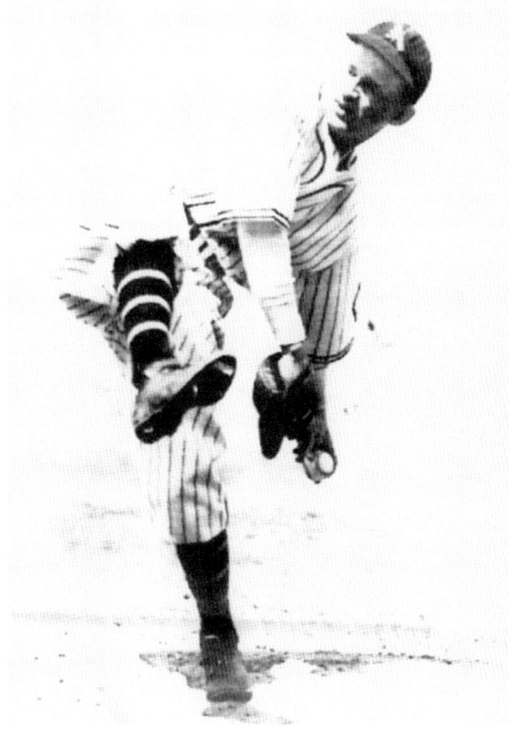

BURTON PERSHING "LEFTY" SWIFT (1918–2008). Akron native and left-handed pitcher Lefty Swift played professional baseball for seven seasons spanning 1938–1946. Starting with Sioux City, he later pitched for the International League Baltimore Orioles in 1943 and 1946. His career was interrupted in 1944 and 1945 by military service during World War II. He was later awarded two Bronze Stars. (Courtesy of Akron Area Museum.)

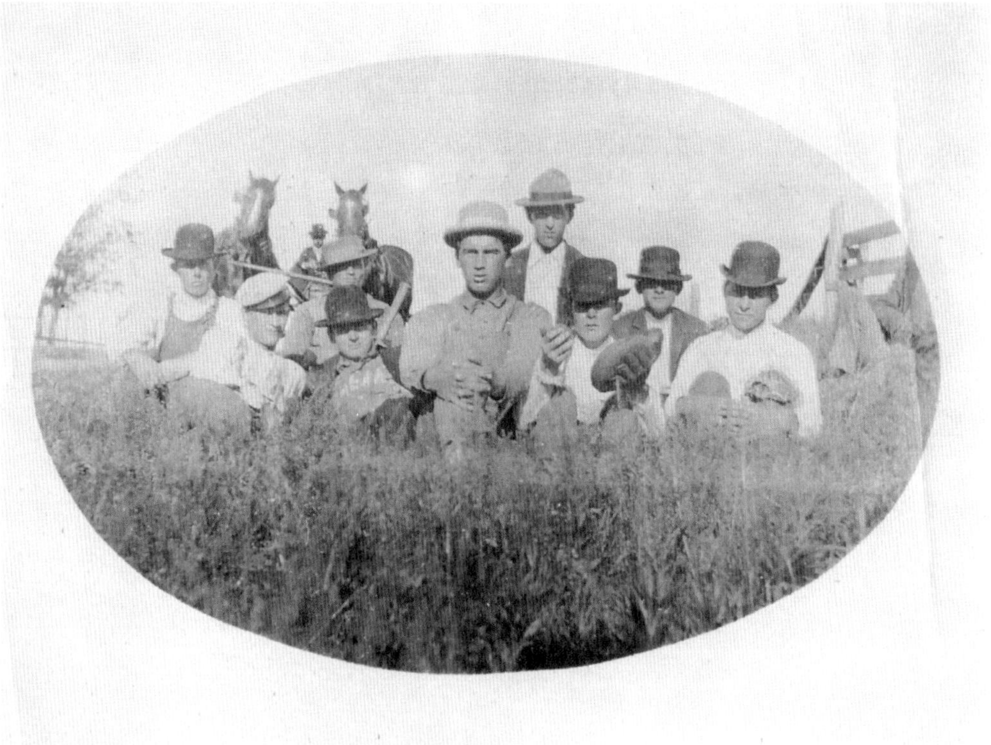

Early Remsen Ballplayers. Living on a farm near Remsen, the Homan family played baseball in a country field. This prized photograph captures the spirit of rural baseball. Identified are, from left to right, (first row) John Homan, Peter J. Homan, unidentified, probably cousin Joe Lotz, and Nicholas Homan; (second row) two unidentified, Louis Homan, and Frank Homan. Peter Homan Sr. is seated in the rear wagon. (Courtesy of the Homan family.)

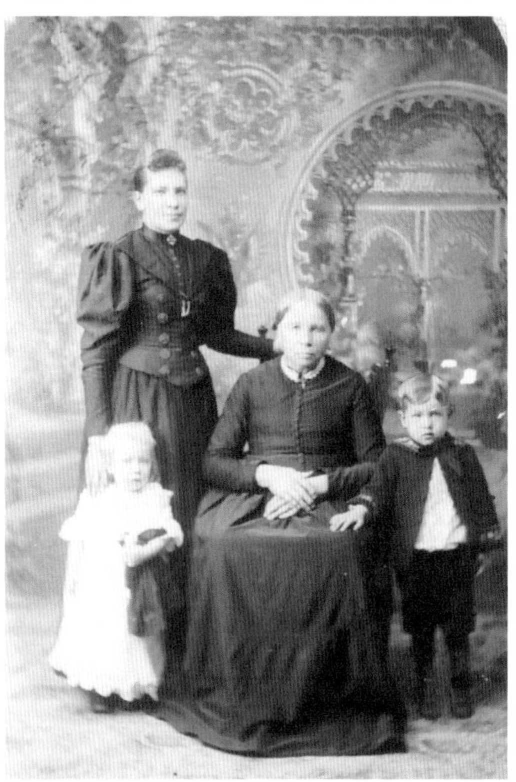

Joe Lotz and Family. This studio photograph shows Joe Lotz, a future professional pitcher from Remsen, with family members. Standing are his mother, Susan Arens Lotz, his sister, Lizzie, and Joe. Seated between the siblings is Joe's grandmother Elizabeth Elringer. (Courtesy of *Remsen Bell-Enterprise*.)

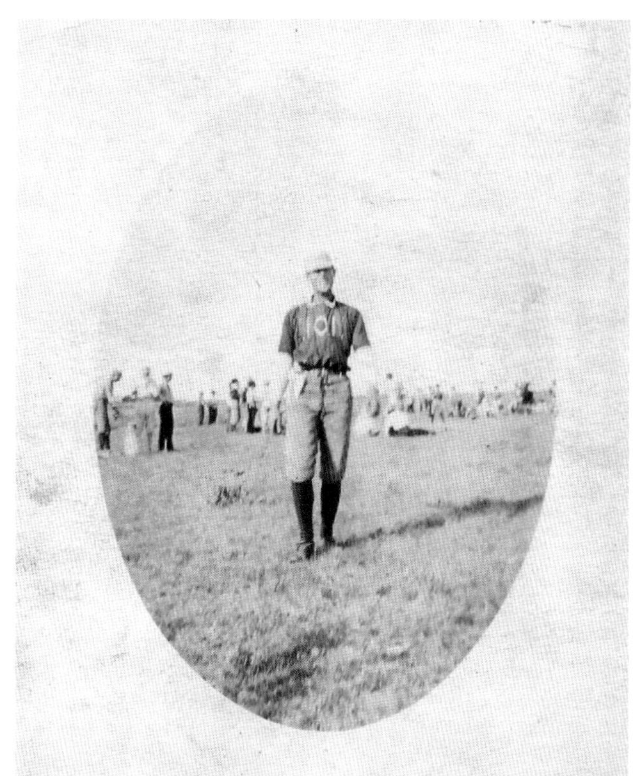

Unidentified Ballplayer in Pasture. This treasured family photograph shows an unidentified ballplayer in the foreground of a group gathering for a baseball game. The playing field is in a pasture on a farm belonging to Peter Homan. Notice the number 101 on the player's jersey, its significance lost in time. (Courtesy of the Homan family.)

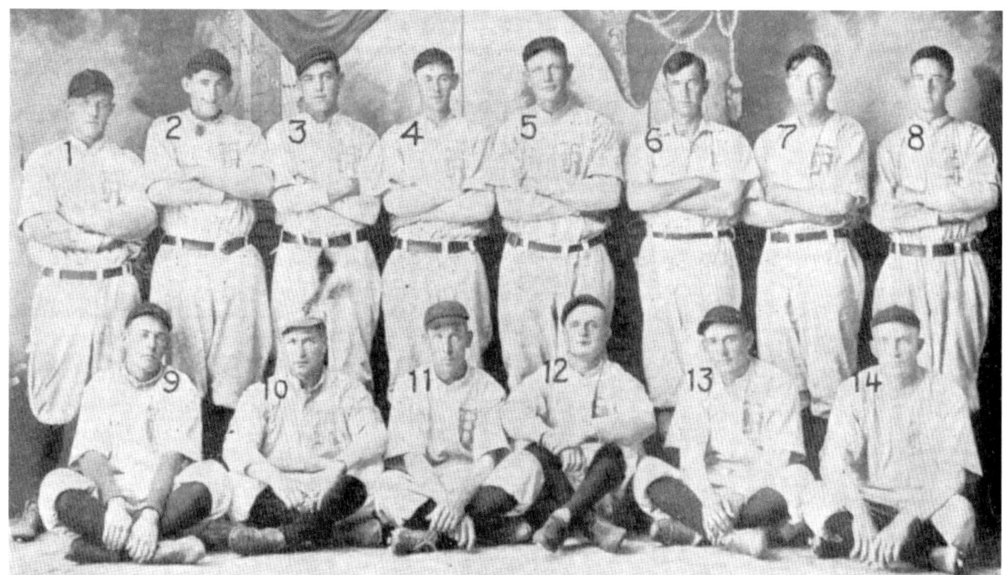

Kearny Kapitalists, 1913. Nebraska State League champions of 1913, this team featured three who made it to the major leagues, including Remsen's Joe Lotz. Rolla Mapel (No. 3) pitched for the St. Louis Browns in 1919, Joe Lotz (No. 10) pitched for the St. Louis Cardinals in 1916, and shortstop Harry Berte (No. 11) played for the Cardinals in 1903. (Courtesy of Library of Congress, Spalding Official Baseball Guide.)

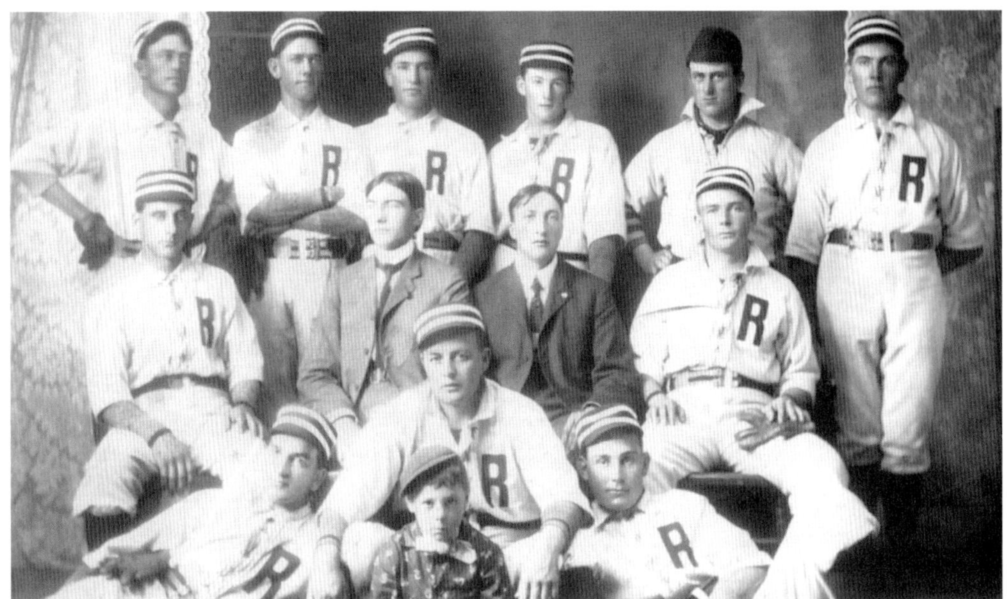

REMSEN BASEBALL CLUB WITH JOE LOTZ. This undated Remsen team photograph includes hometown hurler Joe Lotz, front and center behind the batboy. He started pitching at age 15, playing for amateur, semipro, barnstorming, and minor-league teams and one major-league team before retiring. He was featured in *Ripley's Believe It or Not!* for holding the world's record for number of games pitched: 1,300 games in 21 years. (Courtesy of *Remsen Bell-Enterprise.*)

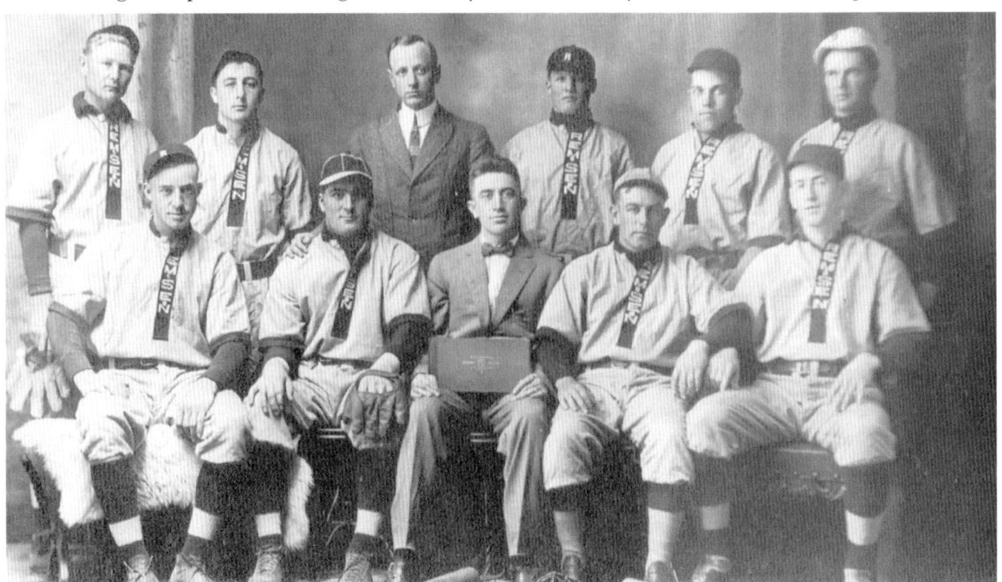

EARLY REMSEN TEAM PHOTOGRAPH. This is another undated Remsen team photograph, but the style of uniform suggests that it is in the first or second decade of the 20th century. Remsen's wealth of baseball talent included M.R. Faber, who managed its early clubs for nearly 20 years. The Remsen Fabers, as well as the Homans, were cousins to baseball hall of famer Red Faber. (Courtesy of *Remsen Bell-Enterprise.*)

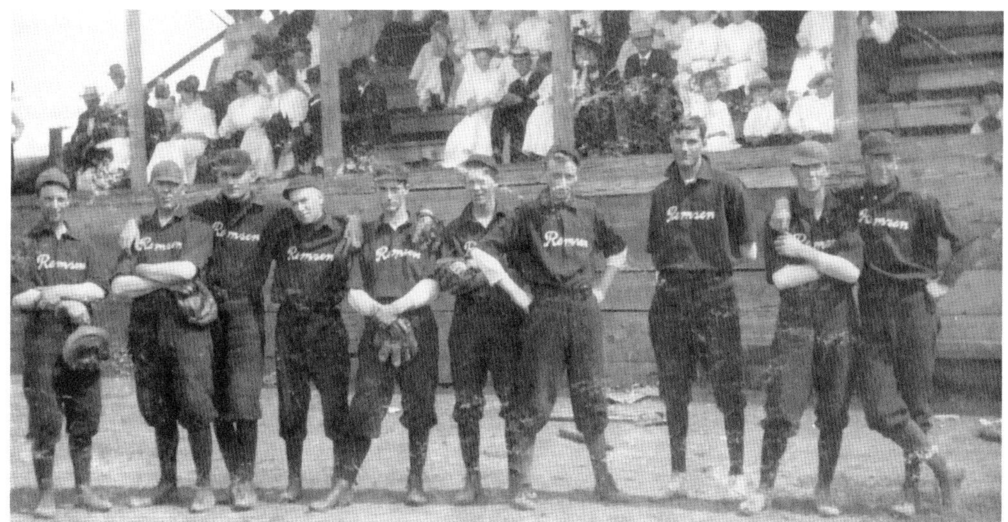

REMSEN TEAM, 1911. Only two players in this 1911 photograph are positively identified: eighth from left is Peter Homan, and second from left is Joe Lotz. Other team members of that year were Nick Faber, Mike Strohbeen, E.F. Kieffer, Ralph Creglow, Mathew Heyman, Henry Hay, F.E. Wentz, and Dr. S.W. Kuster. Notice the dressy clothing worn by the grandstand crowd. (Courtesy of the Homan family.)

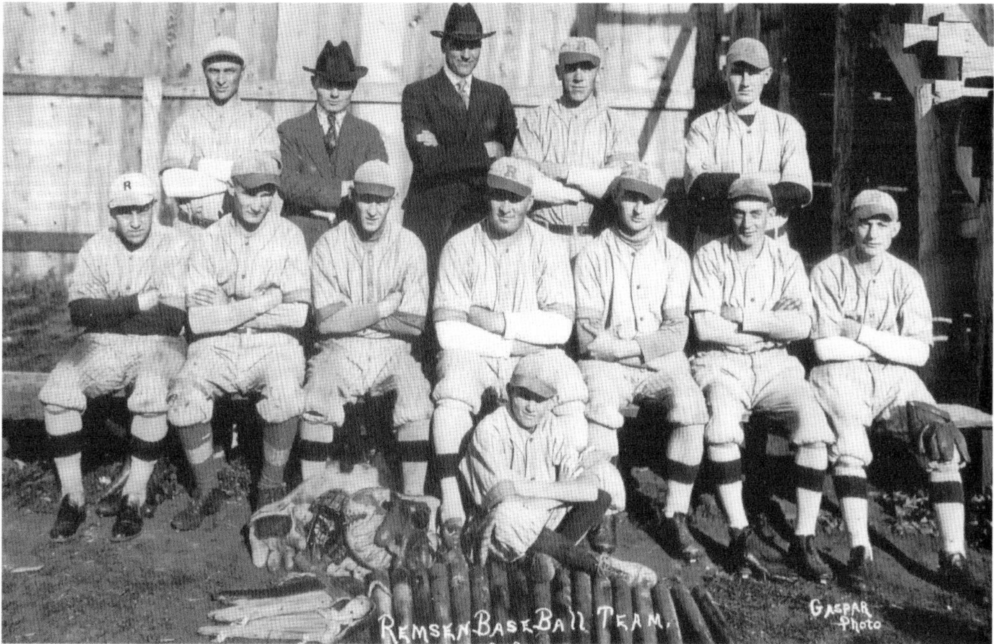

REMSEN BASEBALL TEAM, 1919. This 1919 photograph is the best image of an early Remsen team found to date. The tall man in the back row wearing a dark suit is team manager Peter Homan. Notice the photographer identification on the lower left corner, Gaspar Photo. At that time, former major-league pitcher Harry Gaspar operated his studio in Le Mars. (Courtesy of the Homan family.)

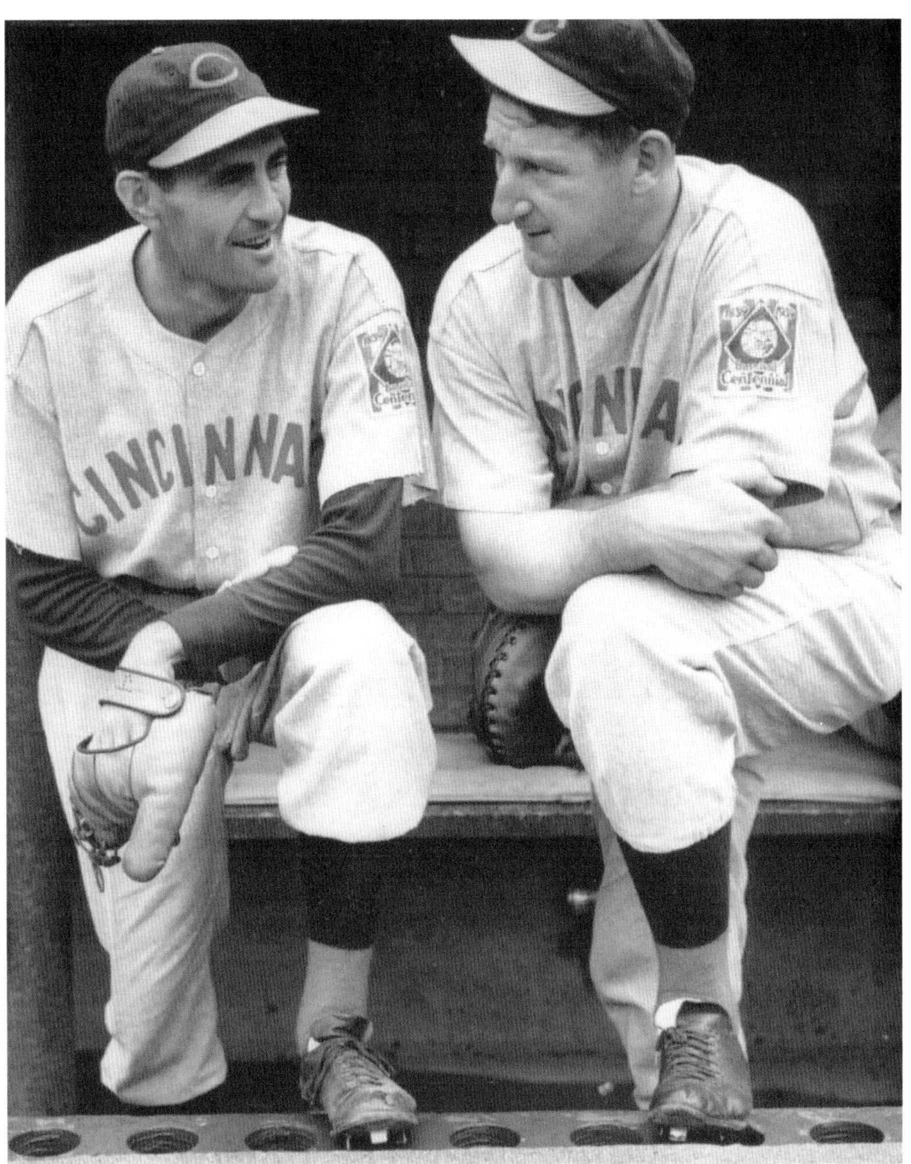

JOHNNY NIGGELING AND ERNIE LOMBARDI, 1939. Pitcher Johnny Niggeling (left) poses with future hall of fame catcher Ernie Lombardi. Both men played for the Cincinnati Reds in 1939. Born and raised in Remsen, Niggeling learned the art of baseball there. Although he sometimes pitched, he was a good hitter and mostly played the infield for his hometown St. Mary's High School. He started pitching regularly around 1929 while with the Class D Waterloo Hawks. He then went on to play in 10 different leagues before he finally secured a steady job as a major-league pitcher. He was well known for his knuckle ball, a pitch batters and catchers alike abhor. After two short stays with big-league clubs, he made a good impression in Cincinnati in 1939 and then pitched for the St. Louis Browns from 1940 to 1943. He went on to the Washington Senators in 1943, playing there until mid-season 1946 and ending the season, and his major-league career, with the Boston Braves.

JOHNNY NIGGELING (1903–1963). When Remsen's Johnny Niggeling got his third major-league opportunity with Cincinnati, he was 35, an old man by professional athlete standards. But he played in the majors for another eight years and then signed with the Western League Sioux City Soos, where he won 12 games in 1947. He then retired and went back to barbering, his longtime off-season occupation.

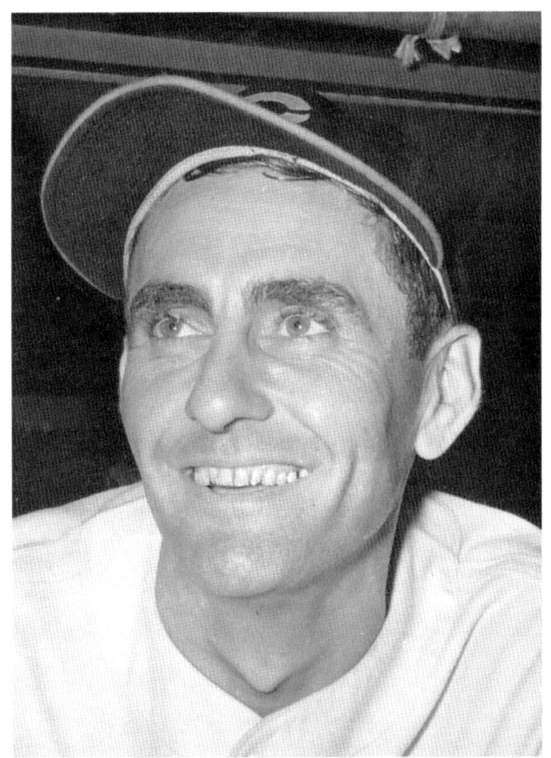

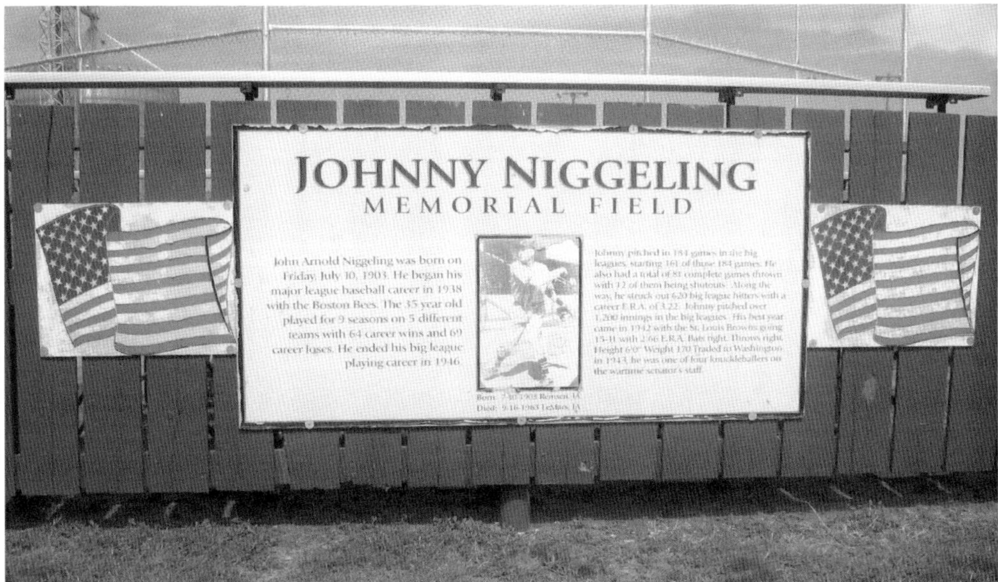

JOHNNY NIGGELING MEMORIAL FIELD. Following Johnny Niggeling's death in 1963, a Remsen ballpark was named for its most notable son. Located at the site of the town's first baseball field, originally carved out of a cornfield, it lies on the edge of town in the shadow of several imposing grain elevators. A small city with a rural character, Remsen maintains the aura of the idyllic American country town.

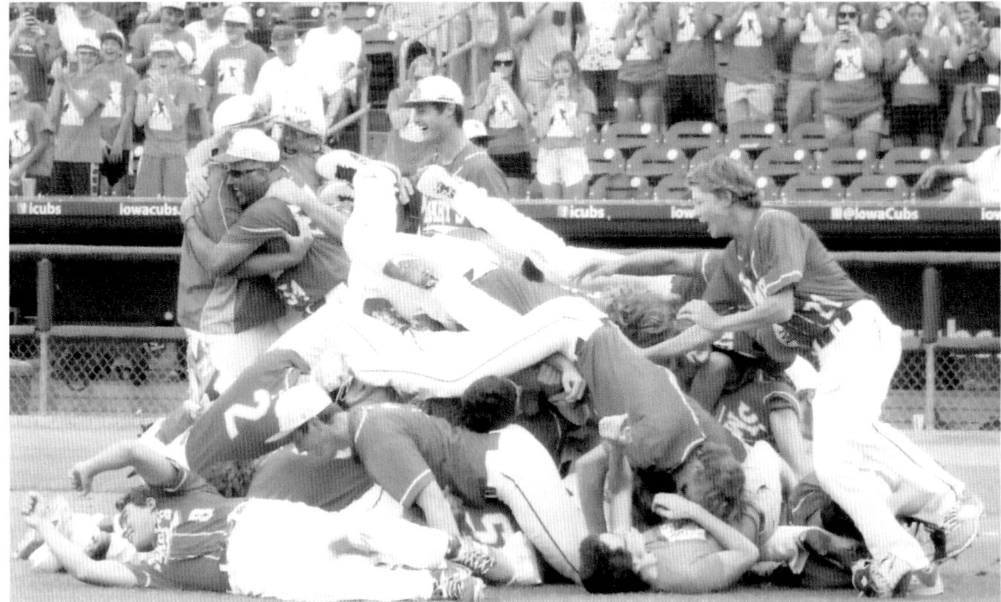

State Champions, 2016. Remsen's St. Mary's Hawks baseball players celebrate in a heap after winning the Class 1A state championship in 2016. They won at Des Moines against West Sioux, a team from the same War Eagle Conference, both clubs from Northwest Iowa. (Courtesy of *Le Mars Daily Sentinel*; photograph by Michael Haller.)

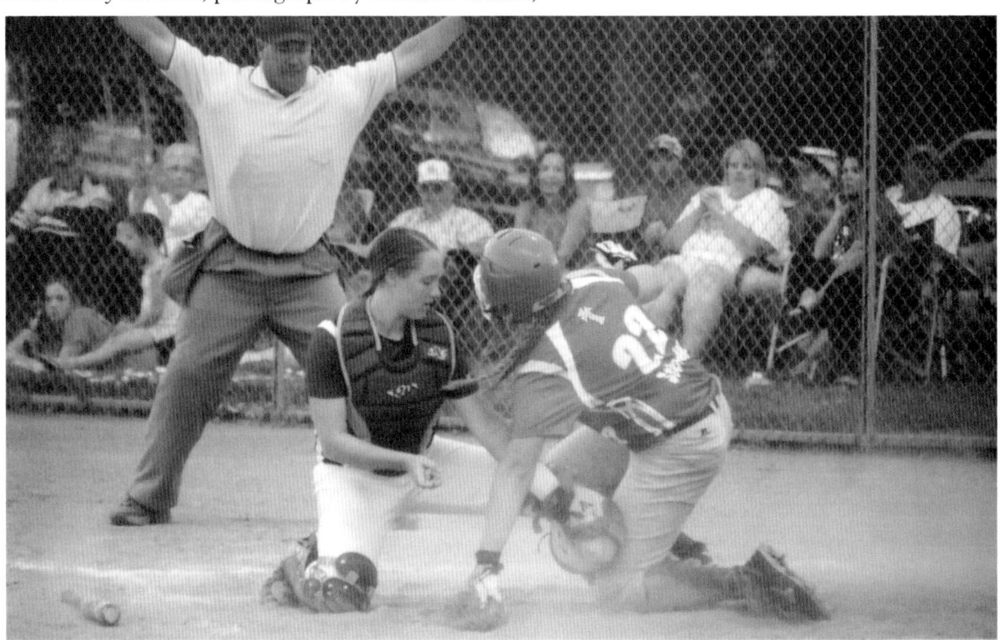

War Eagle Conference Softball. Le Mars Gehlen Catholic catcher Jolee Linden (center) tags Remsen St. Mary's runner Shelby Schroeder during a softball game in Le Mars on June 20, 2016. High school softball teams in Northwest Iowa play with just as much intensity as their baseball counterparts. (Courtesy of *Le Mars Daily Sentinel*; photograph by Michael Haller.)

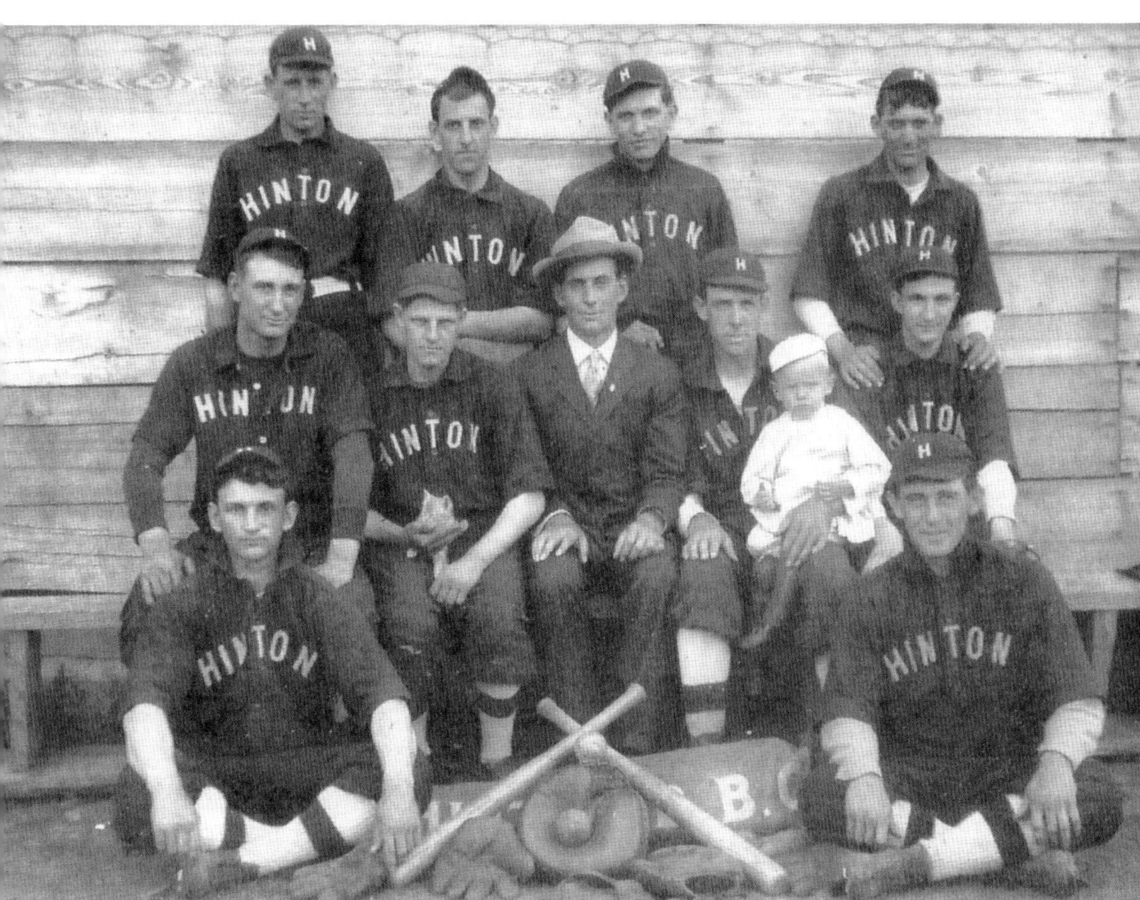

HINTON BASEBALL TEAM, 1908. A town of under 1,000, Hinton has a strong tradition of sports. Today, its sprawling Blackhawk Sports Complex, seen from the highway while driving by the town, supports football as well as youth softball and baseball programs. Seen in this 1908 team photograph are, from left to right, (first row) Clyde Brown and Roy Bogenrief; (second row) Joe Cook, Robert Crouch, John Snyder (coach and owner), Joe Levins (with unidentified child), and Clare Levins; (third row) Sam Weinrich, Jacob Hadab, Tom Gozona, and Floyd Crawford. (Courtesy of Plymouth County Historical Museum.)

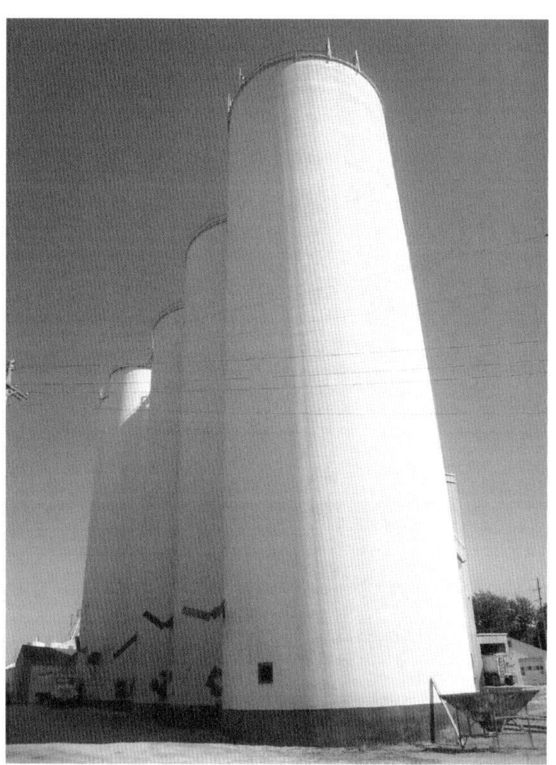

GRAIN ELEVATORS IN LE MARS. A common sight in towns throughout Iowa, grain elevators like these in Le Mars are essential to the grain-producing farmland. The tallest structures seen from a distance in most towns are these, water towers, and church steeples. They are as much a part of the landscape as baseball diamonds.

WIND TURBINES IN POCAHONTAS COUNTY. During the early 21st century, wind turbines began to stud the landscape in some parts of Northwest Iowa. This photograph, shot near the town of Fonda in 2010, shows the flatland in rural Pocahontas County. A flat surface provides for a smooth baseball field.

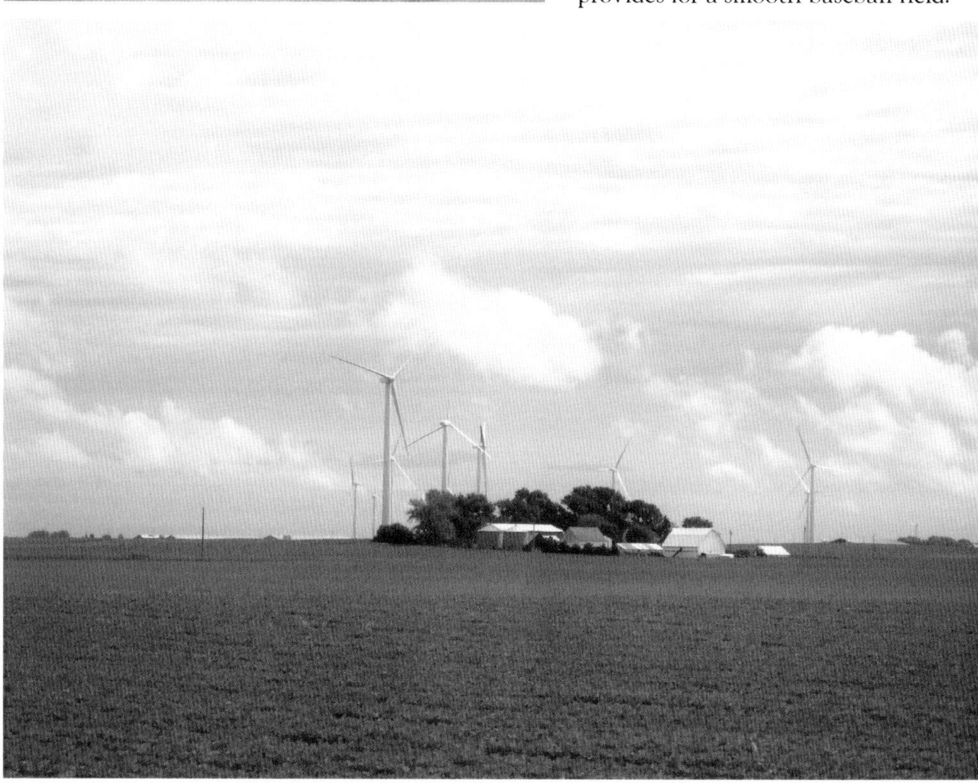

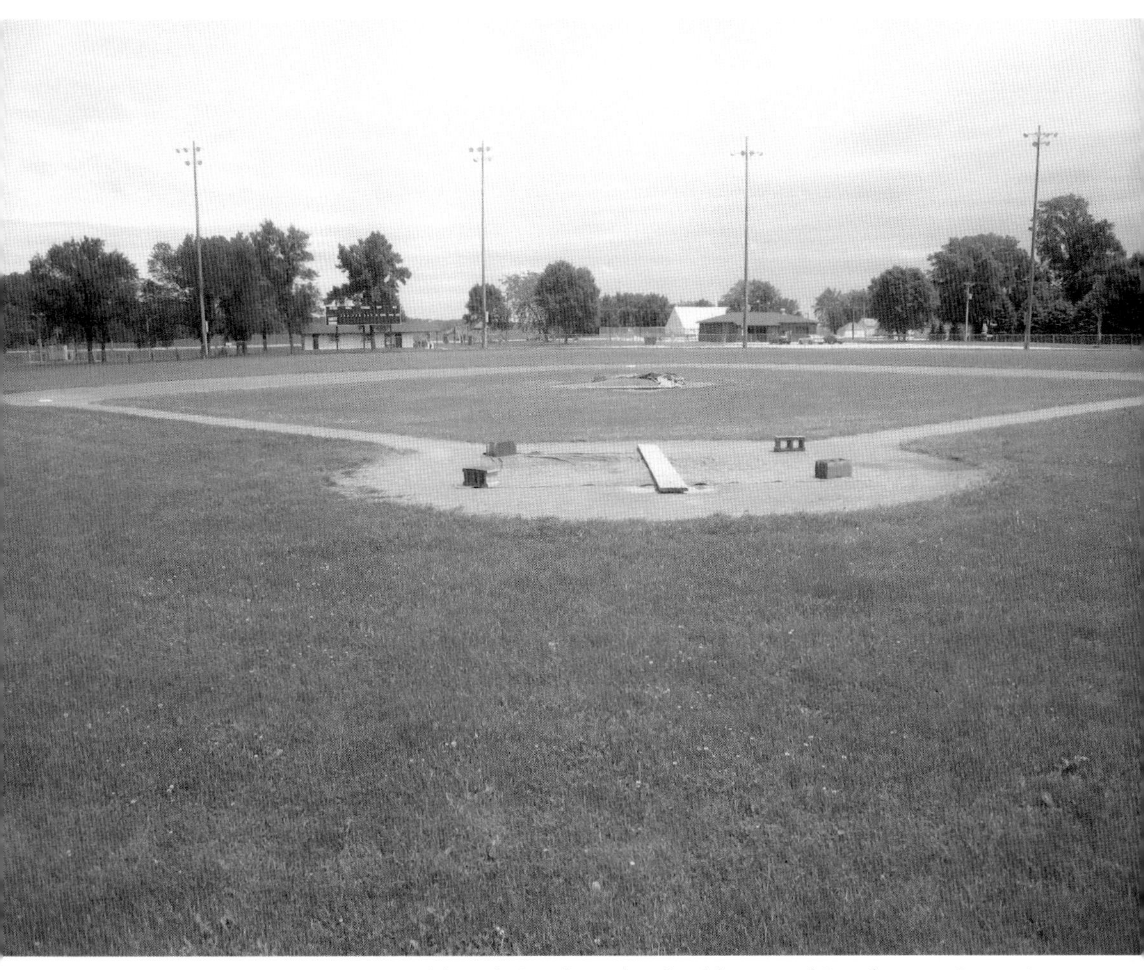

Baseball Diamond in Fonda. Although Fonda is the third-largest of Pocahontas County's nine towns, its population has dwindled to less than 1,000 in recent years. Nonetheless, as seen in this 2010 photograph, its baseball field is just as well kept as ever. Near the edge of town, it is the same park where the semipro Fonda Cubs of the 1950 Iowa State League played. Members of that team were Bob Coon, George Dorr, Tom Boland, Lee Bailey, Bob Trowbridge, Bob Zubeck, Dick Baldrini, Hugh Wise Jr., Herb Kauffman, Ray Dall'Osto, Glenn Honsbruch, Clive Follmer, Don Turek, Cliff Copeland, Bob Evens, Jim Jeter, and Mike Rzadzki. Of the 17-member roster, only two were from Fonda. Some were hired from other Iowa towns, but others, like Wise, came from as far away as Hollywood, Florida.

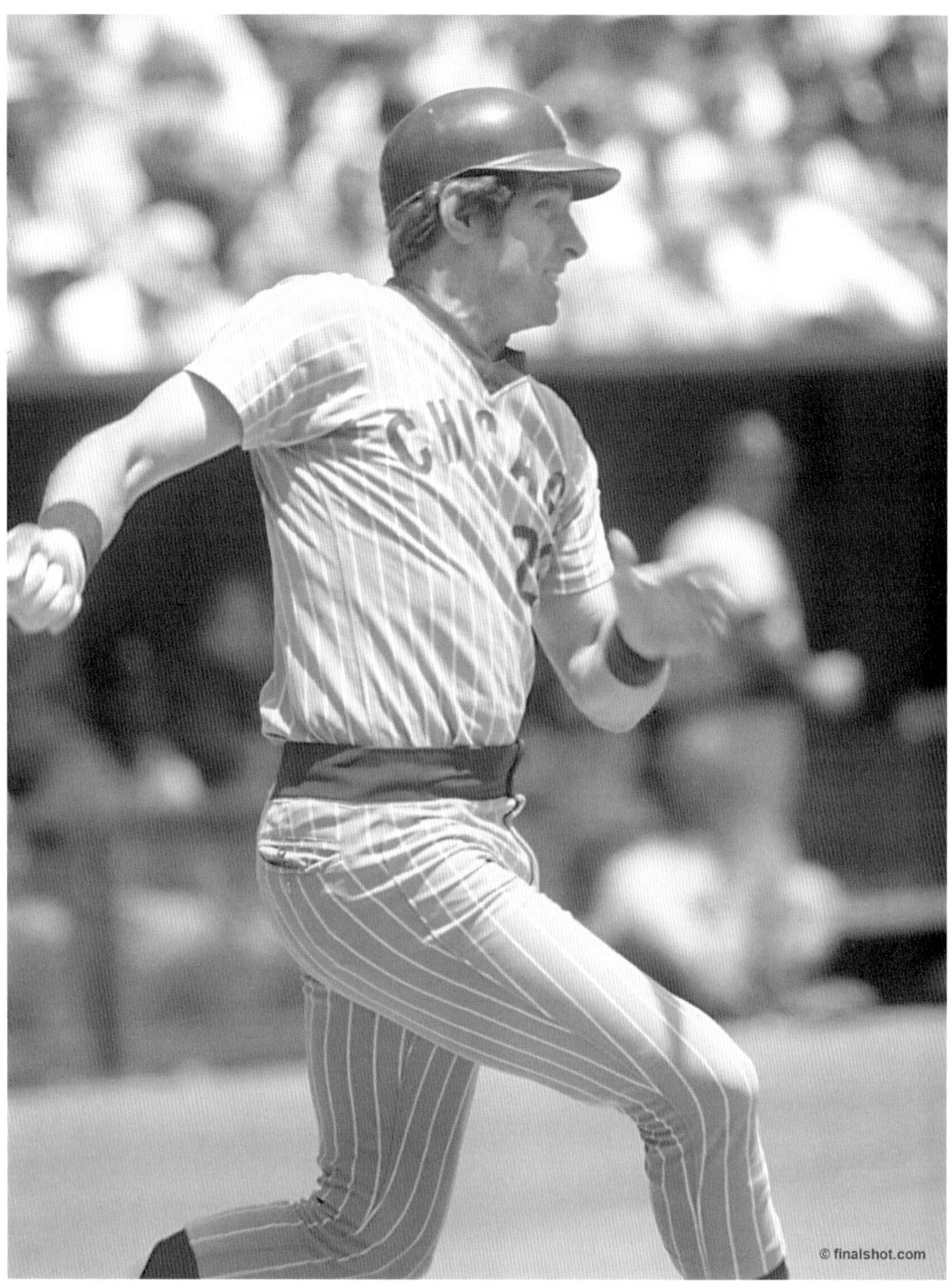

LARRY BIITTNER (1945–). Born in Pocahontas, left-handed throwing and batting Larry Biittner graduated from high school there before beginning his extensive professional baseball career. Playing first base and the outfield, his first major-league assignment was with the Washington Senators in 1970. Between several minor-league stints, he played for the Texas Rangers in 1972 and 1973, and in 1974, he went to the Montreal Expos. From there, he played for the Chicago Cubs for five seasons, followed by Cincinnati in 1981 and 1982, and lastly with Texas again in 1983. (Courtesy of finalshot.com.)

SAC, SIOUX, AND WEBSTER COUNTIES

Like other Iowa communities, Sac County towns built baseball teams before the dawn of the 20th century. In 1896, future big-league pitcher Paul Zahniser was born in the county seat of Sac City. Lake View, the county's second-largest town, had Fats and Leans teams in 1894. Eventually, several county leagues were organized. The one in 1913 consisted of teams from eight towns, and in 1921, there was a Business Men's League. At one point, former Chicago White Sox pitcher Lefty Williams played for Lake View. The town's best diamond was at Lakewood Park, where its team, the Hawks, played.

With 14 towns, Sioux County is more populous than many others in Northwest Iowa. And even its tiniest towns supported baseball from early on. Little Maurice had a team called the Invincibles competing on local farm fields as well as ballparks in area towns in 1891. Mid-sized Hawarden's semipro team of 1908 posted a win-loss record of 49-8. In August 1911, slightly smaller Hull's club lost a game to little Hospers by one run. Naturally, the larger towns of Orange City, the county seat, and Sioux Center have rich baseball histories. Before modern communications, Sioux Center's businessmen hung "Out to the ball game" signs on their doors for customer convenience. In recent times, Orange City's Jordon De Jong pitched for the Toronto Blue Jays. The tradition continues.

Webster County, even more populous than Sioux County, consists of 16 towns, although the county seat of Fort Dodge carries the majority of its residents. Not counting Sioux City, Fort Dodge, with six, had more minor-league baseball clubs in the early 20th century than any other towns in Northwest Iowa. Moreover, major-league baseball benefited from the pitching skills of Fort Dodge–born pitchers Lou Fiene and Gene Ford, and recently, Mike Schwabe and Kevin Wickander. Jimmie Long, who played pro ball for nine seasons, caught for the Chicago White Sox in 1922. But undoubtedly the county's other towns all had ball clubs over the years. That is a given.

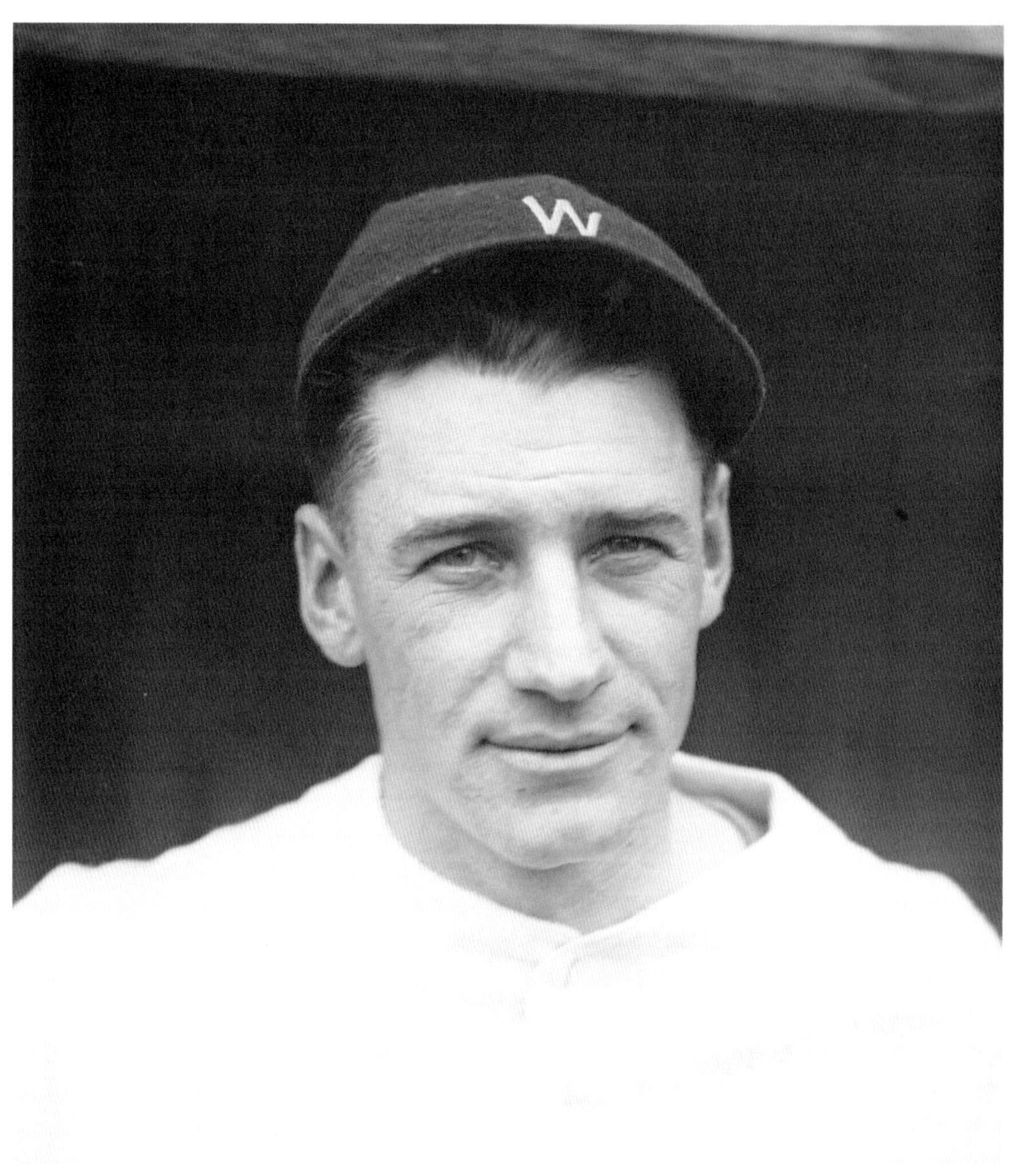

Paul Vernan Zahniser (1896–1964). Born in Sac City, inveterate baseball man Paul Zahniser pitched professionally for 17 seasons, five in the major leagues. Starting out in Columbus, Ohio, in 1918, he posted his best performance in 1921 by winning 22 games for the Class A Southern Association Memphis Chickasaws. His first and best year in the majors was 1923 with the Washington Senators. Although he did not fare as well in 1924, on July 2 he blanked the Boston Red Sox 5-0, inspiring sportswriter Frank Young of the *Washington Post* to quip that "Zahnny's" effectiveness removed the competitive aspect of the contest. Coincidentally, Zahniser found himself pitching for Boston for the next two years. Then, after several minor-league stints, he got his last big-league chance, albeit brief, with Cincinnati in 1929. He spent most of the remainder of his years as a pro with Pacific Coast League clubs.

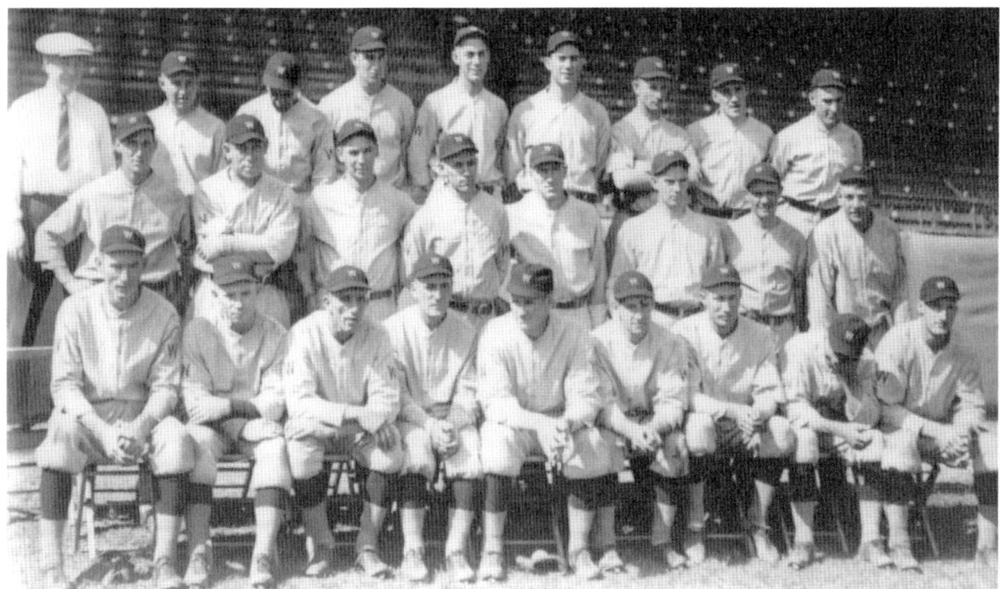

1924 WASHINGTON SENATORS. This Senators team finished first in the American League and won the World Series 4-3 against the New York Giants. Although a member of the Senators that season, Sac City's Paul Zahniser did not play in the series. Nor did Kossuth County's Showboat Fisher, Zahniser's teammate. Zahniser is eighth from left in the back row.

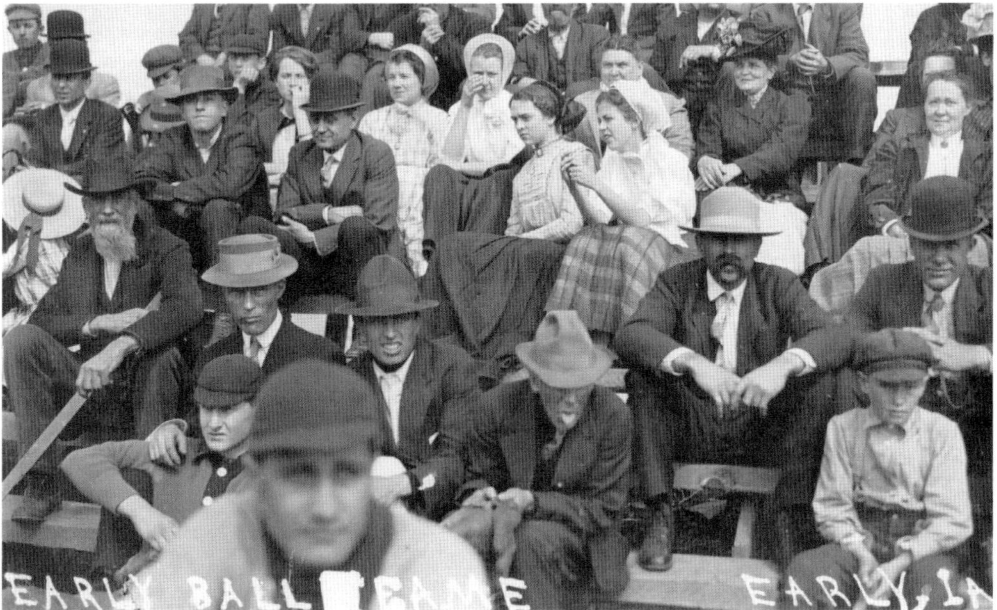

BALL GAME CROWD AT EARLY, IOWA, 1910. Early is sixth in population of Sac County's nine towns, and its numbers have not changed considerably since 1900. Today, the town hosts an annual Crossroad Days in July. Among other activities, softball tournaments are part of the celebration. Onlookers are undoubtedly just as involved as this crowd in 1910. (Courtesy of State Historical Society of Iowa, Des Moines.)

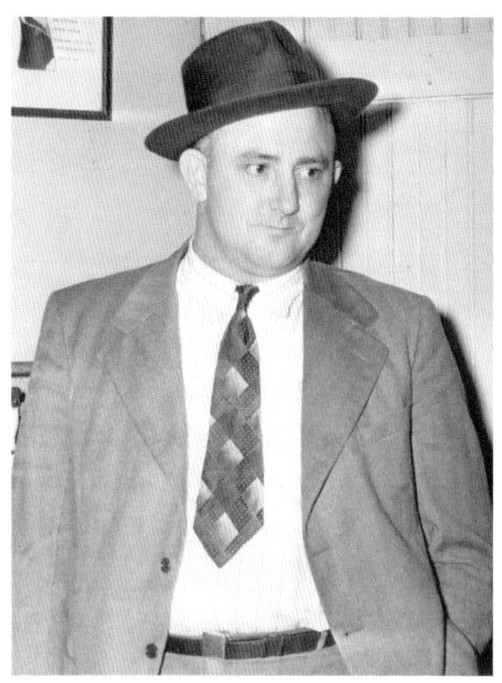

Clarence Higginbotham, Alias Ed Taylor. A popular ballplayer named Ed Taylor caught for the 1937 Lake View Hawks, earning the title "Mighty Taylor" by hitting long balls. Four years later, his photograph appeared in *Real Detective* magazine, identifying him as "the laughing killer." Soon captured in Sioux Rapids by Buena Vista County's sheriff, Higginbotham was exposed as a twice-escaped convict charged with a 1933 Alabama murder.

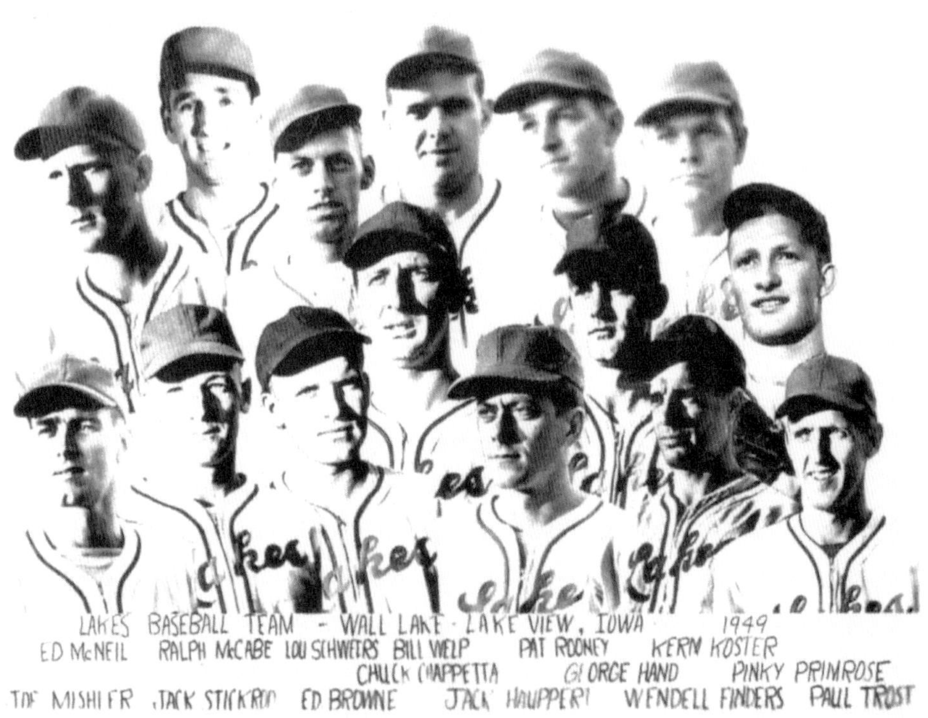

1949 Lake View–Wall Lake Lakes. The Sac County towns of Lake View and Wall Lake organized a team called the Lakes in the late 1940s. When a member of the Iowa State League of 1949, its roster consisted of local talent, outstanding college players, and even a former major-league player, Ralph "Mack" McCabe. (Courtesy of Lake View Historical Society.)

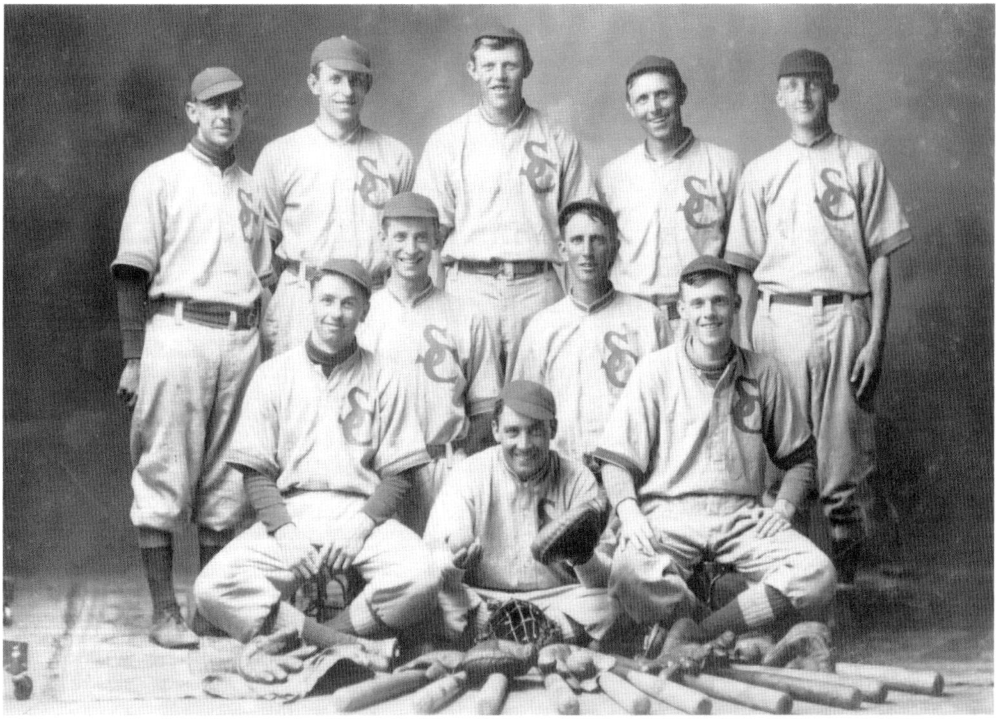

1911 Sioux Center Town Baseball Team. In this team photograph are, from left to right, (first row) Otto Vander Velde, pitcher; ? Highstreet, catcher; and Fred Aue, left field and pitcher; (second row) John Van Steenbergen, second base, and G. De Mots, right field; (third row) John Reimersma, third base; Gerrit Van Steenbergen, first base; ? Hoekstra, center field; George Siemen, manager; and T. De Ruyter, shortstop. (Courtesy of Greater Sioux County Genealogical Society.)

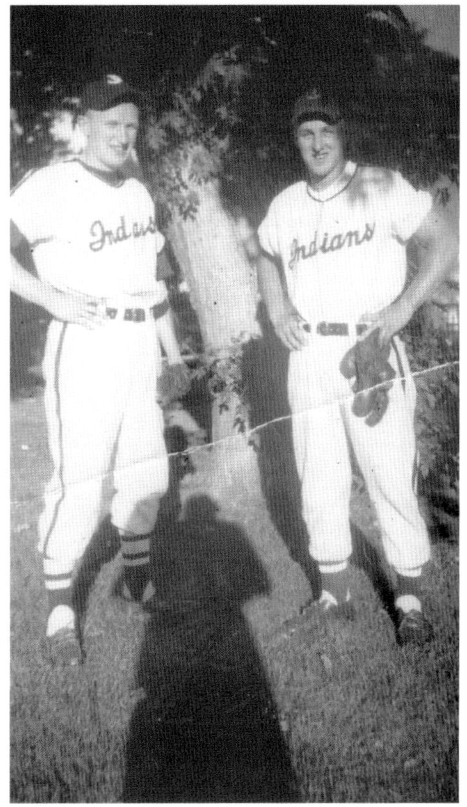

Wayne and David Bruinsma. Brothers Wayne (left) and David Bruinsma played baseball for Sioux Center's high school and Junior Legion clubs. Later, accomplished pitcher David played for and managed a US Army team in Germany. Then he signed with the Duluth-Superior team of the Chicago White Sox farm system, planning to report in April 1959. Tragically, he died of cancer in October 1958. (Courtesy of Greater Sioux County Genealogical Society.)

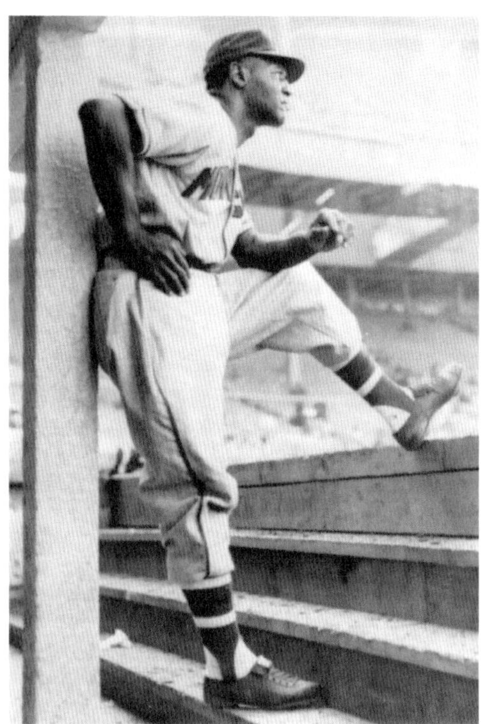

JOHN JORDON "BUCK" O'NEIL (1911–2006). Early in his professional career, renowned Negro League ballplayer Buck O'Neil played first base for the Kansas City Monarchs in a game at Sioux County's Rock Valley. About half the size of Sioux Center, Rock Valley hosted the match between the Monarchs and the barnstorming House of Davids on September 26, 1938. The Monarchs lost 1-0 in the nail-biter.

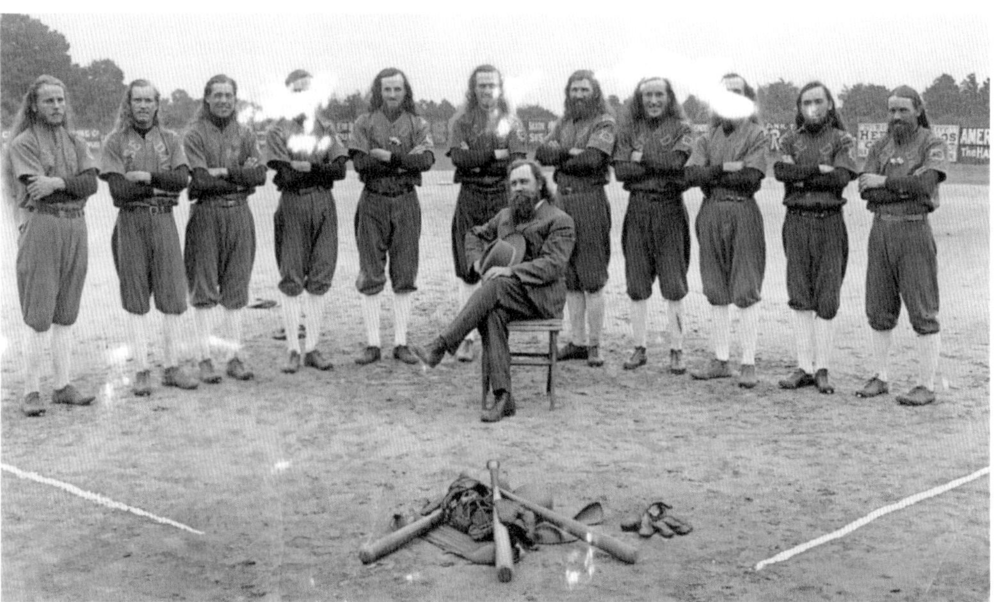

HOUSE OF DAVID BASEBALL TEAM. Initially established by the Israelite House of David, a Michigan religious community, this club started barnstorming across the country in 1920, the year this team photograph was taken. By 1938, when a House of David team played the Kansas City Monarchs at Rock Valley, there were two factions. But they were always identified by their long beards.

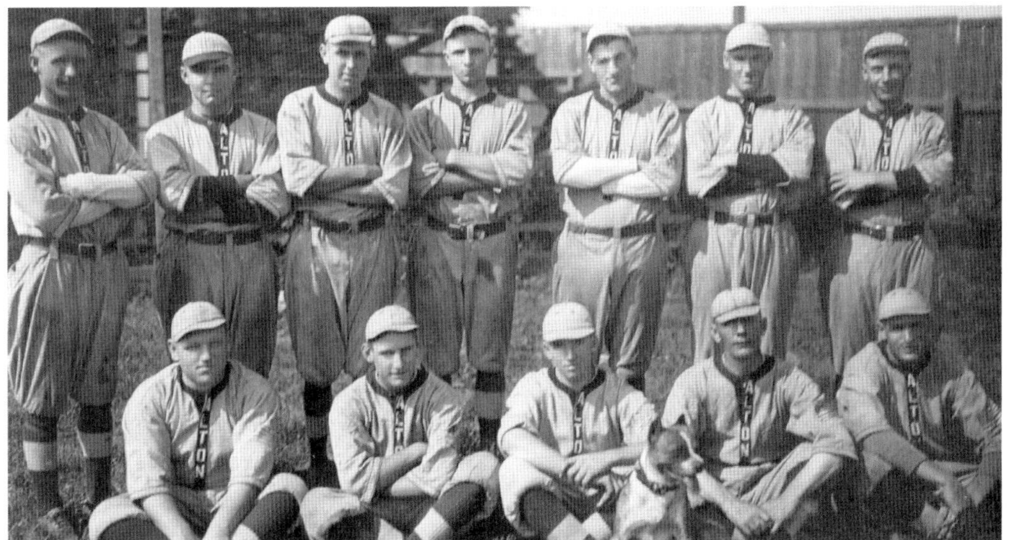

1919 Alton Baseball Team. Sioux County's Alton had two future big-leaguers on its 1919 baseball team, Herman Bell and Roscoe "Wattie" Holm (he grew up in Alton). From left to right are (first row) Bernard "Dekken" Hoxmeier, Holm, C. Keizer, Bob Holmes, and manager John "Bunny" Bonneville; (second row) Bill McGrau, J.T. "Matty" Even, Bill "Lefty" Hyink, Earl Hein, Bell, Gerrit "Spech" Van Nimwegen, and Jack Reuvers. (Courtesy of Alton Historical Museum.)

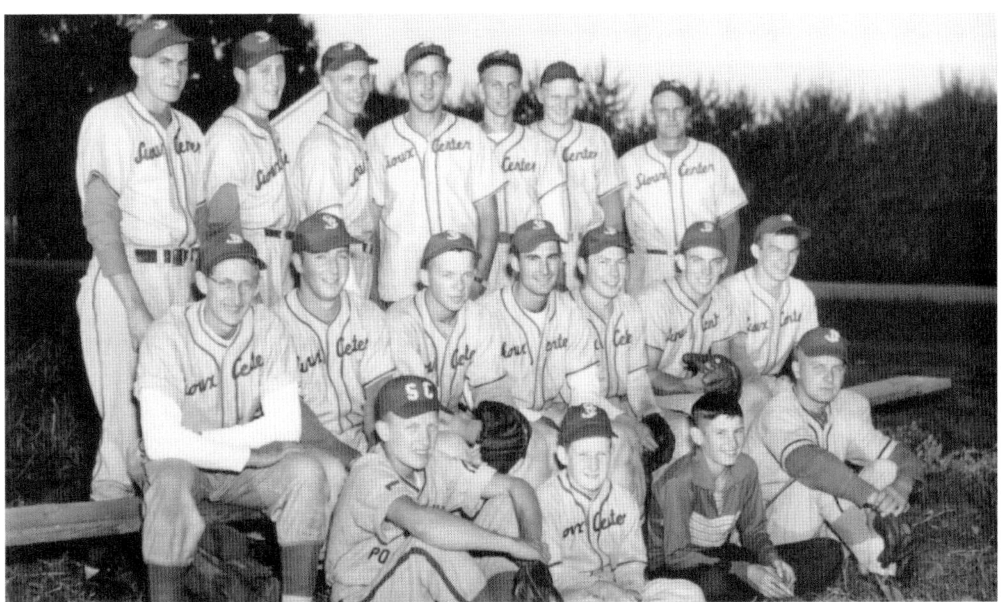

Sioux Center Team, 1940s. This is just one of many teams representing Sioux Center over the years, and two players in this photograph resemble the Bruinsma brothers. On the far left in back row and sitting on the far left in front row, the two are undoubtedly members of the Bruinsma family. Northwest Iowa League champions several times in the late 1940s, Sioux Center's clubs are legend. (Courtesy of Greater Sioux County Genealogical Society.)

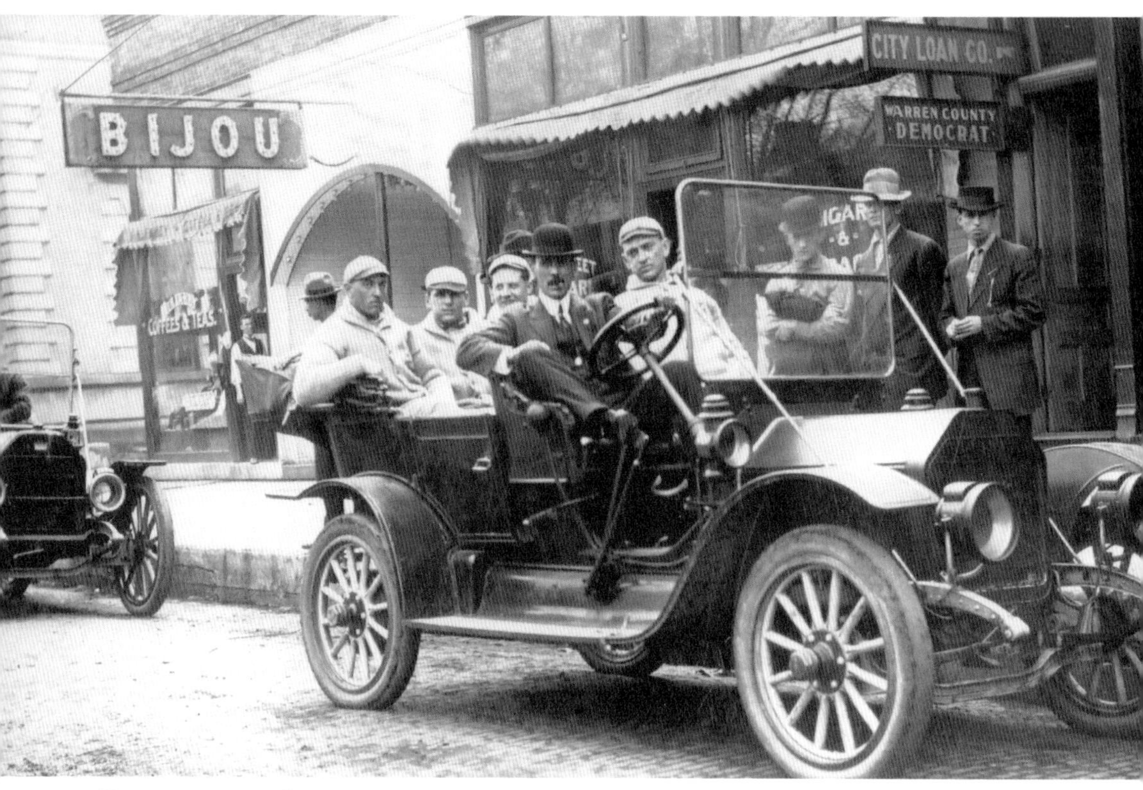

BARNSTORMING BASEBALL TEAM, C. 1912. Seen here in Monmouth, Illinois, the St. Louis Cardinals traveled through Iowa in October 1912. During a similar barnstorming tour, the Cardinals played an exhibition game in Alton on October 6, 1924. In that game, which attracted over 1,700 fans, home-grown Wattie Holm and Herman Bell, Cardinal regulars then, were Alton's battery. The Cardinals won 4-2. (Courtesy of Only Classics Collection.)

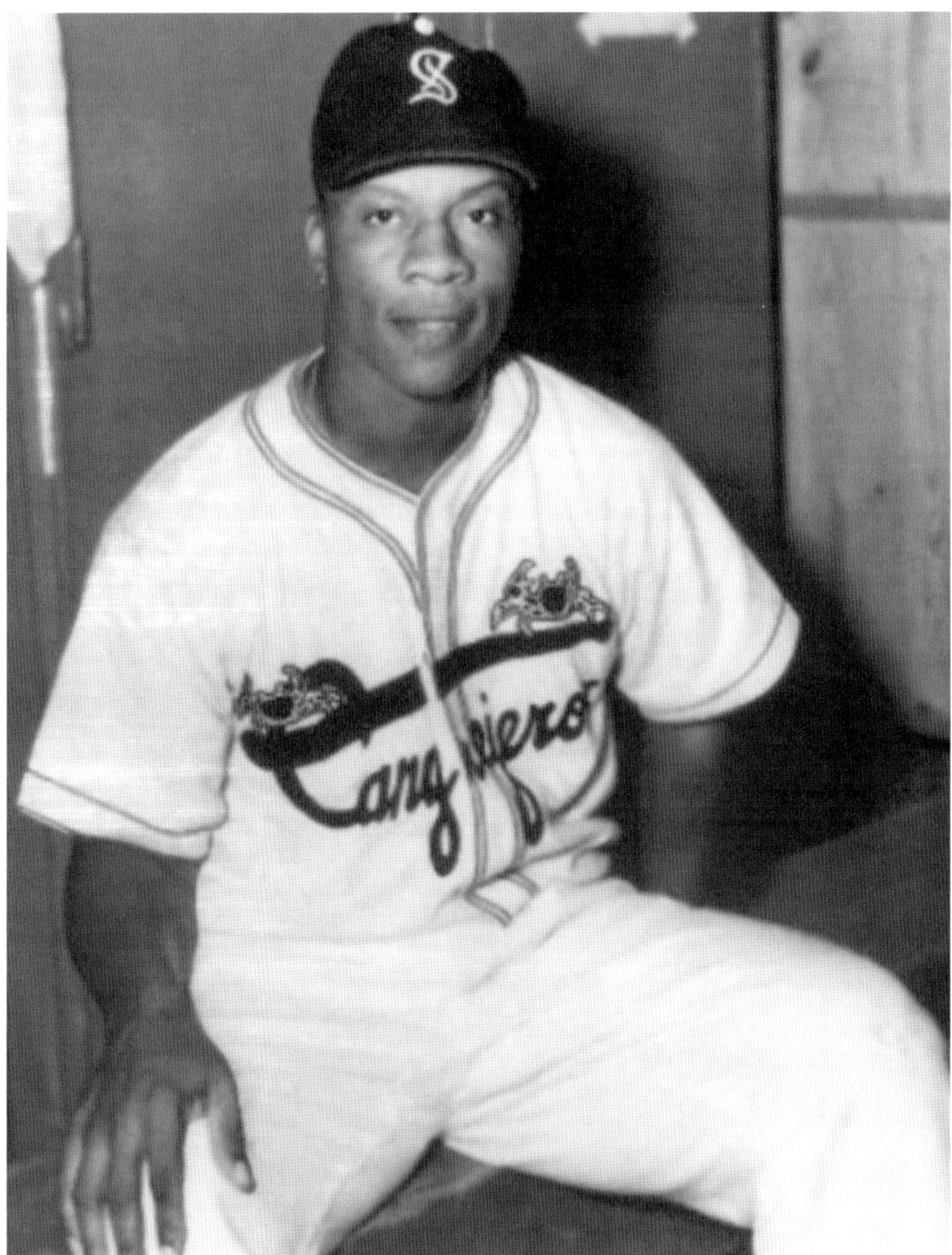

WILLARD BROWN IN PUERTO RICO. In 1947, Willard Brown briefly played for the St. Louis Browns, becoming the first African American to hit a home run in an American League game. In St. Louis's Sportsman's Park on August 13, 1947, he hit an inside-the-park homer. Playing winter ball in Puerto Rico in 1949–1950, Brown won the Triple Crown, earning the nickname "Ese Hombre." Nonetheless, he went hitless at Rock Valley in 1938. He played left field for the Kansas City Monarchs in a game against the House of David there that year.

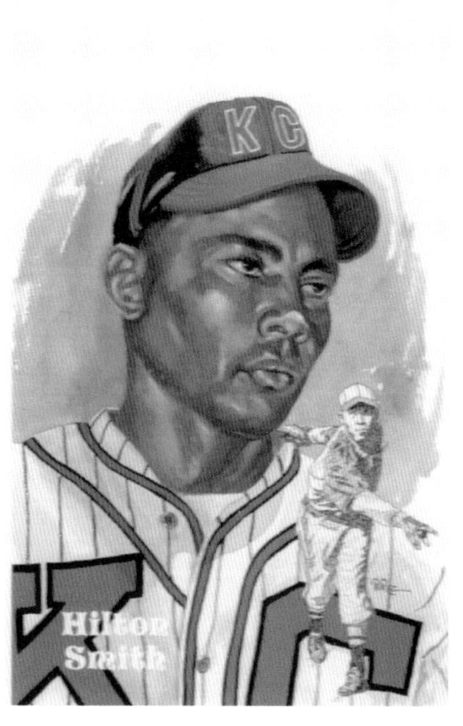

HILTON SMITH (1907–1983). Hilton Smith relieved the Monarchs' starting pitcher in the 1938 game at Rock Valley, striking out one and giving up one hit in one inning. Little did the enthusiastic crowd on hand that day know that they were witnessing a future hall of famer in action. Starting with the storied Kansas City Monarchs in 1936, Smith was inducted into the National Baseball Hall of Fame in 2001. (Courtesy of Dick Perez, Perez-Steele Hall of Fame Postcards.)

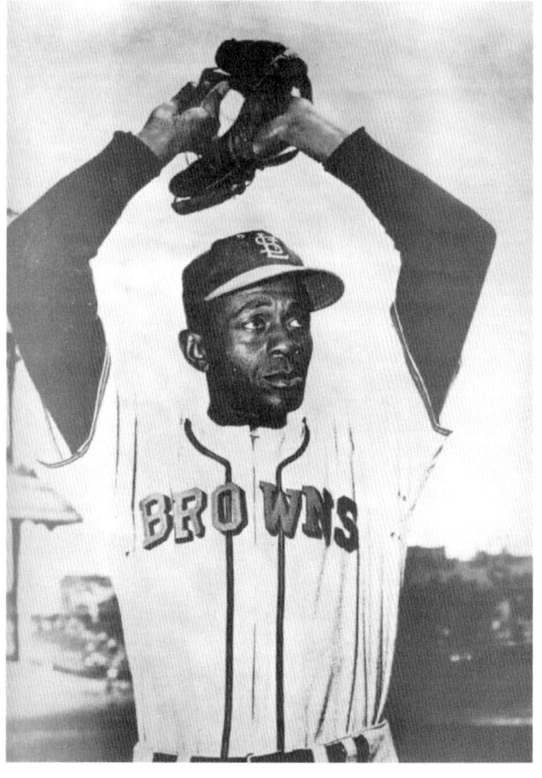

LEROY ROBERT "SATCHEL" PAIGE (1906–1982). Beginning his professional baseball career in the Negro Leagues in 1926, Satchel Paige surfaced as one of the most celebrated pitchers of all time with a number of clubs, including the Monarchs. He later played for three American League teams between 1948 and 1965. On August 29, 1940, he appeared in person with his all-star team at Rock Valley, Iowa.

Satchel Paige and Bob Feller, 1947. Future hall of fame pitchers Satchel Paige (left) and Bob Feller went on a barnstorming tour together in 1947, each choosing his own all-stars. Buck O'Neil and Hilton Smith were on Paige's team. Born in Van Meter in Central Iowa, Feller played in a tournament held at the 1935 Iowa State Fair when he was 16. A Le Mars club competed in that same event.

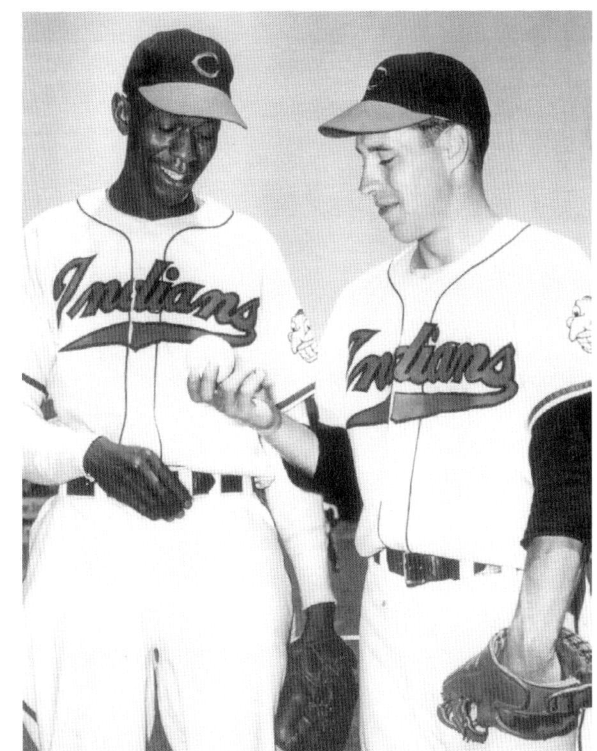

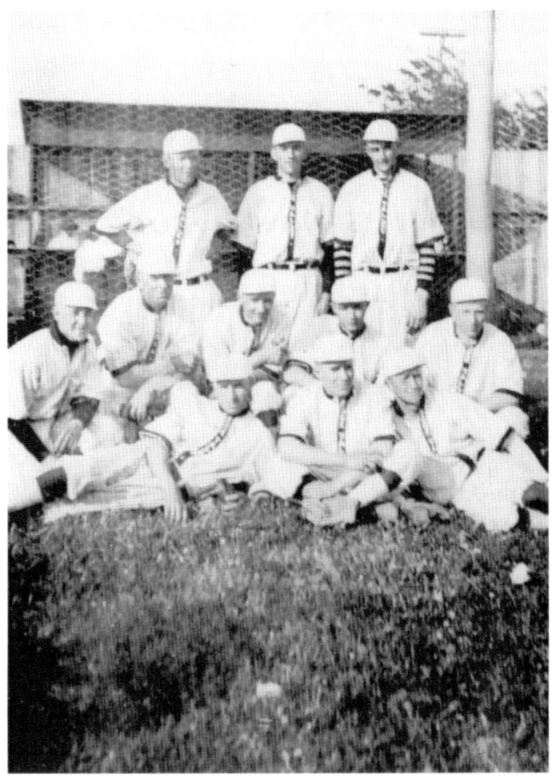

1910 Rock Valley Baseball Team. The identities of the members of this 1910 Rock Valley team are lost in time, but this image is testament to the town's baseball legacy. Today, Rock Valley Baseball Park, built in 1937 with a new grandstand as a WPA project in 1939, is one of the area's most historic ballparks. Used for semipro baseball from 1939 to 1949, it then served Northwest Iowa Amateur Baseball League games.

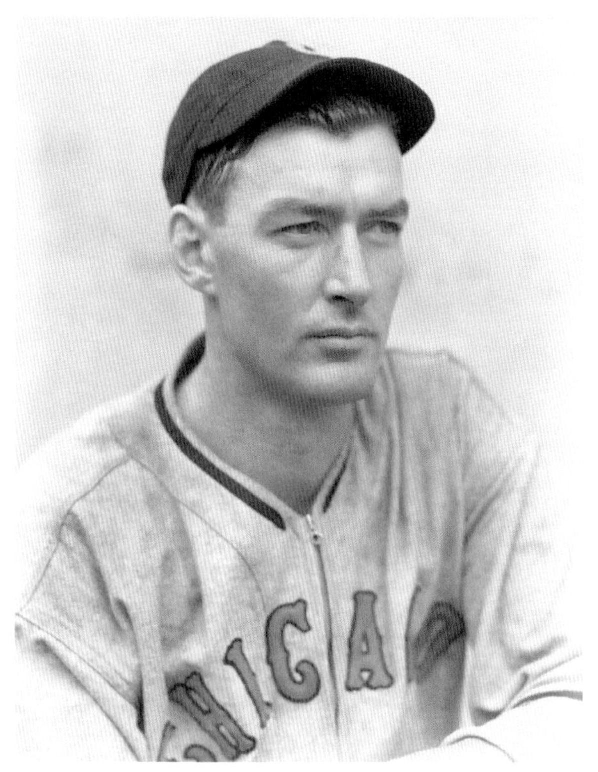

EUGENE MATTHEW "GENE" FORD (1912–1970). Born in Webster County's Fort Dodge, Gene Ford lived in Iowa towns throughout his life. The tall, right-handed pitcher played for two minor-league clubs and then the National League Boston Bees in 1936 and the Chicago White Sox in 1938. Later living in Emmetsburg, he was president of the Palo Alto County Farmers' Union and active in the Democratic Party. (Courtesy of findagrave.com.)

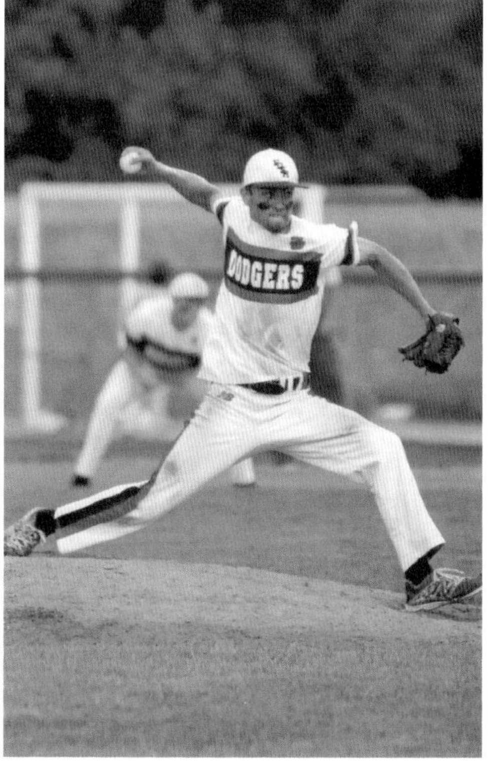

FORT DODGE BASEBALL, 2016. In a game with Sioux City East before a packed house at McNeil Field, Fort Dodge high school senior Sam Kolacia pitches in a Class 4A sub-state final. The Dodgers won the game 5-1. Named in 1995 for former Dodger coach Ed McNeil, the winningest high school baseball coach in Iowa history, the ballpark hosted its first game in 1942—a contest between the Chicago Cubs and the Chicago White Sox. (Courtesy of *Messenger News*; photograph by Britt Kudla.)

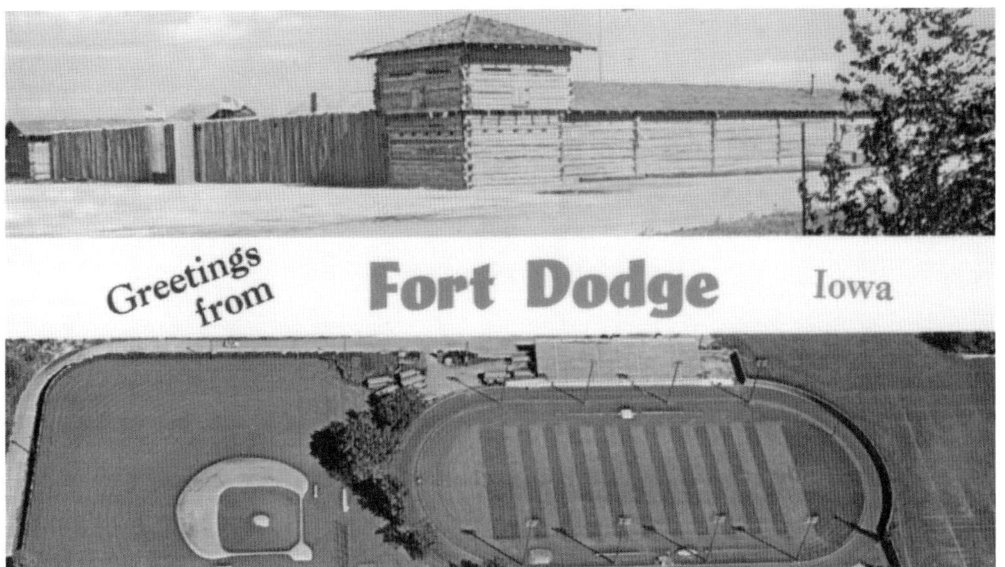

Fort Dodge Dodger Stadium. This dual-image postcard shows the replica of the original Fort Dodge, built in 1850. Also pictured is Dodger Stadium, now used by Fort Dodge High School and other educational institutions for football, track, soccer, tennis, and baseball. Built in 1939–1940, it is one of the state's best athletic facilities. McNeil Field is the baseball diamond on the left. Echoing Wrigley Field history, lights were first installed there in 2015.

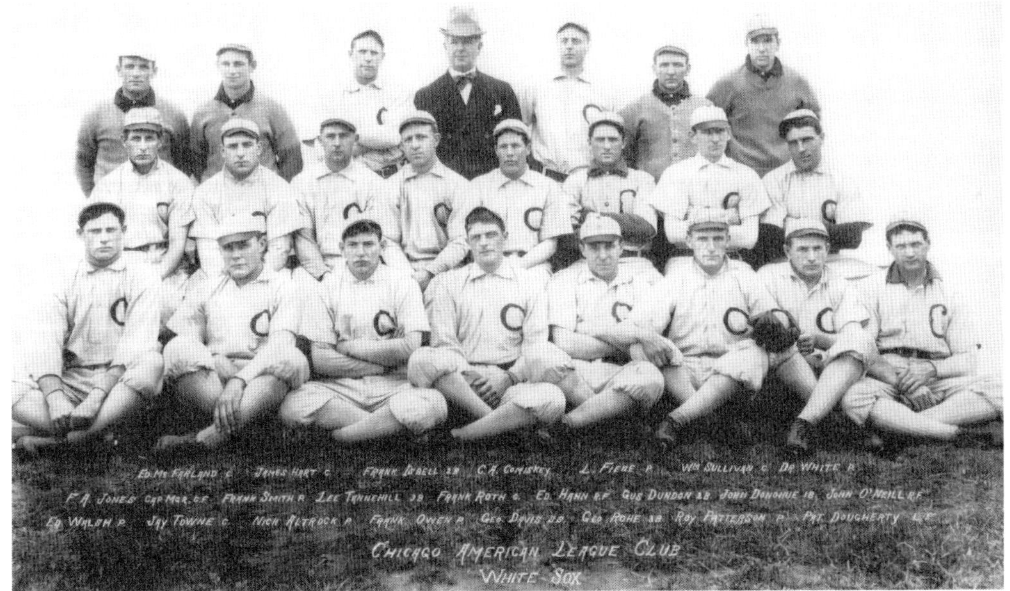

1906 Chicago White Sox with Lou Fiene. Born in Fort Dodge, Lou Fiene (1884–1964) pitched four seasons for the Chicago White Sox, 1906–1909. Seen here posing with the team that won the World Series against the Chicago Cubs, he stands fifth from left in the back row, next to legendary team owner Charlie Comiskey. Nicknamed "Big Finn," Fiene tallied a respectable 3.85 ERA during his major-league career.

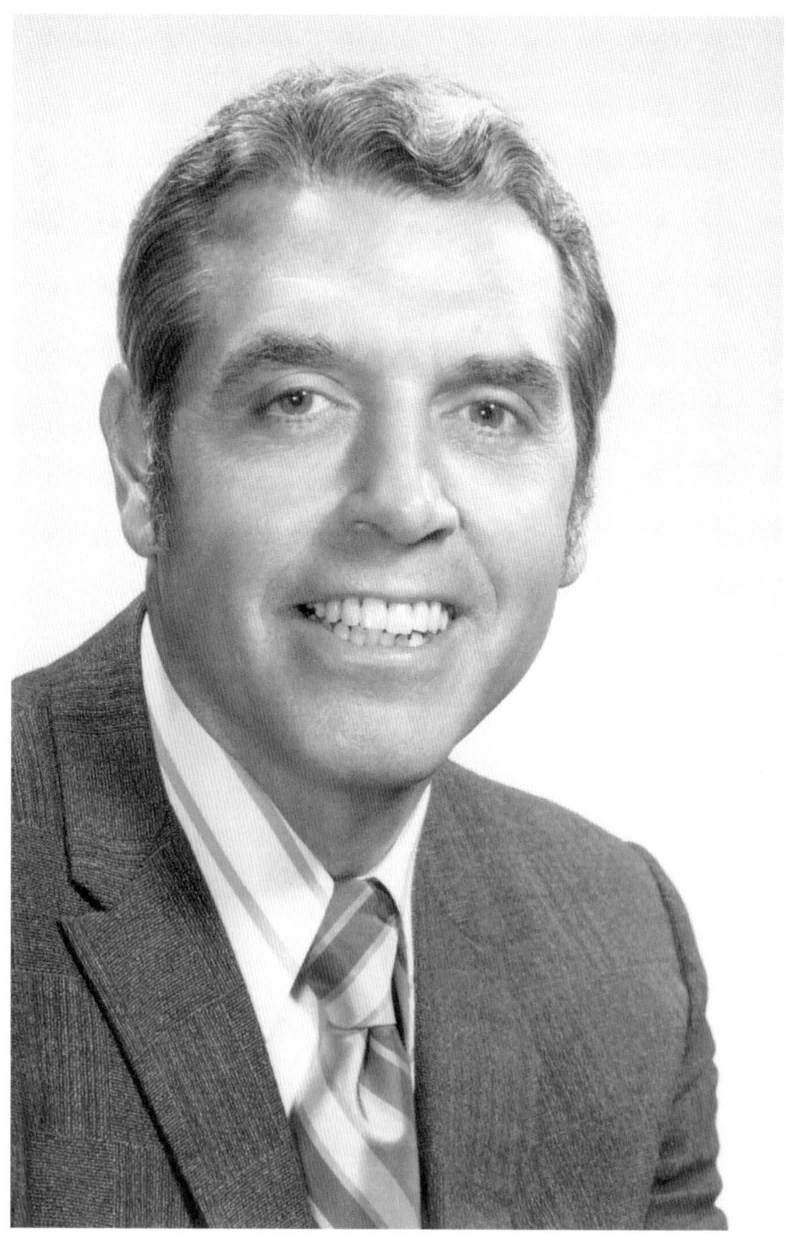

ROBERT GENE ELSTON (1922–2015). In 1941, Fort Dodge native Gene Elston began his extensive broadcasting career by announcing high school basketball games in his hometown. Before long, he graduated to minor-league baseball games. By 1954, he was the number two radio announcer for the Chicago Cubs. Four years later, he was announcing the nationally broadcast *Game of the Day* with fellow Iowan and retired pitcher Bob Feller. Then, in 1961, Elston started his long run with the Houston baseball franchise, first the Colt .45s and then the Astros. Starting in 1987, he again did national broadcasts such as *The Game of the Week*. After his retirement in 1998, Elston received the Ford C. Frick Award from the National Baseball Hall of Fame in Cooperstown, New York. (Courtesy of Adam A. Penale, findagrave.com.)

Woodbury County

The annals of Woodbury County's baseball history cannot be recounted in one illustrative chapter. Northwest Iowa's most heavily populated county due to the inclusion of its seat of Sioux City, it contributed 75 minor-league clubs and at least 11 home-grown major-league talents between 1888 and 2016. That does not count the untold number of future major-league players from other areas who were groomed by Sioux City and other Woodbury County teams. During that span, six different historic baseball parks have been used for professional baseball in Sioux City alone. Moreover, one gifted player from Sioux City is now a member of the National Baseball Hall of Fame in Cooperstown.

Historians naturally focus on Sioux City when covering Woodbury County baseball. The city lies along the Nebraska–South Dakota border, greatly enhancing the number of fans and players drawn from the greater metropolitan area. And the county's 16 towns have always participated in the sport. Four Woodbury County–grown big-league players came from towns other than Sioux City. Moreover, it is important to recall the countless clubs fielded by schools, churches, businesses, and amateur leagues. Many youngsters who rose to the ranks of professionals started out in such organizations. In recent times, Dave Edler, who played the infield for the Seattle Mariners from 1980 to 1983, and pitcher Don Wengert, with six big-league clubs from 1995 to 2001, were both born in Sioux City.

This chapter highlights some of the most significant people, places, and events that formed Woodbury County's baseball past.

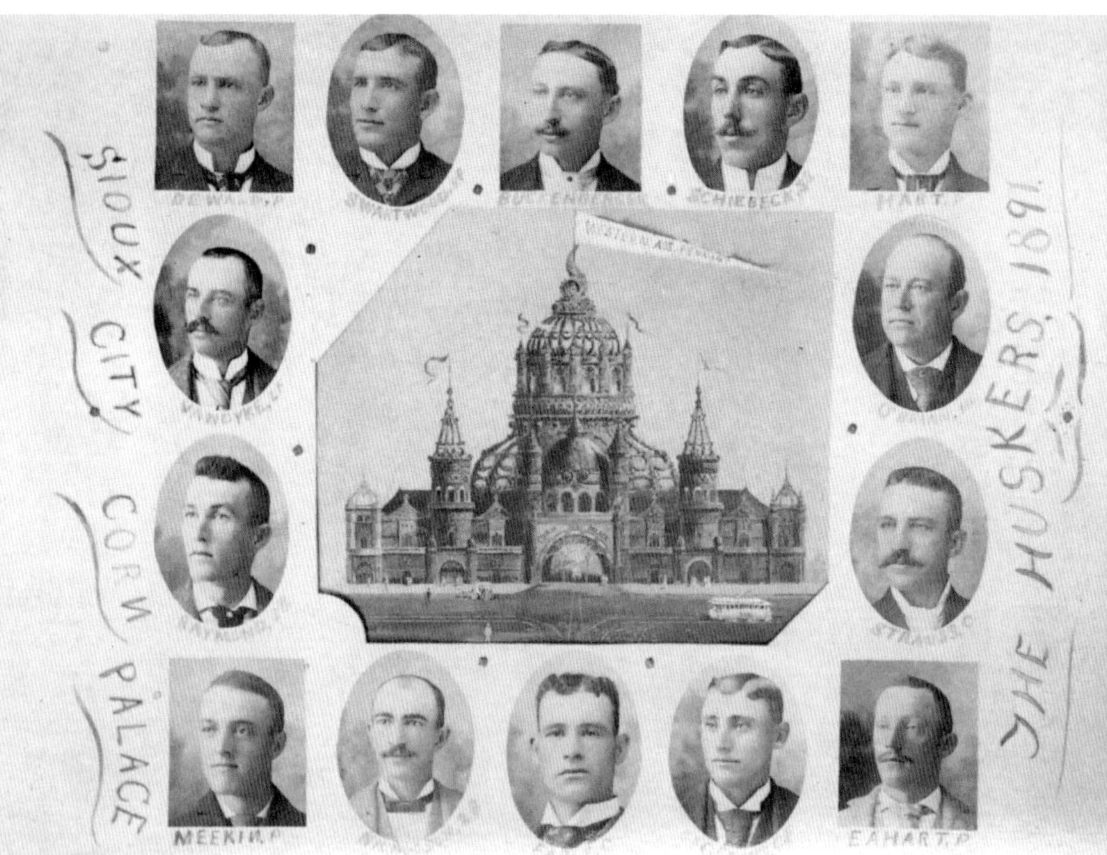

1891 SIOUX CITY CORN HUSKERS. Sioux City formed its first professional baseball club, the minor-league Western Association Corn Huskers, in 1888. The team of 1891 took four of a postseason six-game series with the Chicago Colts (forerunners of the Cubs), a National League team led by Cap Anson. Born in Central Iowa's Marshalltown, Anson was later dubbed "the greatest player-manager of the 19th century" by the National Baseball Hall of Fame. Held at Sioux City's Evans Park, the contest took place during the city's annual Corn Palace Festival. After defeating Chicago, the Huskers arranged an exhibition match with the major-league American Association St. Louis Browns. Sioux City swept the five-game series. That gave rise to the erroneous notion that the Huskers won the World Series that year. That was because Chicago disputed Boston's National League championship title that year. (Courtesy of Sioux City Public Museum.)

PETER W. WEBBER. Little is known about this ballplayer, other than he did pitch and play outfield for the Sioux City Corn Huskers of 1888 and 1889. He did have a five-year professional career. This vintage cigarette card spells his last name "Weber." (Courtesy of Library of Congress.)

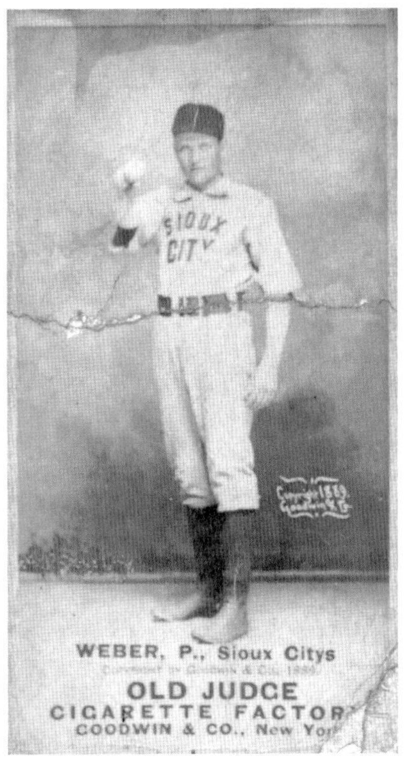

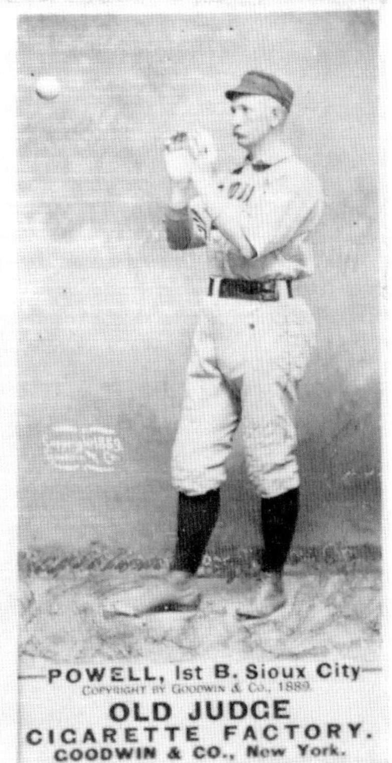

JAMES EDWIN "JIM" POWELL (1859–1929). Sioux City Corn Huskers manager and first baseman from 1888 to 1890, Jim Powell started playing professionally for his hometown of Richmond, Virginia, in 1884. From then to 1900, he played for seven different cities. (Courtesy of Library of Congress.)

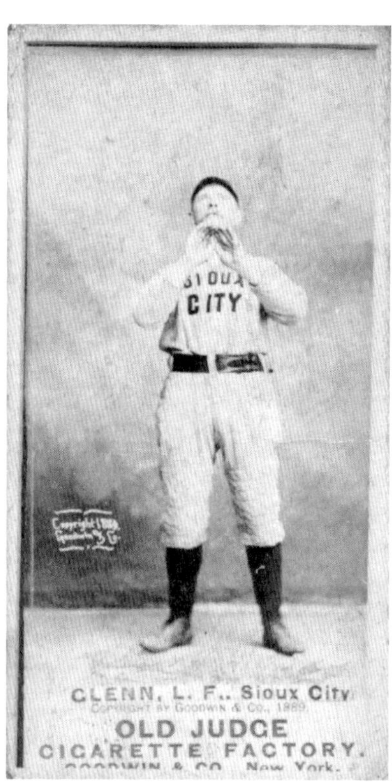

EDWARD C. "MOUSE" GLEN (1860–1892). At the end of his professional career, Ed Glen played left field for the Cornhuskers in 1889 and 1890. Like manager Jim Powell, Glen was born in Richmond, Virginia. Beginning with Richmond, he played for several other clubs, including the National League Boston Beaneaters in 1888. (Courtesy of Library of Congress.)

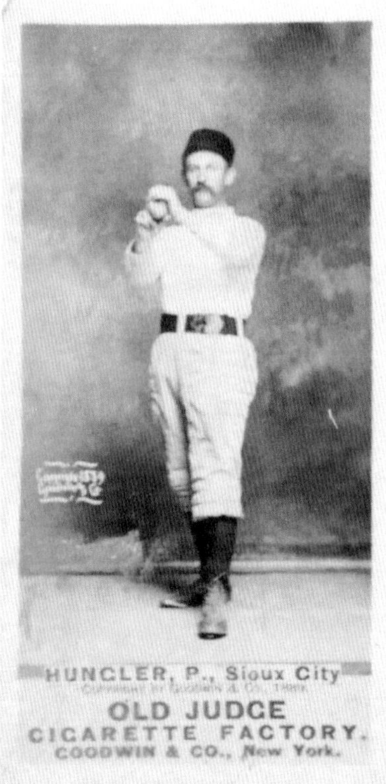

ALBERT "AL" HUNGLER (1860–1893). Born in Cincinnati, pitcher and right fielder Al Hungler played in the minor leagues from 1887 to 1890. During his one season with Sioux City in 1889, he tallied a 3-3 win-loss record. (Courtesy of Library of Congress.)

Joseph P. Crotty (1859–1926). Catcher and right fielder Joe Crotty was born in Cincinnati and began his professional baseball career in 1882, appearing in eight games with the St. Louis Brown Stockings that year. He then played for 10 other teams before his one year with the Sioux City Corn Huskers in 1889. Crotty spent his last season with the Canton, Ohio, Deubers in 1893.

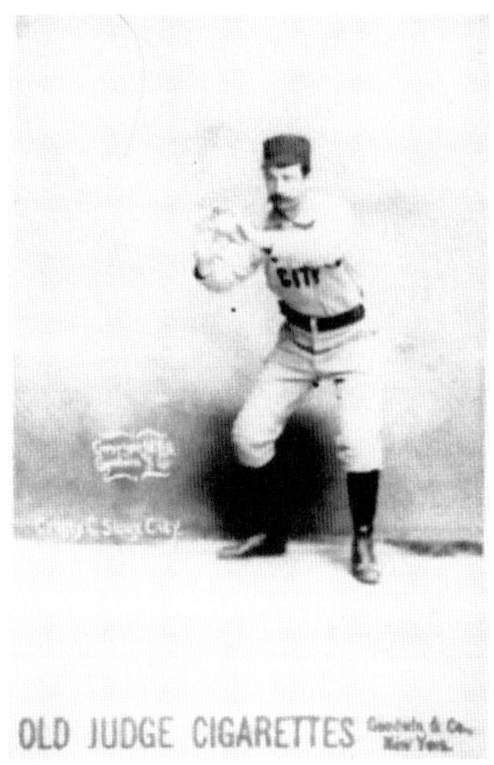

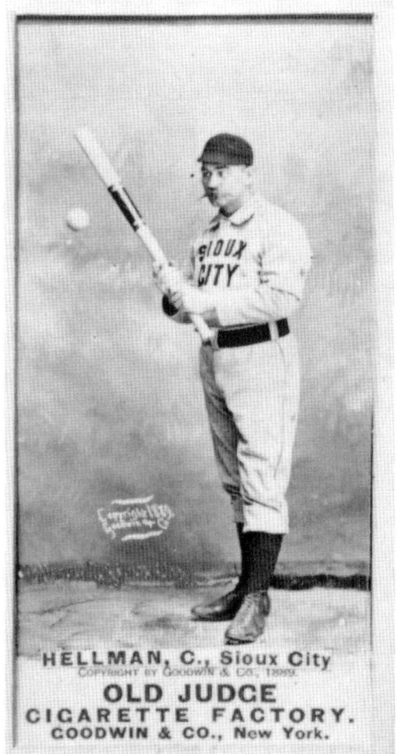

Anthony Joseph "Tony" Hellman (1861–1898). Also born in Cincinnati, catcher and outfielder Tony Hellman spent 1889, his last year as a professional ballplayer, with Sioux City. He started out in Terre Haute in 1884. Were it not for the Old Judge cigarette trading cards, individual Corn Huskers images of 1889 would be nonexistent. (Courtesy of Library of Congress.)

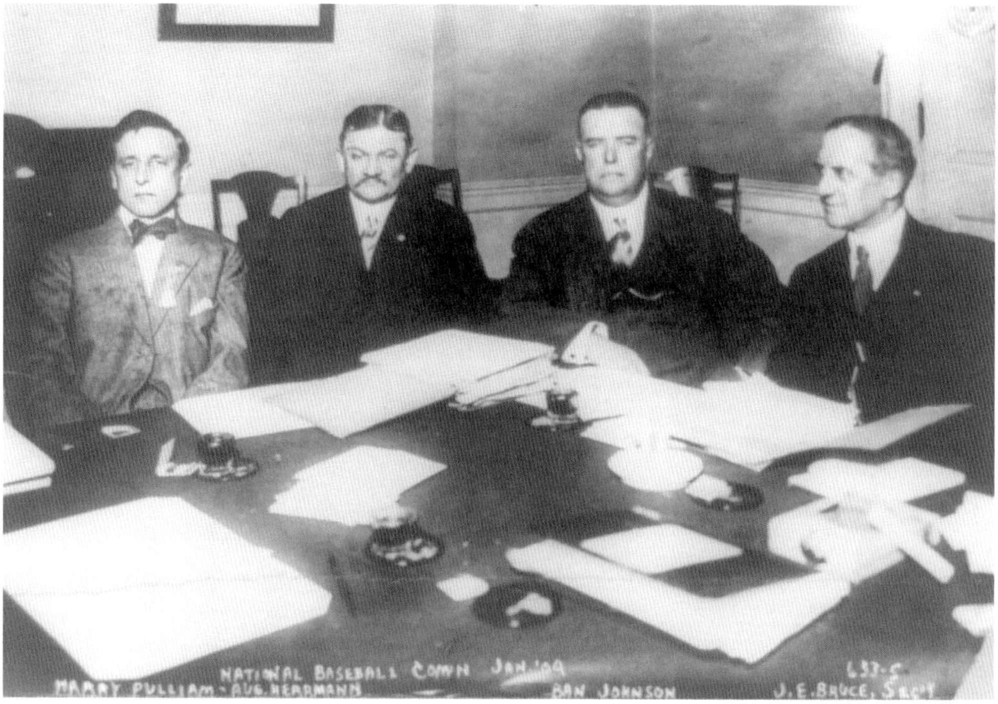

BAN JOHNSON AND ASSOCIATES. Elected president of the Western League in 1893, Ban Johnson converted it into the still-existing American League by 1901. During the transition period, the Sioux City Cornhuskers became the St. Paul Apostles and then the Chicago White Sox. In this 1909 photograph, Johnson, third from left, attends a big-league executive meeting. (Courtesy of Library of Congress.)

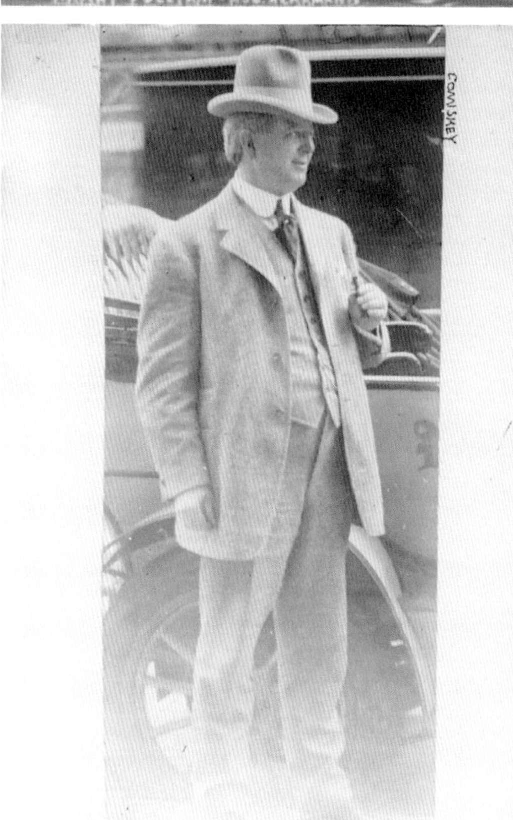

CHARLES ALBERT COMISKEY (1859–1931). Chicago-born Charlie Comiskey, "The Old Roman," bought and managed the Western League Sioux City Cornhuskers (one word by then) in 1895. The team then moved to St. Paul, where it became the Apostles. It then moved to Chicago, surfacing as the American League White Sox in 1901. (Courtesy of Library of Congress.)

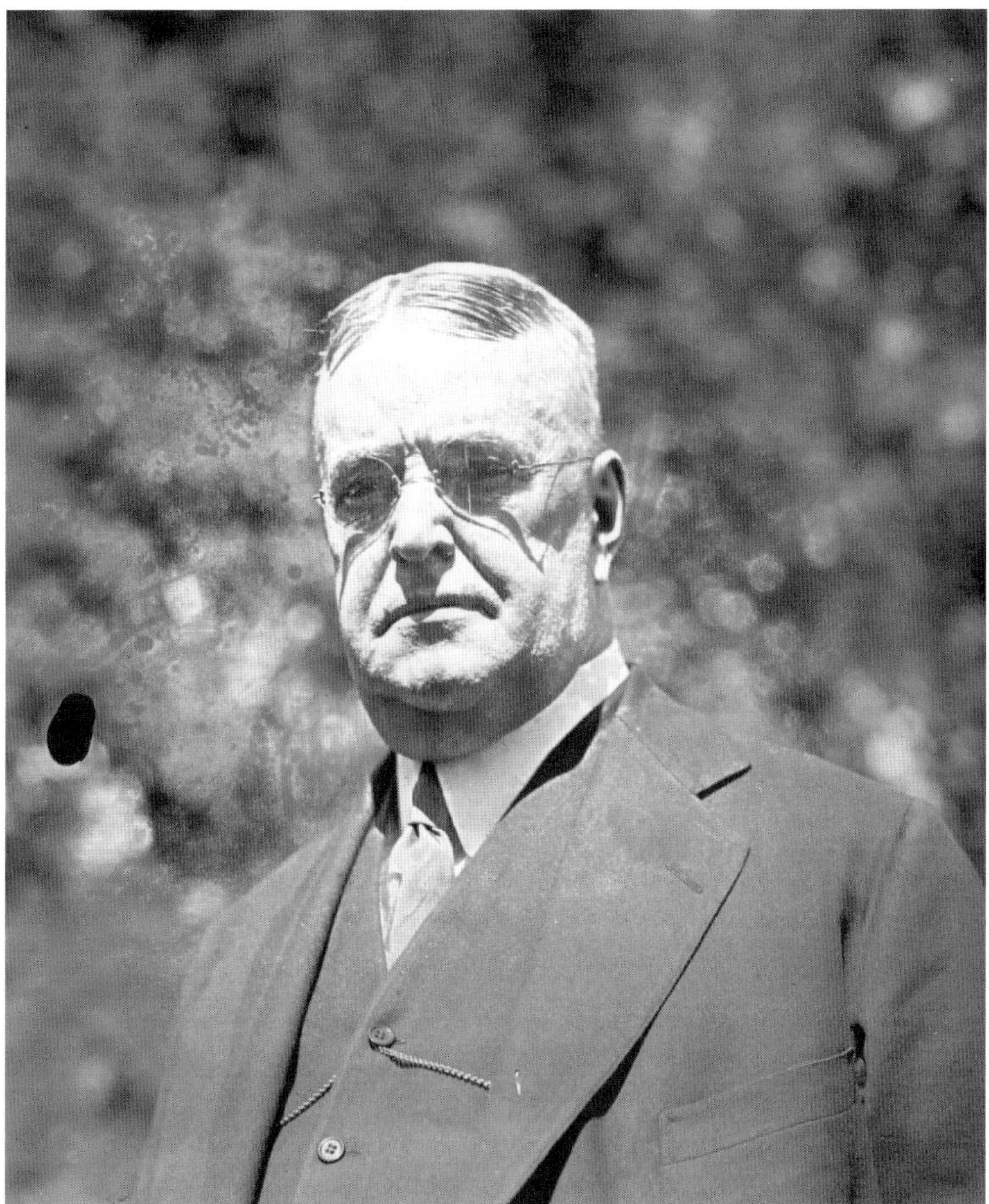

BYRON BANCROFT "BAN" JOHNSON (1865–1931). When baseball's National League reduced its number of teams from twelve to eight in 1900, Western League president Ban Johnson sent the former Cornhuskers, then the St. Paul Apostles, to Chicago and the Columbus team to Cleveland. He then renamed the league the American League. The 1901 season began with the two major leagues that still exist today. (Courtesy of Library of Congress.)

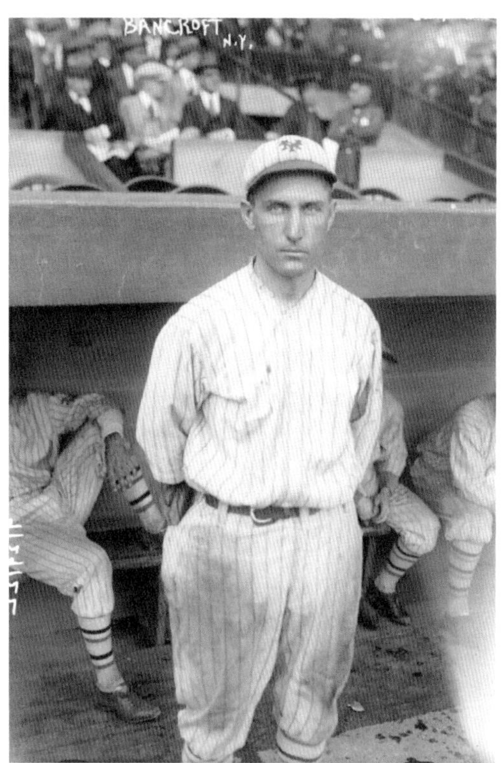

DAVID JAMES "BEAUTY" BANCROFT (1891–1972). Sioux City–born shortstop Dave "Beauty" Bancroft honed his baseball prowess playing sandlot ball and starring on Sioux City's Central High School team. From there, he played with several minor-league clubs until 1915. Signing with the Philadelphia Phillies then, he played for National League clubs for 16 years. He was inducted into the National Baseball Hall of Fame in 1971. (Courtesy of Library of Congress.)

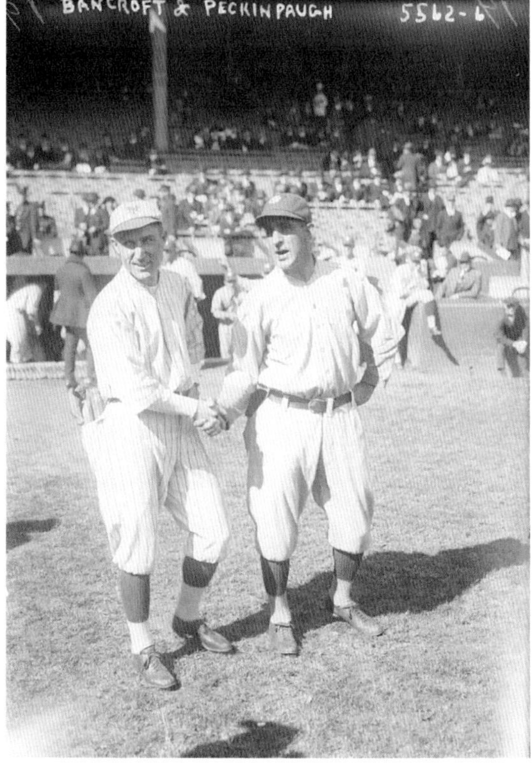

DAVE BANCROFT (LEFT) AND ROGER PECKINPAUGH, 1920. Starting 1920 with the Phillies, Bancroft spent most of the season with the New York Giants. Here, he shakes hands with fellow shortstop Roger Peckinpaugh of the New York Yankees. Bancroft played for the Giants through 1923. Although this photograph is dated 1920, it was most likely shot in 1921 during the World Series. (Courtesy of Library of Congress, Bain Collection.)

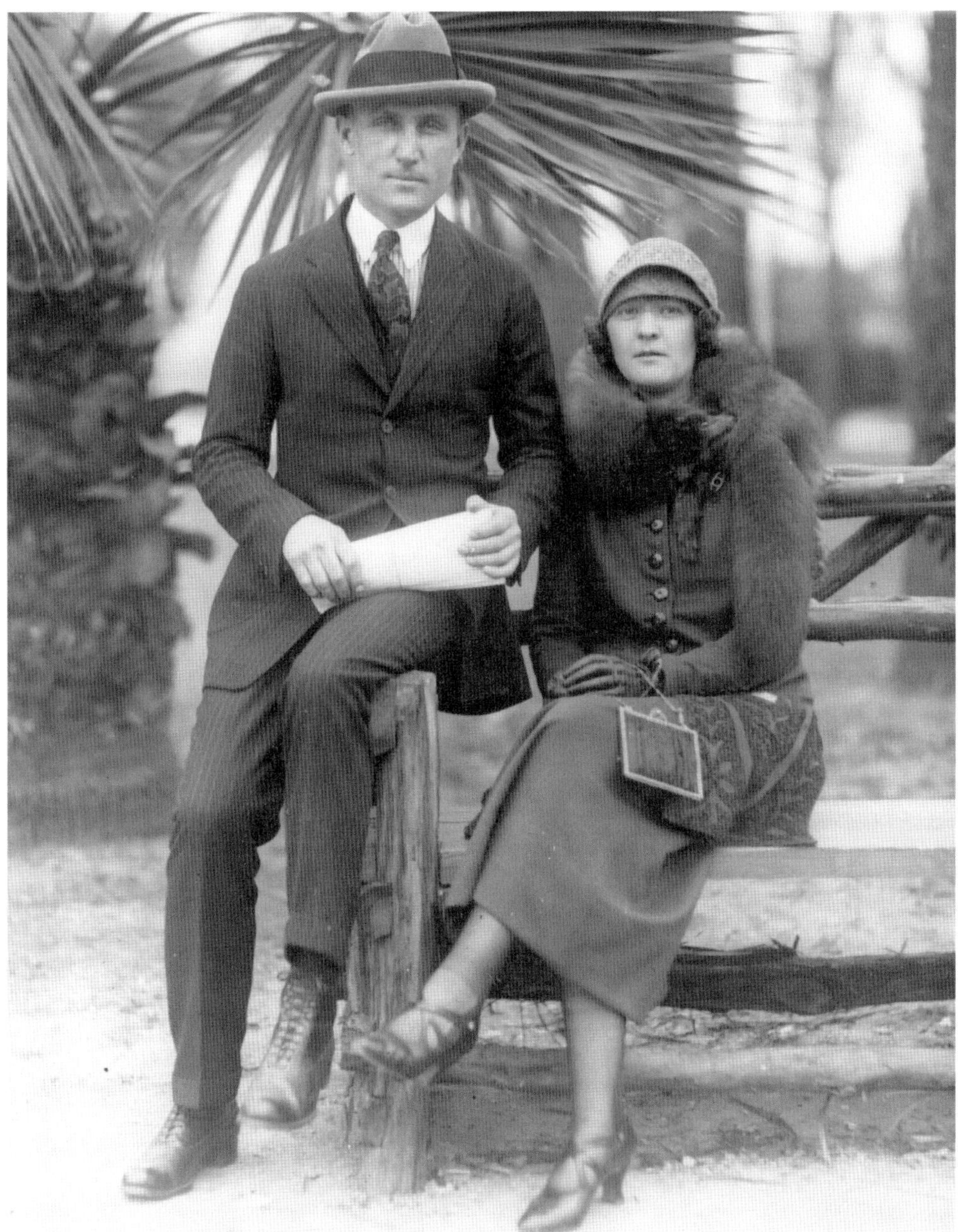

Dave Bancroft and His Wife, Edna, 1922. In 1909, Bancroft started his professional baseball career playing for the Duluth White Sox of the Minnesota-Wisconsin League. Halfway through the season, he was sent to the Superior, Wisconsin, Blues of the same league. Playing there again the following year, he met and married Edna Harriet Gisin. The couple made Superior their home, but Dave went to play for Portland in the Pacific Coast League from 1912 to 1914. Faring well there, he gained the notice of the Phillies and started with that club in 1915. That began his epic major-league career. His marriage never produced children, but the devoted couple lived in Superior for the rest of their lives.

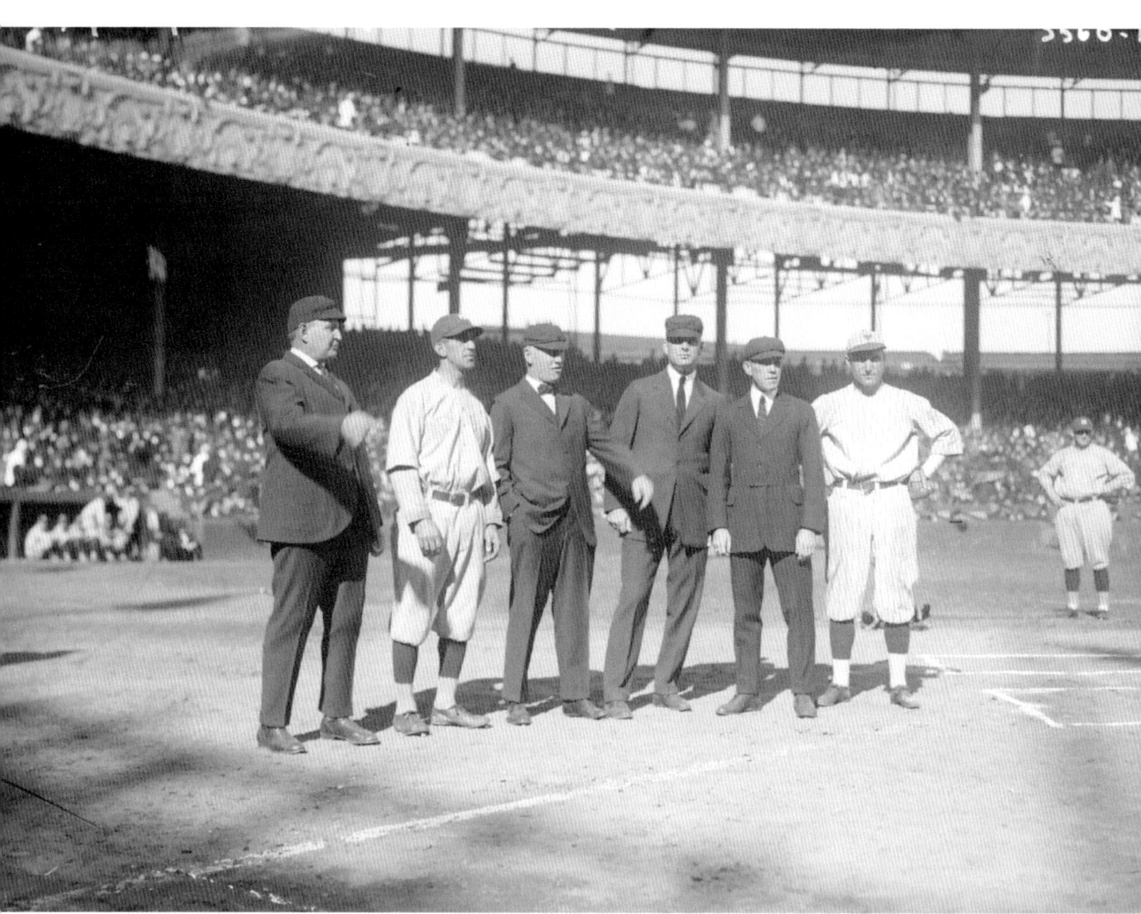

Peckinpaugh, Bancroft, and Umpires at Polo Grounds, 1921 World Series. After coming to the New York Giants in 1920, Dave "Beauty" Bancroft was with the team in 1921 when it defeated the New York Yankees 5-3 in the World Series. With Bancroft as its captain and star shortstop, the club went on to win the National League pennant the following two seasons, winning the World Series against the Yankees again in 1922 and losing to the Yankees in 1923. By then, Beauty had gained a reputation as one of the greatest shortstops who ever lived. Following the series of 1923, he went to the Boston Braves as player-manager for the next four years and the Brooklyn Robins in 1928 and 1929. He finished his big-league playing days back with the Giants in 1930. (Courtesy of Library of Congress, Bain Collection.)

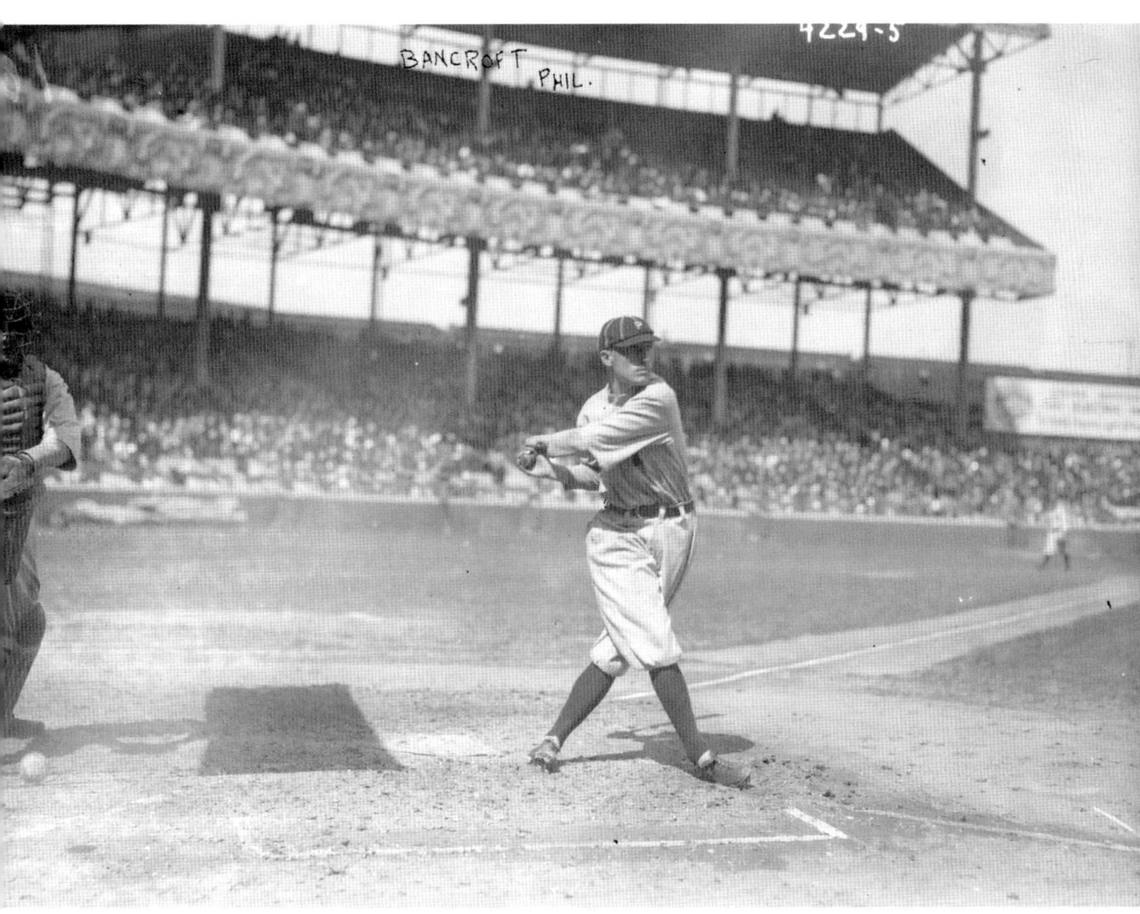

Dave "Beauty" Bancroft, 1917. At bat for Philadelphia during his third year in the major leagues, Bancroft was at the beginning of a long career that eventually earned him a plaque at Cooperstown. When he could no longer play after the 1930 season, he stayed on with the Giants as an assistant manager for several years. Then he managed a number of minor-league clubs, including the Western League Sioux City Cowboys of 1936 and later a barnstorming all-girls team. Inducted into the National Baseball Hall of Fame in 1971, he died the following year. It is well known that he got his nickname "Beauty" because that's what he called a good pitch. (Courtesy of Library of Congress, Bain Collection.)

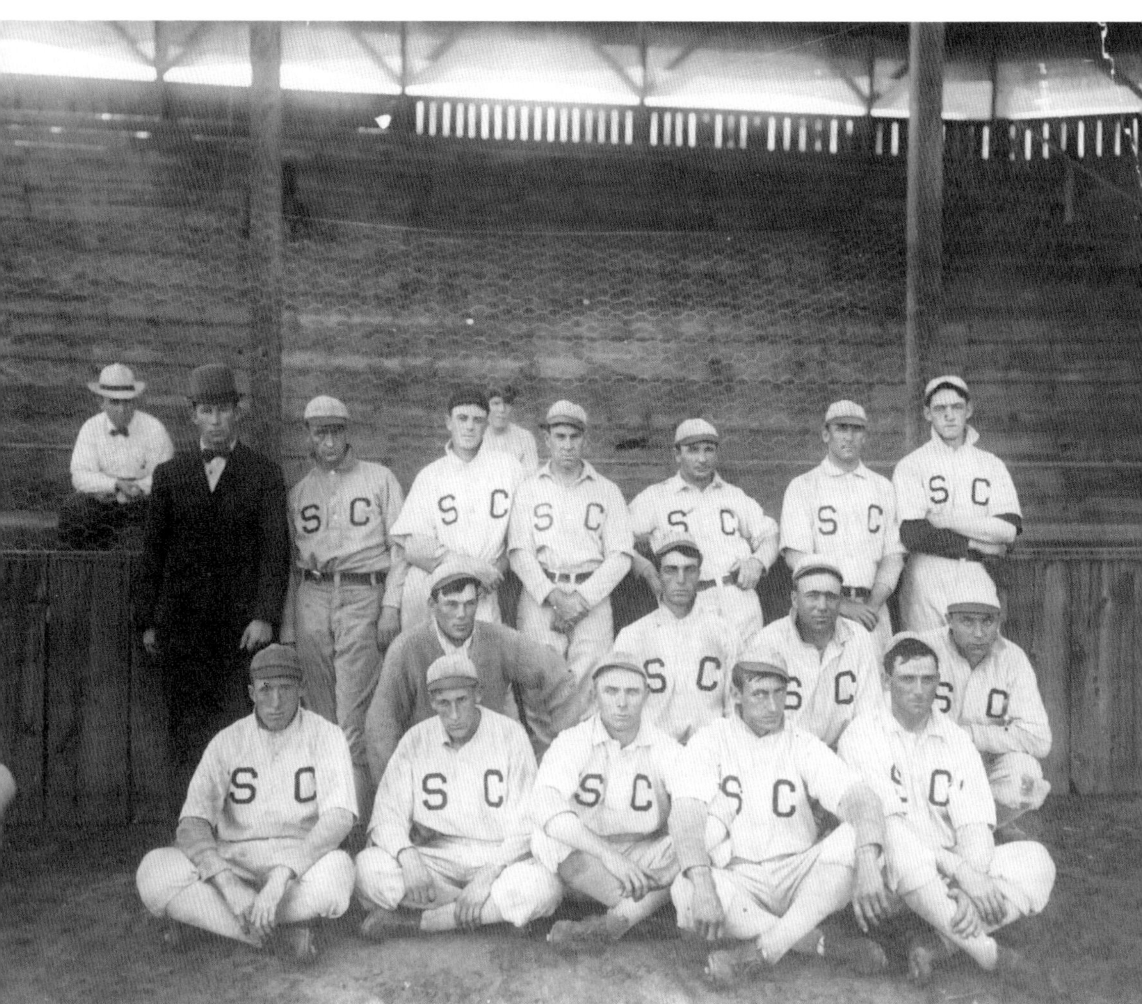

SIOUX CITY PACKERS, 1908. Sioux City's Class A club of 1908, the Packers, ended the season as Western League champions. Five members of that team played for major-league clubs at one time or another. Seen here fifth from left in the top row is player/manager Ducky Holmes, who caught for the St. Louis Cardinals in 1906. Others were pitcher Dick Crutcher (not pictured), with the Boston Braves in 1914; outfielder Danny Green (left of Holmes), with the Chicago Cubs from 1898 to 1901 and the White Sox from 1902 to 1905; pitcher Reeve "Rip" McKay (far left, middle row), with the St. Louis Browns in 1915; and catcher Hank Severeid (not pictured), with four big-league clubs between 1911 and 1926, mostly with the St. Louis Browns but also Cincinnati, Washington, and in 1926, the New York Yankees. (Courtesy of Sioux City Public Museum.)

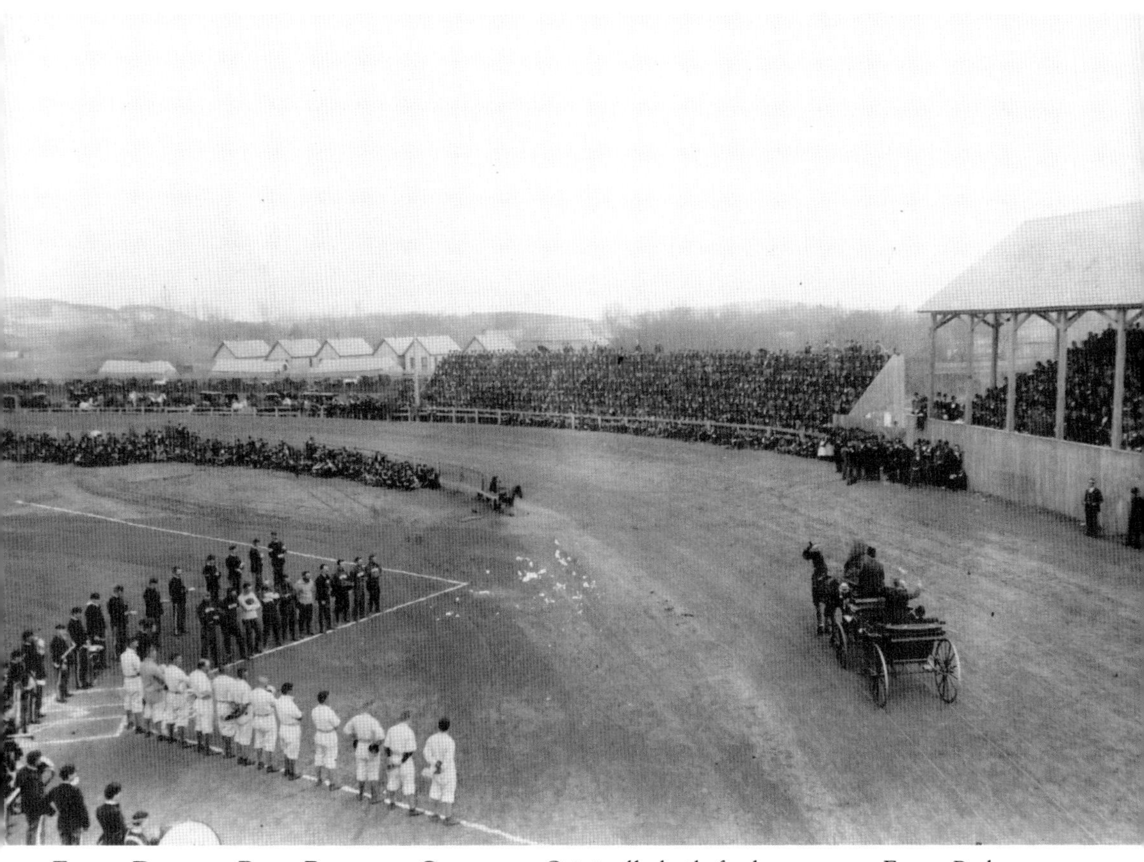

Evans Driving Park Baseball Grounds. Originally built for horse races, Evans Park was equipped with fences, grandstands, and a dirt track. According to historians, the racetrack crossed Perry Creek. Located in the Crescent Park area of Sioux City, it is the earliest known ballpark where the Corn Huskers played. They used Evans from at least 1890 until about 1895, when they played at Riverside Park. The date and occasion of this photograph are unknown. It is obvious that some dignitary was being honored, as a man is waving to the crowd from the horse-driven carriage. Playing for the Huskers in 1890 and 1891 was inveterate baseball man Bob Black. Although born in Cincinnati, he was a well-known figure in Northwest Iowa. Outfielder, pitcher, and shortstop for a number of minor-league clubs beginning in 1883, he eventually moved to Le Mars, where he managed the Blackbirds. (Courtesy of Sioux City Public Museum.)

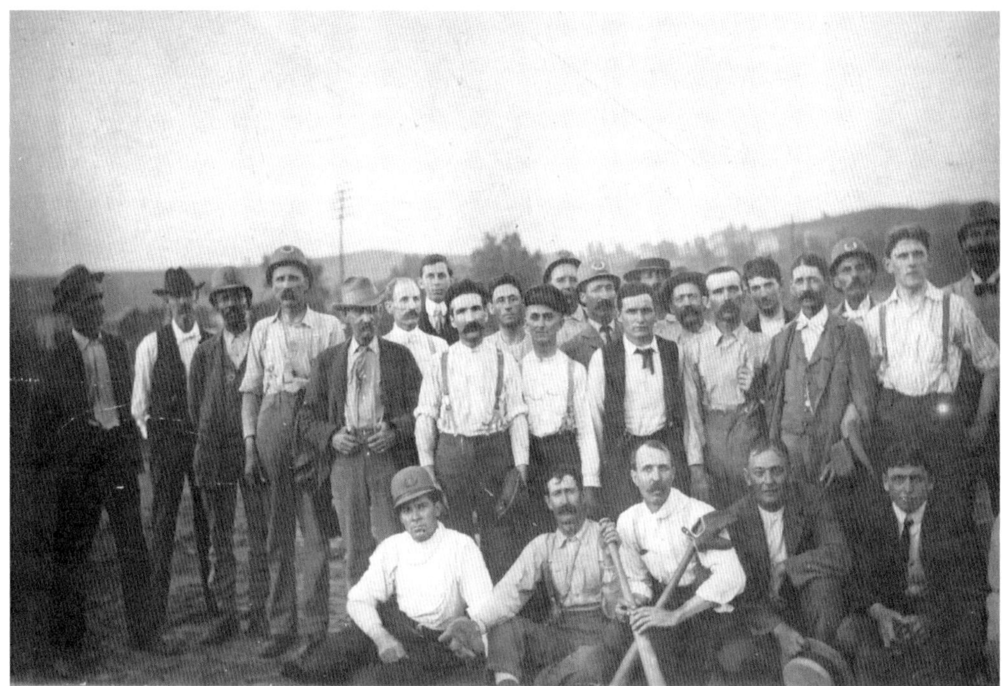

Sioux City Postal Employees Team, 1902. The individuals in this 1902 photograph are unidentified. Nonetheless, the image projects an aura of the times. The sport of "base ball" took precedence in group portraits. The man in shirtsleeves front and center displays bats and glove. (Courtesy of Sioux City Public Museum.)

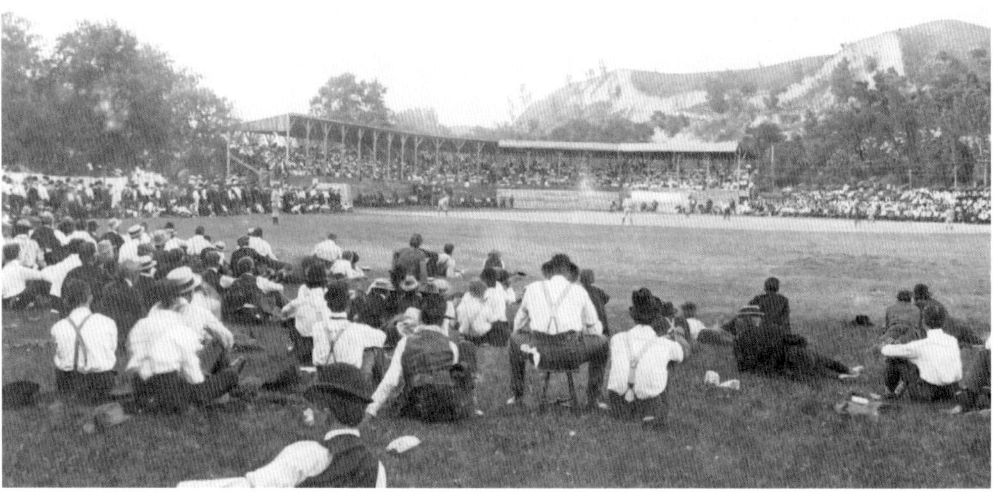

Riverside Baseball Grounds. From 1895 to 1900, Sioux City had no minor-league clubs, but the teams it did have played here. From 1900 until 1919, its professional clubs called the Riverside Grounds or Park home. Located along the Big Sioux River in the Riverside area of Sioux City, it hosted baseball for the Huskers, the Soos, the Packers, and the Indians. (Courtesy of Sioux City Public Museum.)

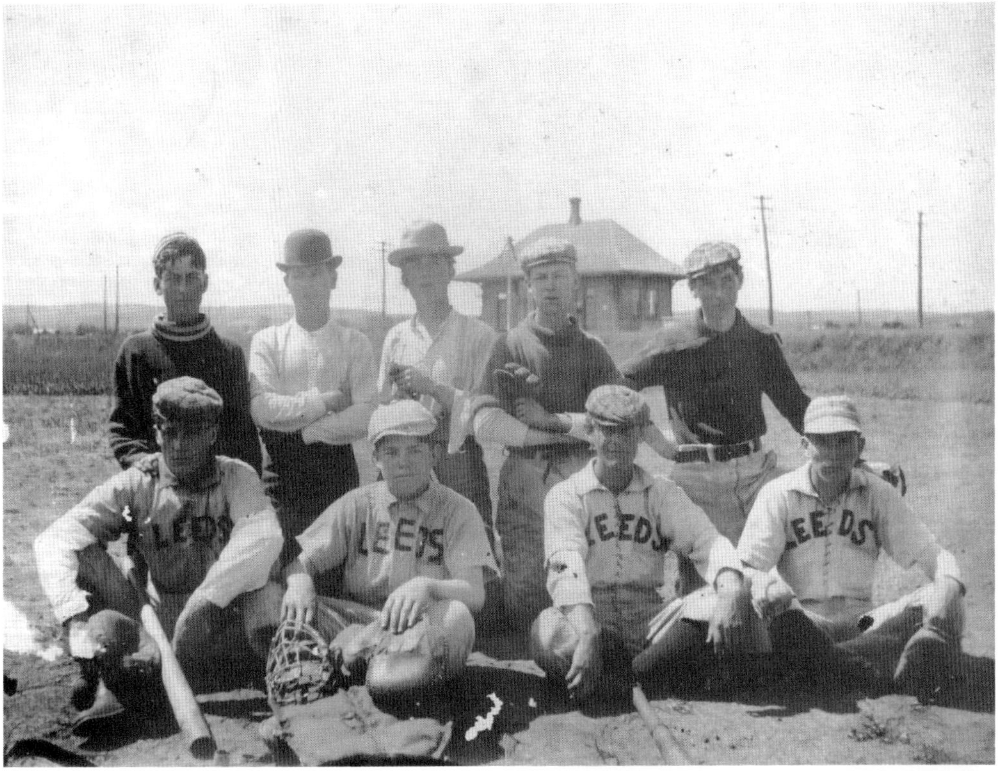

LEEDS TEAM, 1900. Founded in 1889 and then annexed by Sioux City, Leeds is now mostly a residential neighborhood. This baseball club of 1900 reveals an early independent character, considering the array of headgear. On July 24, 1912, the barnstorming All Nations team, which included one woman, played two exhibition games at Leeds. (Courtesy of Sioux City Public Museum.)

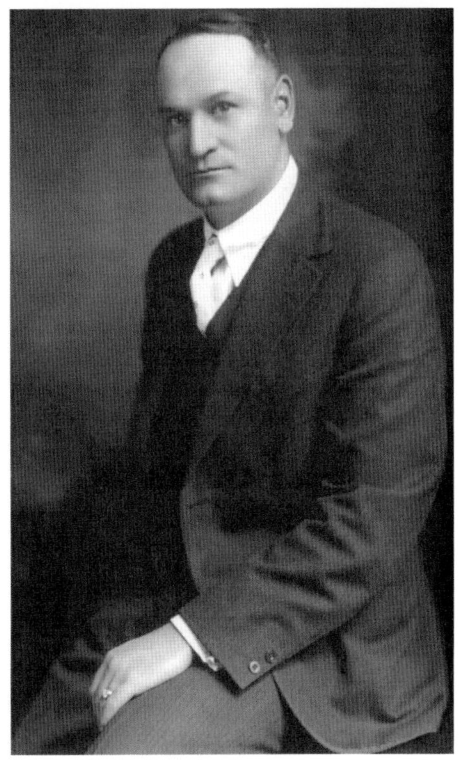

WALTER HENRY "JUDGE" MCCREDIE (1876–1934). Born in Manchester, Delaware County, Walt McCredie moved to Sioux City sometime during his youth. There, he developed his baseball acumen. As an outfielder and shortstop, he began his professional playing days with Des Moines, and by 1900, he was with the Sioux City Cornhuskers. In 1903, McCredie played right field for the Brooklyn Superbas (later Dodgers). He eventually became part-owner and player-manager for the Portland Beavers of the Pacific Coast League.

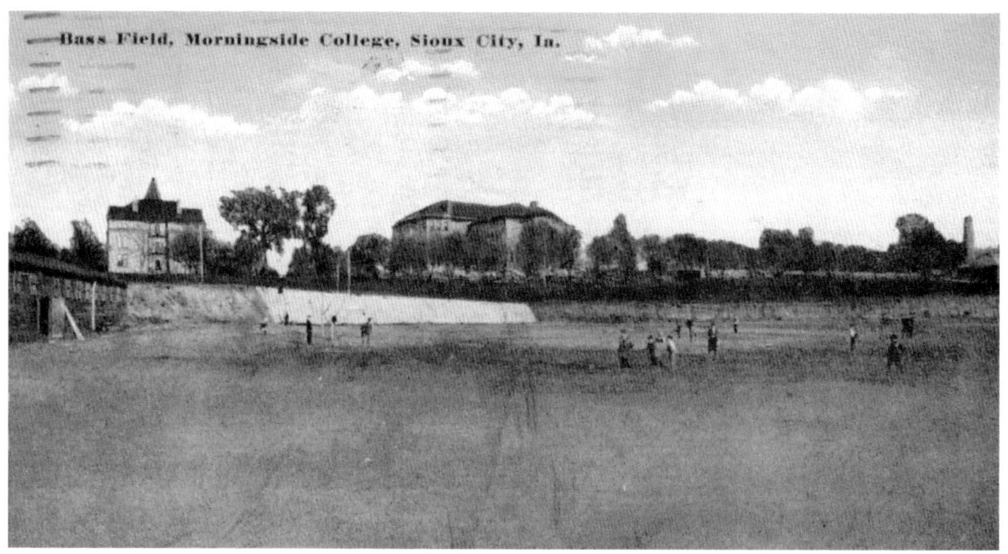

BASS FIELD AT MORNINGSIDE COLLEGE. Founded in 1894, Morningside College in Sioux City has always encouraged sports. Its Mustangs baseball team's Brian Drent has a 165-107 career record as its head coach. Bass Field, shown in this vintage postcard, is still in use. A new softball complex now occupies a third of its property.

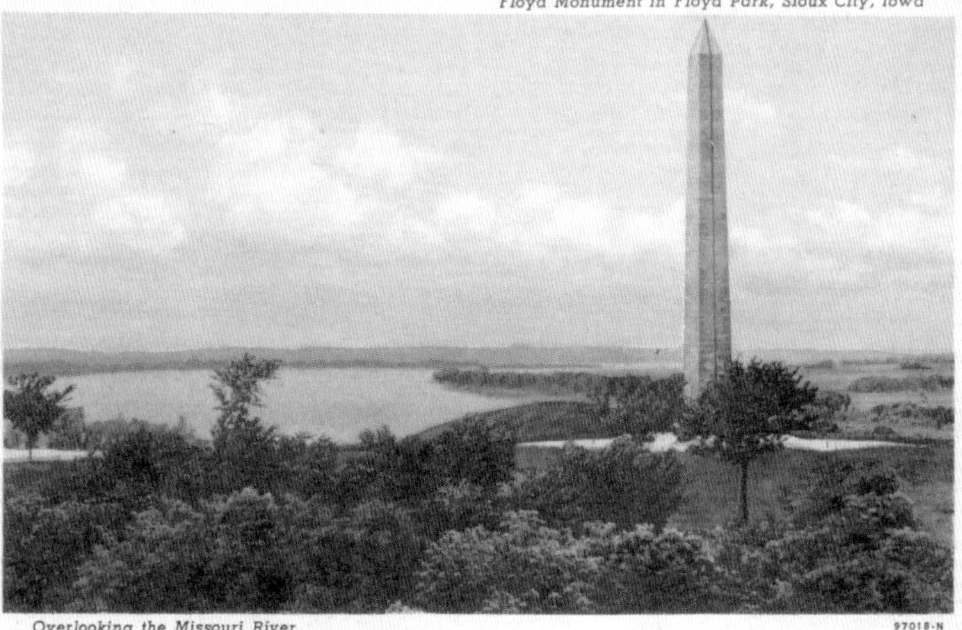

FLOYD MONUMENT IN SIOUX CITY. The Sergeant Floyd Monument commemorates Sgt. Charles Floyd Jr., the only member of the Lewis and Clark Expedition to die during the journey. His remains were buried on a bluff overlooking the Missouri River. The 100-foot sandstone obelisk was completed in May 1901, the year that baseball's American League, germinated by the Sioux City Cornhuskers, emerged.

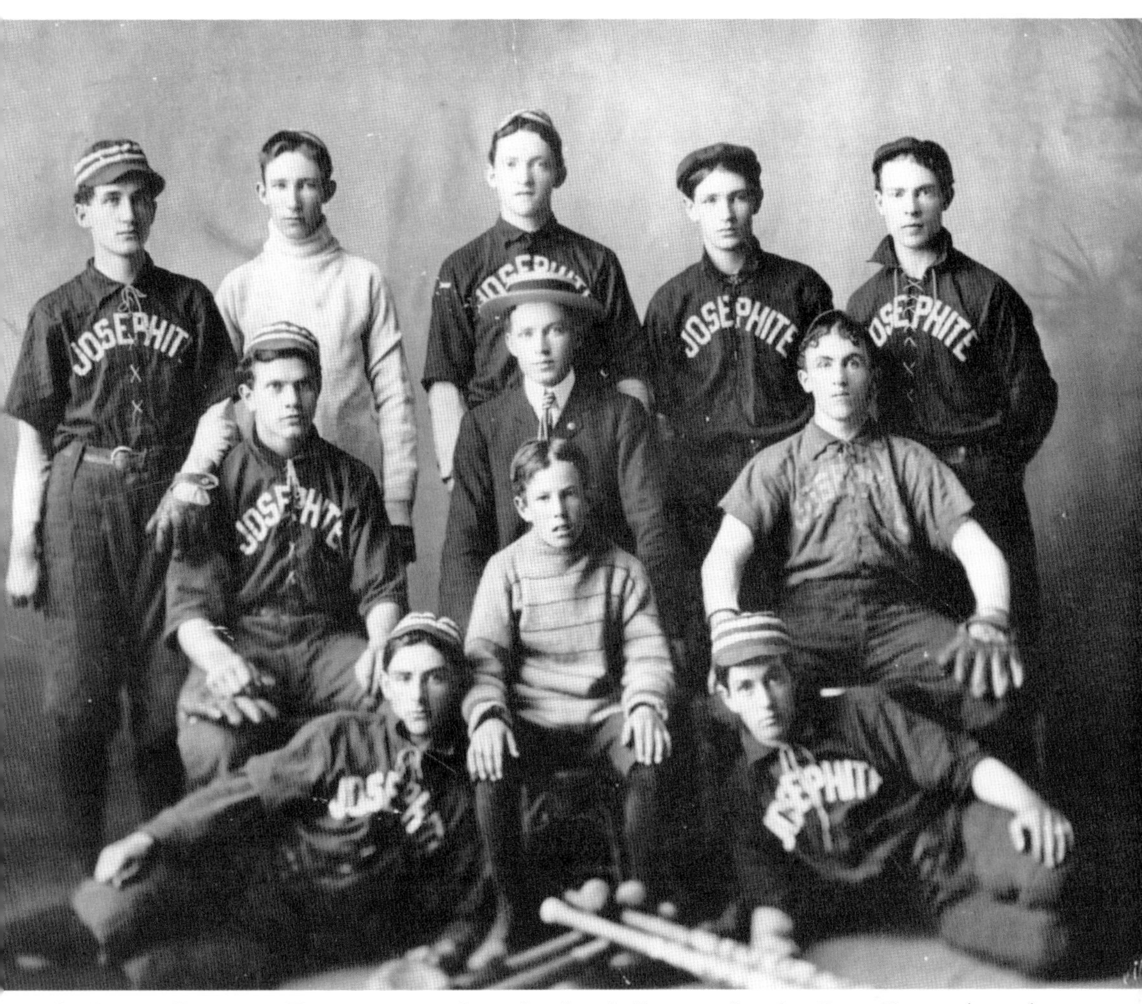

St. Joseph Baseball Team, c. 1900. Countless baseball teams played in Sioux City in the early years. Members of this church or school team, called the Josephites, are, from left to right, (first row) Mark Higney, mascot Willie Kerley, and William Gearen; (second row) George Ghizzoni, manager J.T. Brennan, and Jimmie Coine; (third row) M.J. Kerley, Frank Nicholson, John Nicholson, S.E. Keane, and Leo Brennan. (Courtesy of Sioux City Public Museum.)

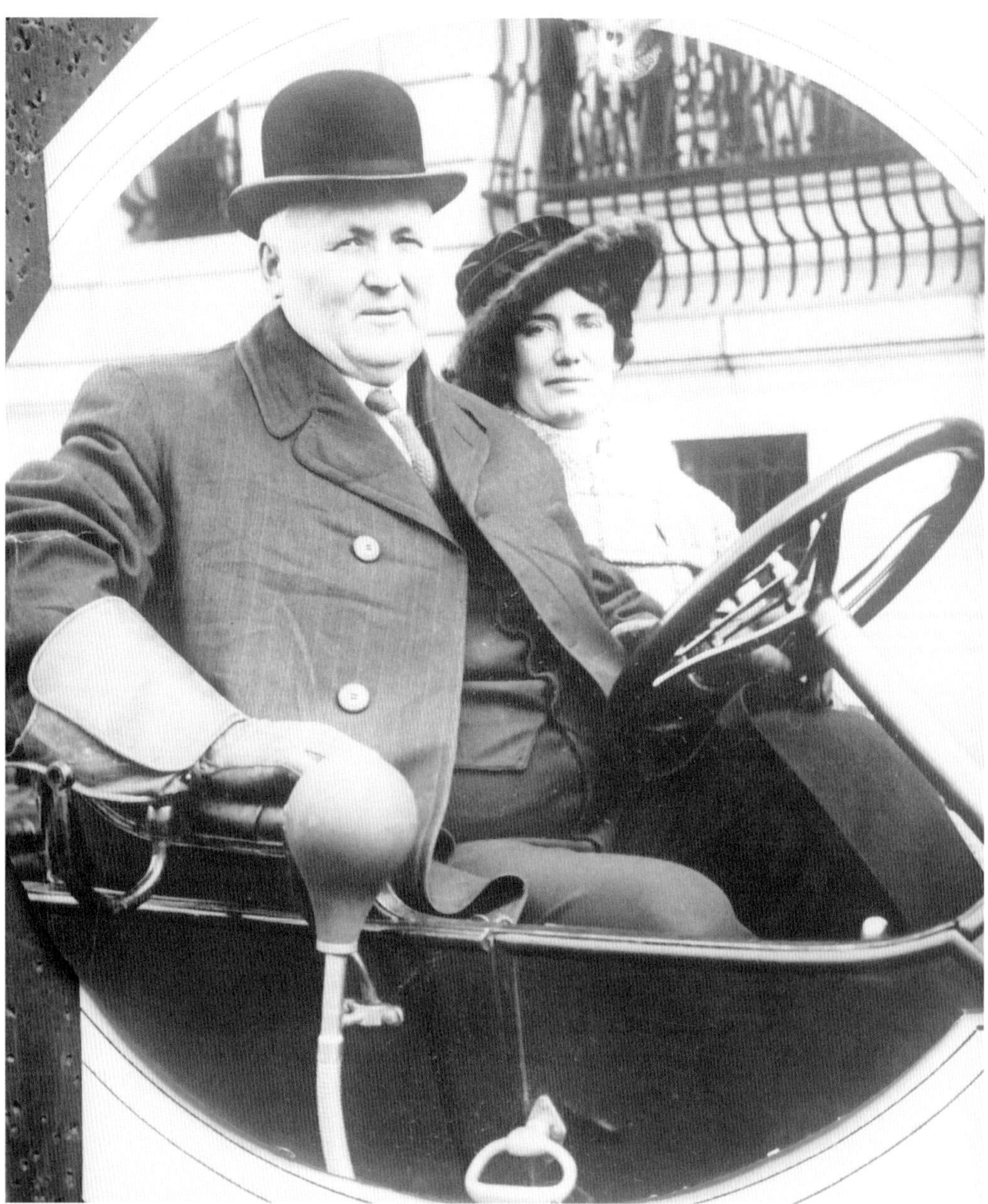

William Wallace McCredie and Wife, c. 1913. Uncle to Walt McCredie, "Judge" William Wallace McCredie became part owner of the minor-league Pacific Coast League Portland baseball club in 1904. He hired his nephew Walt to be the team's player/manager and then took him on as part owner. A highly successful manager, Walt led the club until 1921. His team of 1914 included future hall of famer Dave "Beauty" Bancroft, who made his major-league debut the following year. It is a good possibility that Walt acquired the nickname "Judge" because of his uncle. (Courtesy of Library of Congress, Bain Collection.)

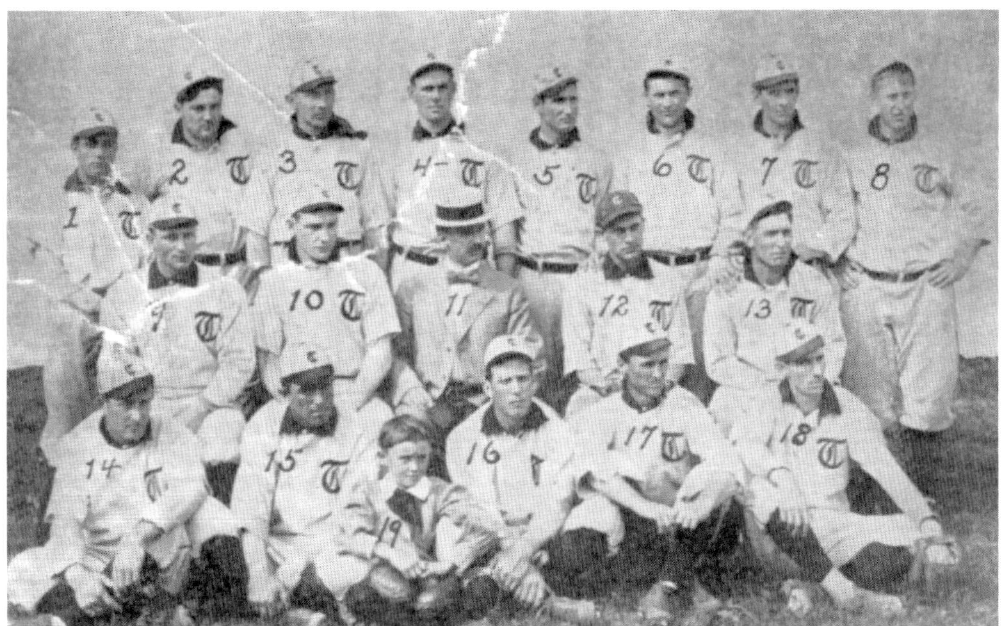

1907 Toledo Mud Hens with Harry Eells. Born in Woodbury County's Danbury in 1880, pitcher Harry "Slippery" Eells played professionally for five years, 1903–1907. His only big-league assignment was with the Cleveland Indians in 1906. Although his win-loss record was 4-5, his ERA was an impressive 2.61. In this image, he is No. 10 with the minor-league Toledo club of 1907. (Courtesy of Spaldings Official Baseball Guide.)

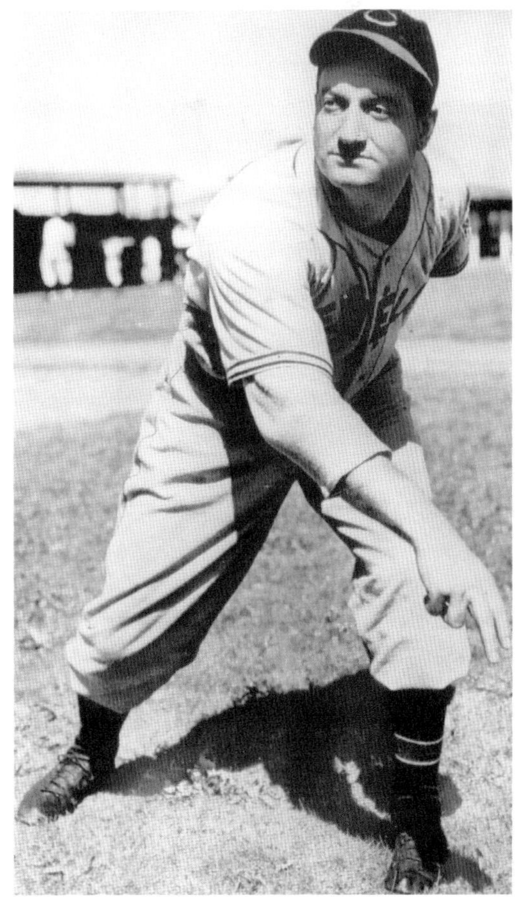

Donald Paul "Don" Black (1916–1959). Born in Salix, Woodbury County, Don Black started pitching professionally in 1937 and spent 1941 and 1942 with minor-league teams. His major-league career began in 1943 with the Philadelphia Athletics. After three years there, he spent his last three professional seasons in Cleveland (with an interlude in Milwaukee).

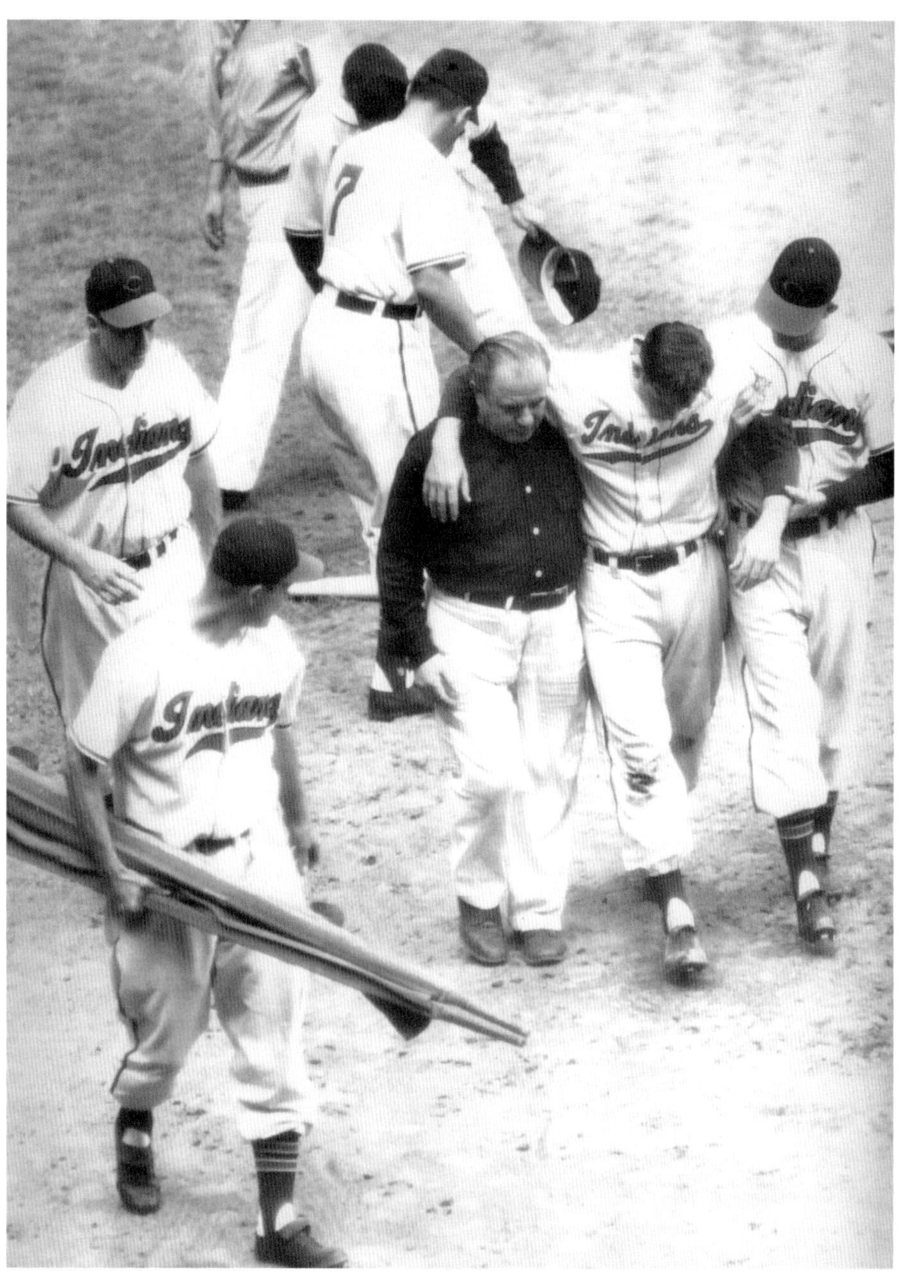

DON BLACK CARRIED OFF THE FIELD, SEPTEMBER 13, 1948. The season of 1947 was pitcher Don Black's best. On July 10, he threw a no-hitter against Philadelphia, his former team. He ended the year with 10 wins, his best since 1944. Engaged in a pennant race in 1948, Cleveland used Black as a spot starter. Tragically, during his 10th start on September 13, he suffered a cerebral hemorrhage and collapsed while at bat against the Browns. After being helped off the field, he lost consciousness and lay in a coma for three weeks. He recovered, but his career was over. The Indians won the World Series that year and voted him a full share of the series money. (Courtesy of Cleveland Memory Project, Cleveland State University, Michael Schwartz Library, John Nash.)

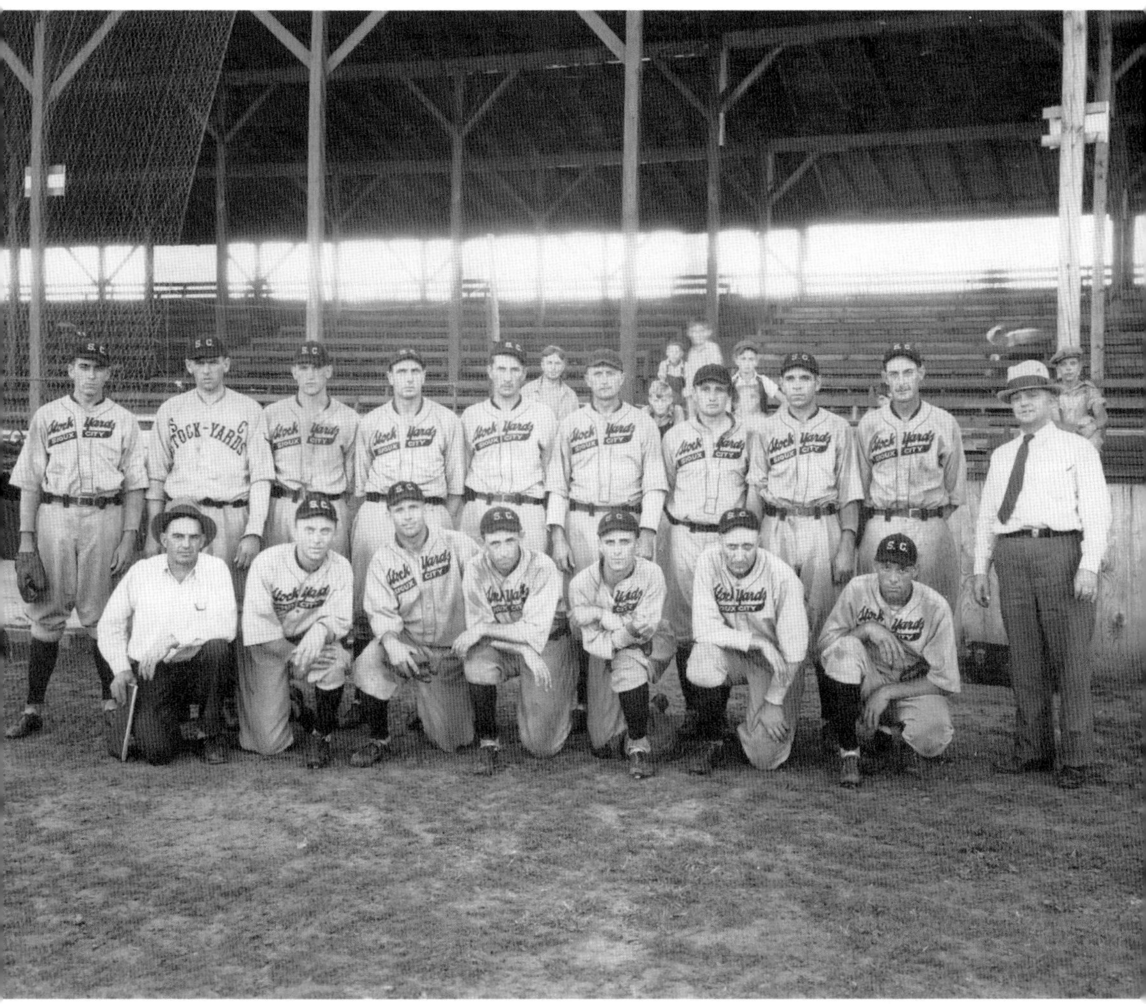

STOCKYARDS PARK, 1932. The Western League Sioux City Indians, and then the Packers, played at Mizzou Park from 1919 until around 1923. That ballpark was on the banks of the Missouri River between Pierce and Douglas Streets. Stockyards Park opened in 1922 and was rebuilt in 1927. It was leased to the Western League and also used for high school and college games. Sioux City did not have a minor-league team from 1925 through 1933, so the Stockyards club shown here may have represented the nearby stockyards. In 1927, Babe Ruth played there during a barnstorming tour. He appeared with Lou Gehrig just days after the Yankees won the World Series. After the Western League Cowboys were organized in 1934, Sioux City's minor-league clubs of different names called Stockyards Park home until 1941.The park was dismantled after that. A Western League Sioux City club did not exist again until 1947, when the Soos began play at Soos Park. (Courtesy of Sioux City Public Museum.)

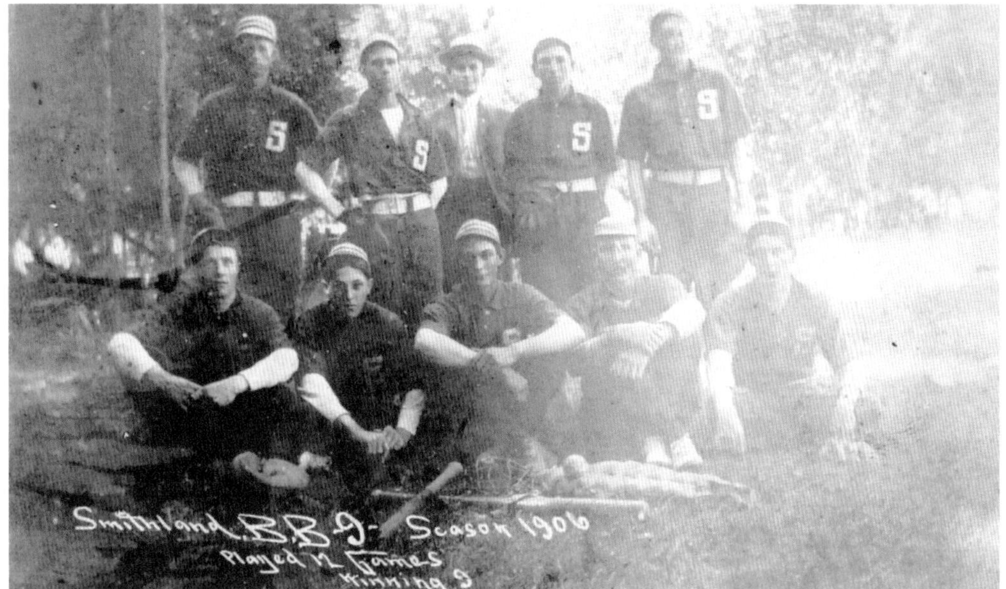

1906 Smithland Baseball Team. A small town in Woodbury County, Smithland is the birthplace of left-throwing pitcher George Myron Clark. Born in 1891, he appeared in 11 games with the New York Yankees in 1913. He then played for several Western League teams in 1914. The players in this photograph are unidentified, but Clark could be one of them.

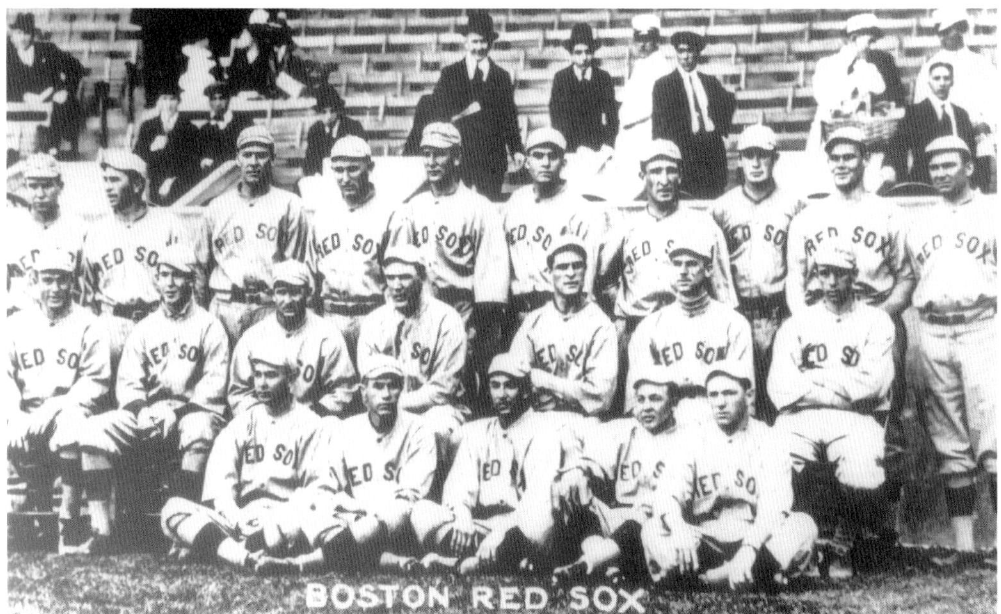

1915 Boston Red Sox with Raymond Haley. Seen here seventh from left in the top row, Raymond Timothy "Pat" Haley was born in Woodbury County's little Danbury in 1891. A skilled catcher, he played professional baseball from 1911 through 1931. His big-league career spanned 1915 through 1917, first with Boston and then with the Philadelphia Athletics. The Red Sox won the World Series in 1915, but Haley was not used.

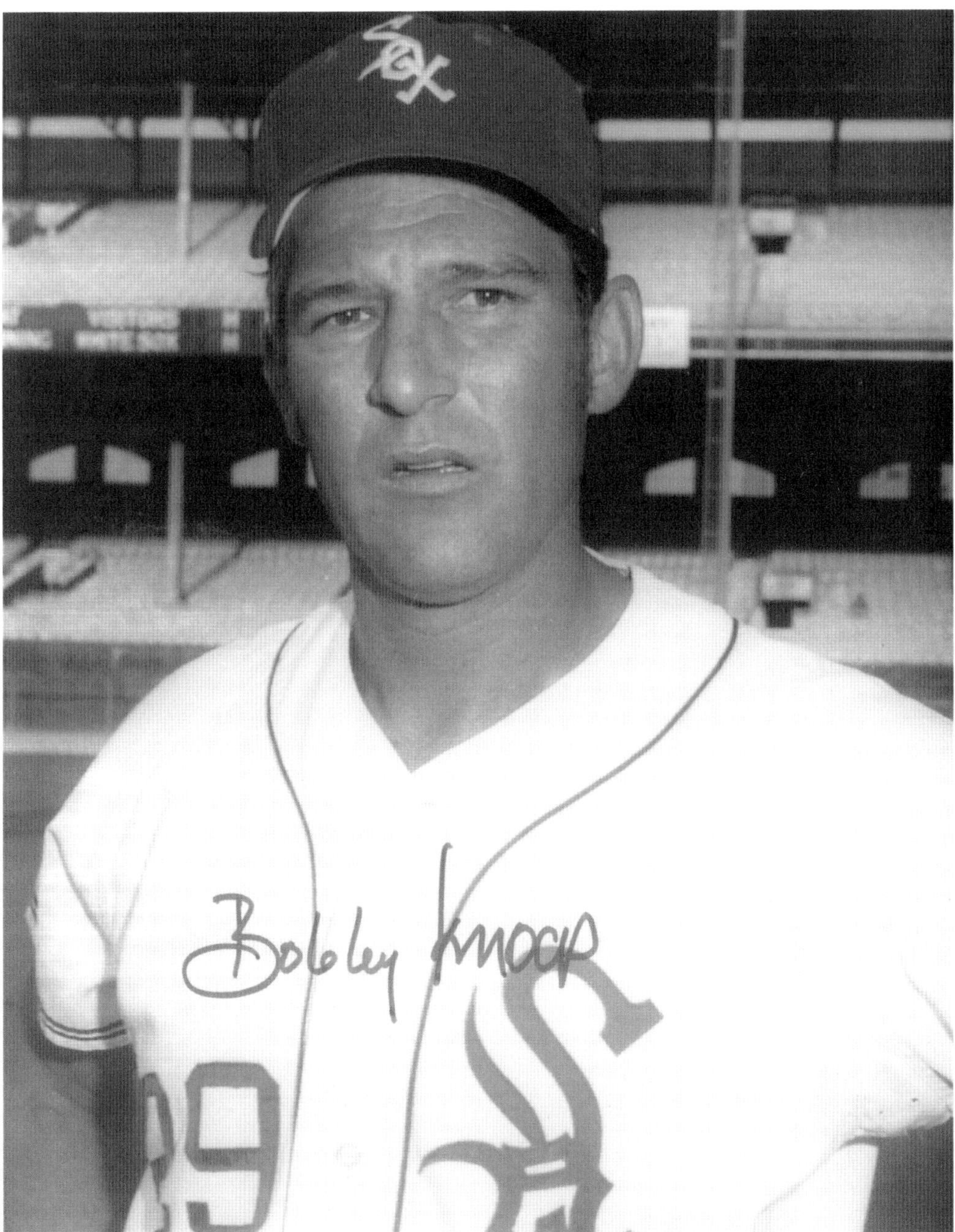

ROBERT FRANK "BOBBY" KNOOP (1938–). Sioux City–born Bobby Knoop began his extensive baseball career at the age of 17, playing second base for a number of minor-league clubs until 1964. That's when he landed with the Los Angeles Angels. With the Angels, he won three Gold Gloves from 1966 through 1968 and was selected to play in the 1966 All-Star Game. He was also voted team MVP three times. In 1969 and 1970, he played for the Chicago White Sox, and he spent 1971 and 1972 with the Kansas City Royals. Known for his great defensive ability, he was elected into the Angels Hall of Fame in 2013.

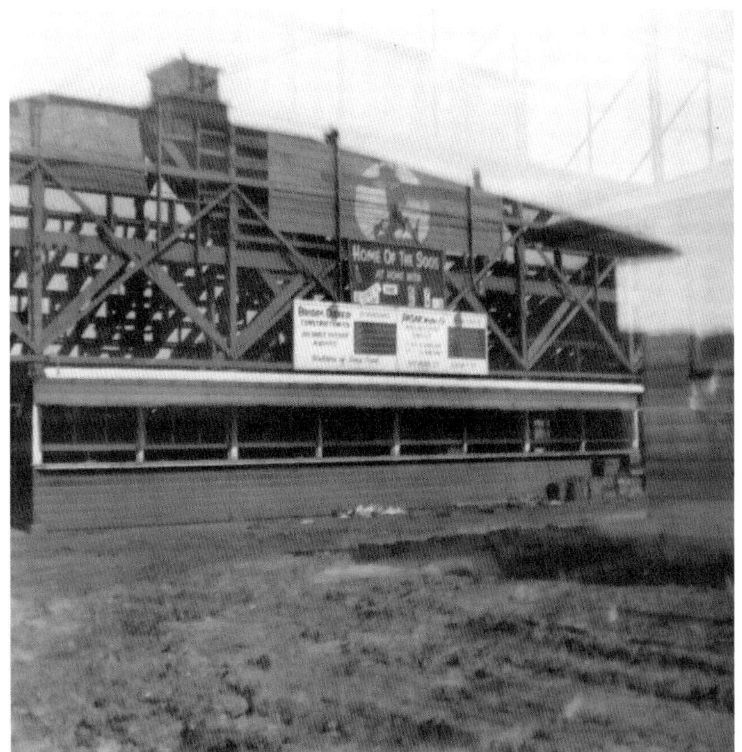

Soos Baseball Park. From 1947 until 1961, the Sioux City Soos played at Soos Park. Its capacity changed over time, but at most it seated 6,500 in 1950. In 1947, Plymouth County's Johnny Niggeling, after retiring from the major leagues, won 12 games for the Soos there. (Courtesy of Sioux City Public Museum.)

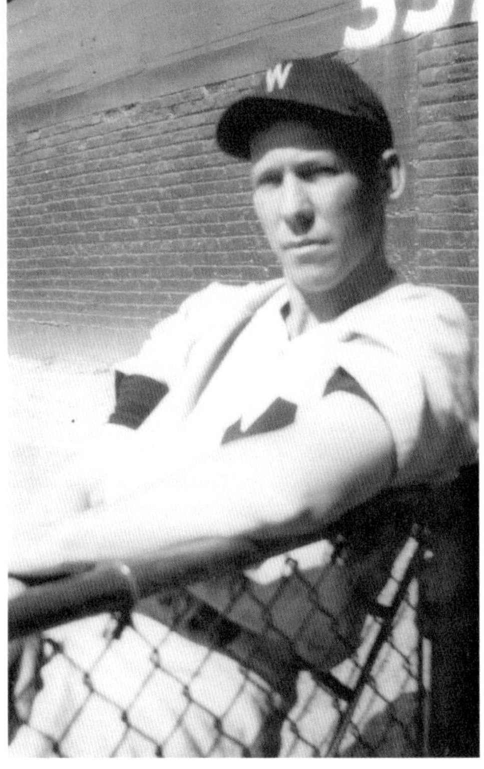

Arnold Revola "Red" Anderson (1912–1972). Born in Lawton, near Sioux City, pitcher Red Anderson's professional playing days spanned 1936 to 1946, interrupted by service in the US Navy in 1943 and 1944. His big-league years were 1937, 1940, and 1941 with the Washington Senators, during which time he tallied a 5-8 win-loss record.

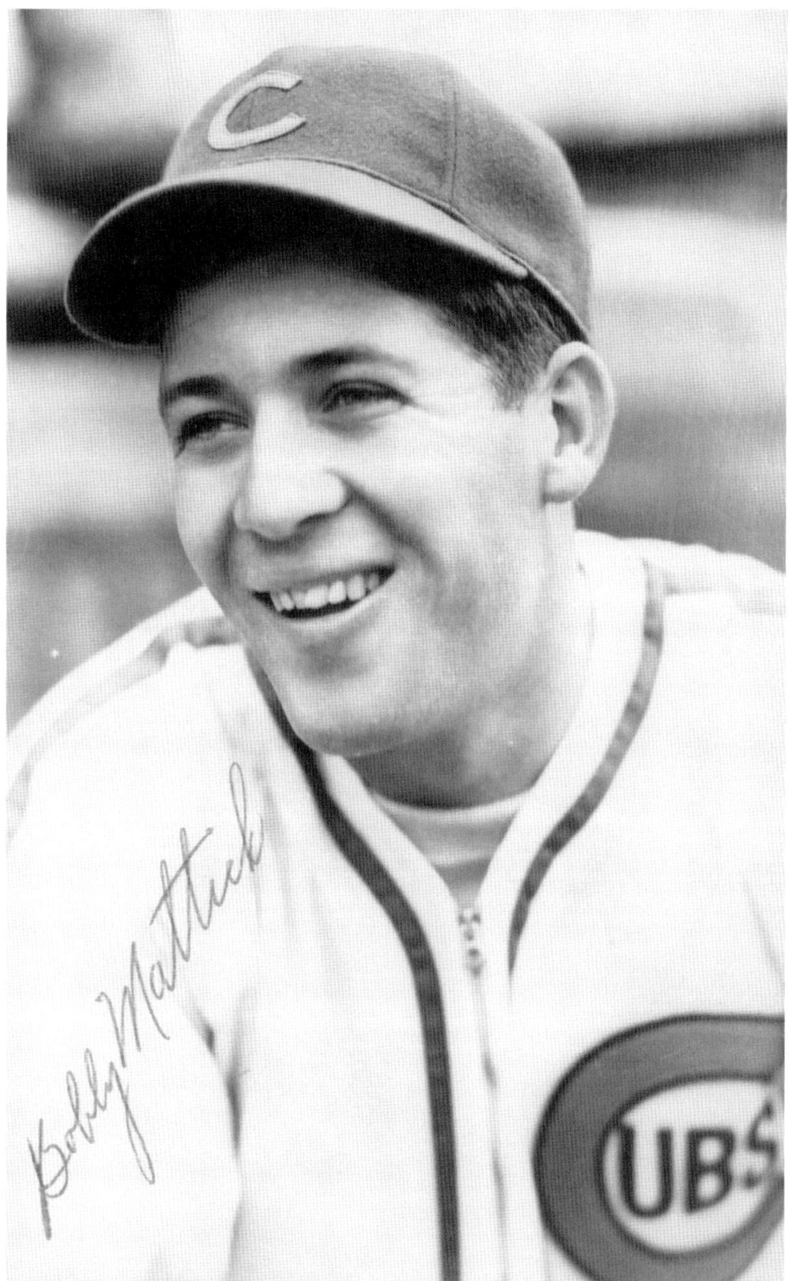

Robert James "Bobby" Mattick (1915–2004). Born in Sioux City, shortstop Bobby Mattick started with the Pacific Coast League Angels in 1934, playing for several other minor-league clubs until going to the Chicago Cubs in 1938. After starting in the minors the next season, he went back to the Cubs and played there through 1940. With Cincinnati in 1941 and part of 1942, Mattick then retired from playing. Later, he became a major-league baseball scout and managed the Toronto Blue Jays in 1980 and 1981. His father, Wally "Chink" Mattick, co-owned and was player-manager for the Sioux City Packers in 1922.

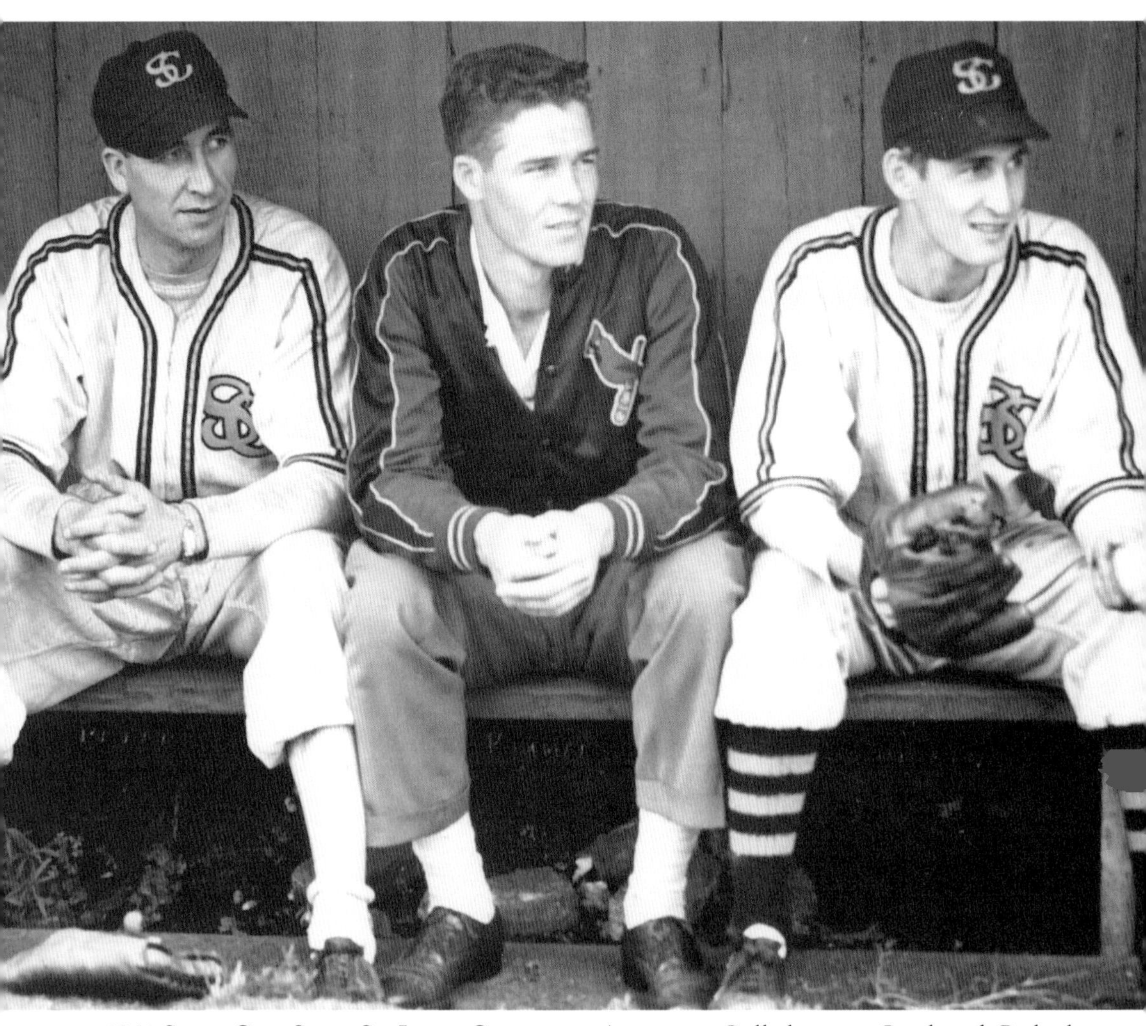

1941 Sioux City Soos, St. Louis Cardinals Affiliate. Still playing at Stockyards Park, the 1941 Sioux City Soos were a farm club of the St. Louis Cardinals. That explains the Cardinal logo jacket. The player on the far left is marked only as "Peters," but there is no one by that name on the recorded roster. The other two are pitchers Charles Kimmel (center) and Al Dickens. Kimmel won 11 and Dickens won 12 that year. (Courtesy of Sioux City Public Museum.)

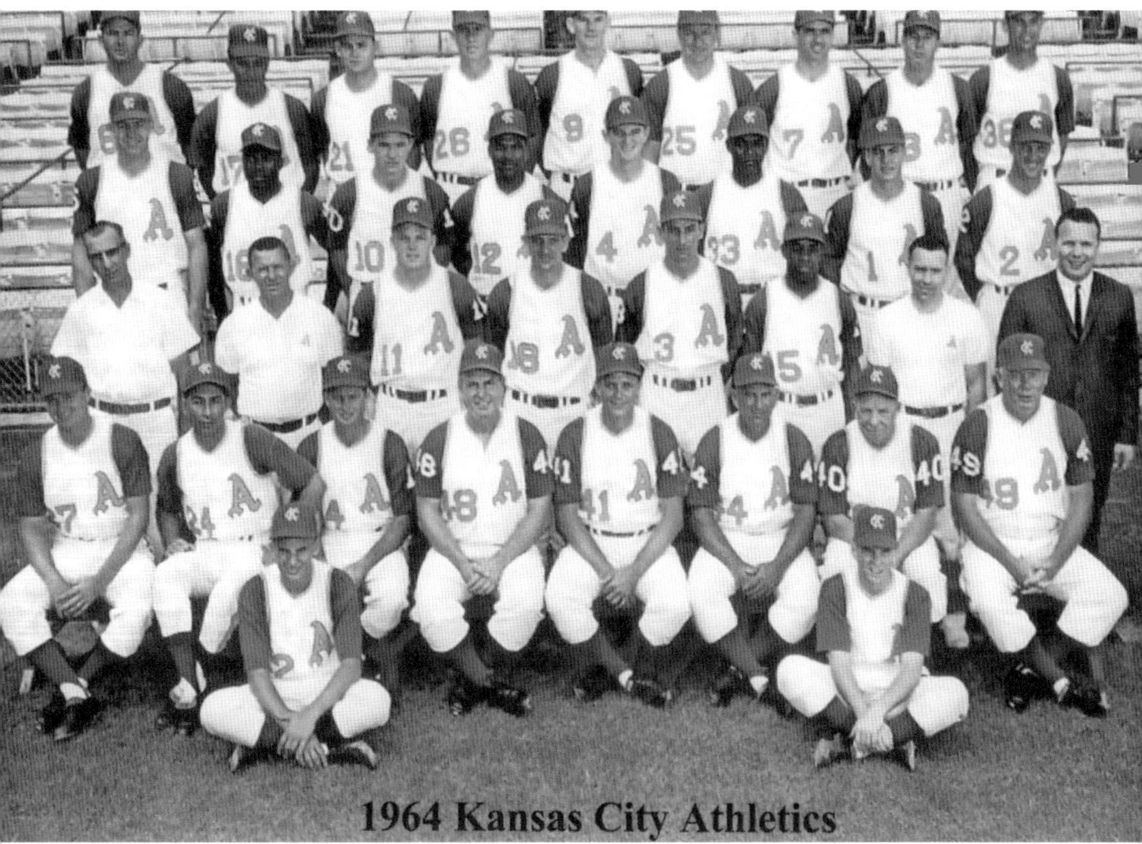

1964 Kansas City Athletics with Dick Green. Infielder Richard Larry "Dick" Green was born in Sioux City in 1941. At third base, shortstop, and second base, he played in the minor leagues for four years before going to Kansas City in 1963. There through 1967, he then spent the remainder of his big-league career with Oakland. In California, he had the opportunity to help the Athletics win the World Series three years in a row, 1972–1974, the last three years of Green's big-league playing days. In this 1964 team photograph, he is no. 1, seventh from left in the third row

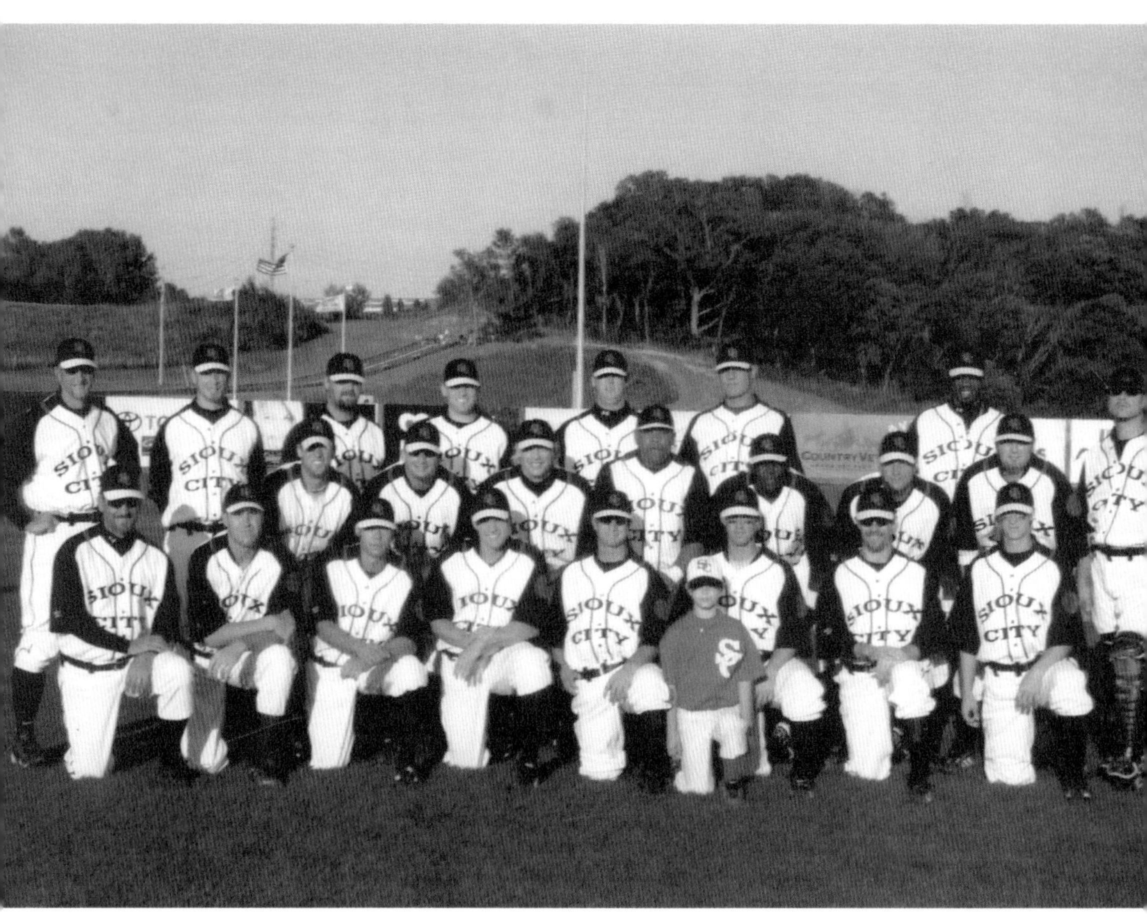

2004 Sioux City Explorers. During the last two years of the Soos' existence, 1959 and 1960, the club belonged to the Class B Illinois-Indiana-Iowa League. After that, Sioux City did not have a professional team until 1993, when the Explorers club was formed. Always in independent leagues, in 2006, it became a member of the American Association. The club of 2004, shown here, belonged to the Northern League. The Explorers play at Lewis and Clark Park, which opened on the team's maiden year. As of 2016, the Explorers' best season was 2015, when they posted a 75-25 record. (Courtesy of Sioux City Public Museum.)

8

Neighboring Counties

This chapter is not an afterthought but a need to include the rest of the state. It would take at least six more works to cover it all. Northwest Iowa teams have always competed with those from neighboring counties. Moreover, area teams' lineups often included players from other parts of the state and the country. Significantly, in addition to the minor-league teams formed in Northwest Iowa, an additional 24 Iowa towns have hosted such clubs.

Cedar Rapids, Linn County, in the northeast, tops the list with number of clubs at 111 since 1890. Polk County's Des Moines, the state capital, is a close second with 109 beginning with the 1887 Hawkeyes. As did many ballplayers from all over the area, Plymouth County's knuckleball pitcher Johnny Niggeling once played for a Des Moines club. Before hurling for the Cincinnati Reds, Harry Gaspar helped Black Hawk County's Waterloo club win the 1907 Iowa League pennant. And over time, various professional leagues comprised Iowa teams from different sections of the state. For instance, the Iowa–South Dakota League of 1903 included a team from Council Bluffs, a city in Southwest Iowa's Pottawattamie County. A number of Northwest Iowa teams belonged to that same group. These inclusions are a result of baseball's cultural importance to generations of Iowans from early childhood on.

The people who organized the clubs, the talented athletes who comprised the teams, and the many fans who came to see them play grew up with baseball. Children living on farms who often had only one ball and one bat would get together with the neighbors and play in the yard or in an open field. Sometimes an especially strong youth would hit the ball into the corn field and they would spend part of the day searching for the lost sphere. Kids growing up in the towns would play on vacant lots or inside their yards, sometimes accidentally knocking the ball through a neighbor's window. To grow up and play with a clean ball and a special bat most likely inspired many a youngster to choose baseball as a career. That could be any child from any part of Iowa or the rest of the country.

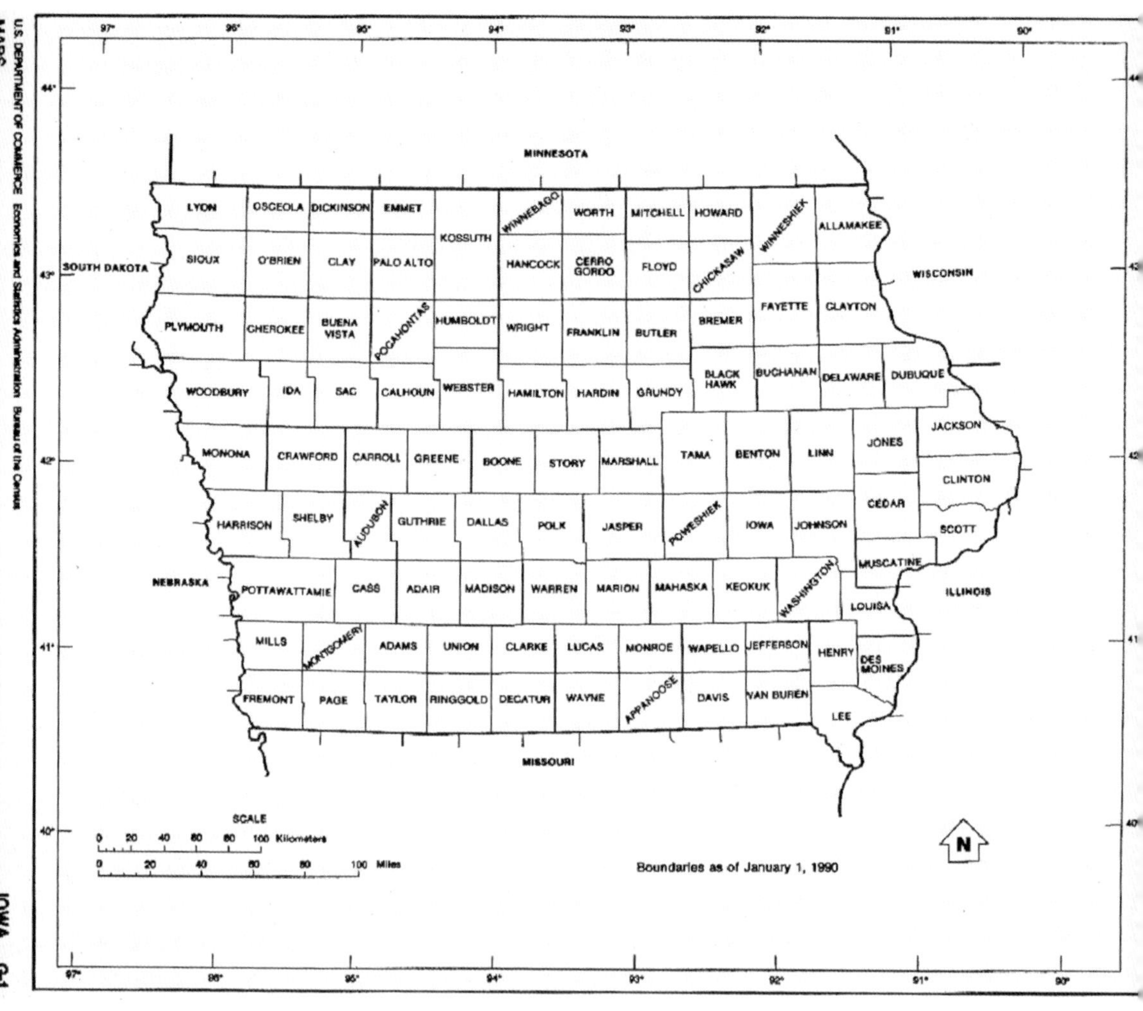

Iowa Map Showing Counties. This book is about baseball history of the northwest corner of Iowa, from Woodbury south to Webster and then north to Kossuth. This map shows those counties in relation to the rest of the state. Other counties are mentioned throughout, so this will allow a perspective. (Courtesy of yellowmaps.com.)

Students Play Ball during Recess, 1939. This postcard photograph shows a boy and girl playing ball in front of their country schoolhouse. Located in Grundy County, the third county straight west of Webster, this captures the spirit of baseball that still exists. (Courtesy of Library of Congress; photograph by Arthur Rothstein.)

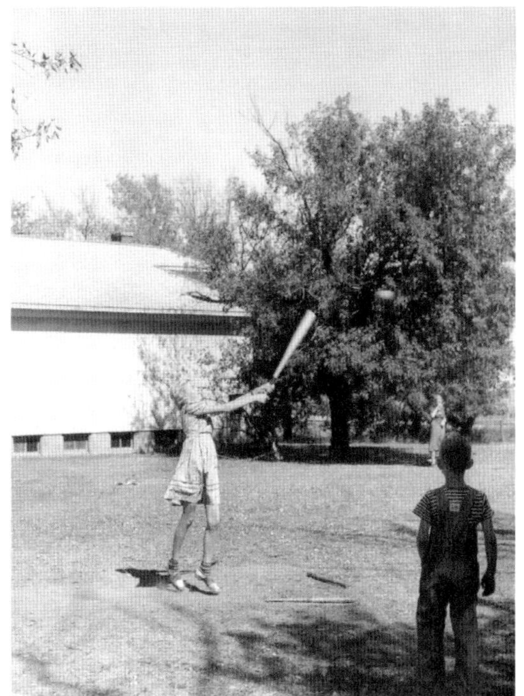

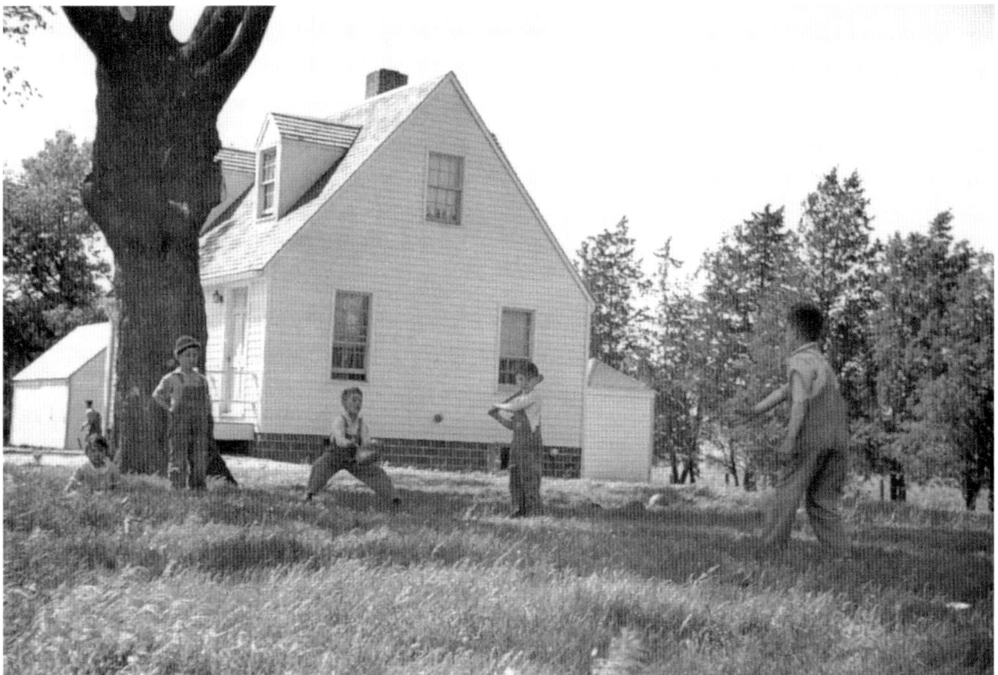

Children at Play, Granger Homesteads, 1936. In Dallas and Polk County, south of Webster County, Granger was the site of the Granger Homesteads, a Depression-era New Deal–sponsored resettlement effort for underemployed coal miners. (Courtesy of Library of Congress; photograph by Carl Mydans.)

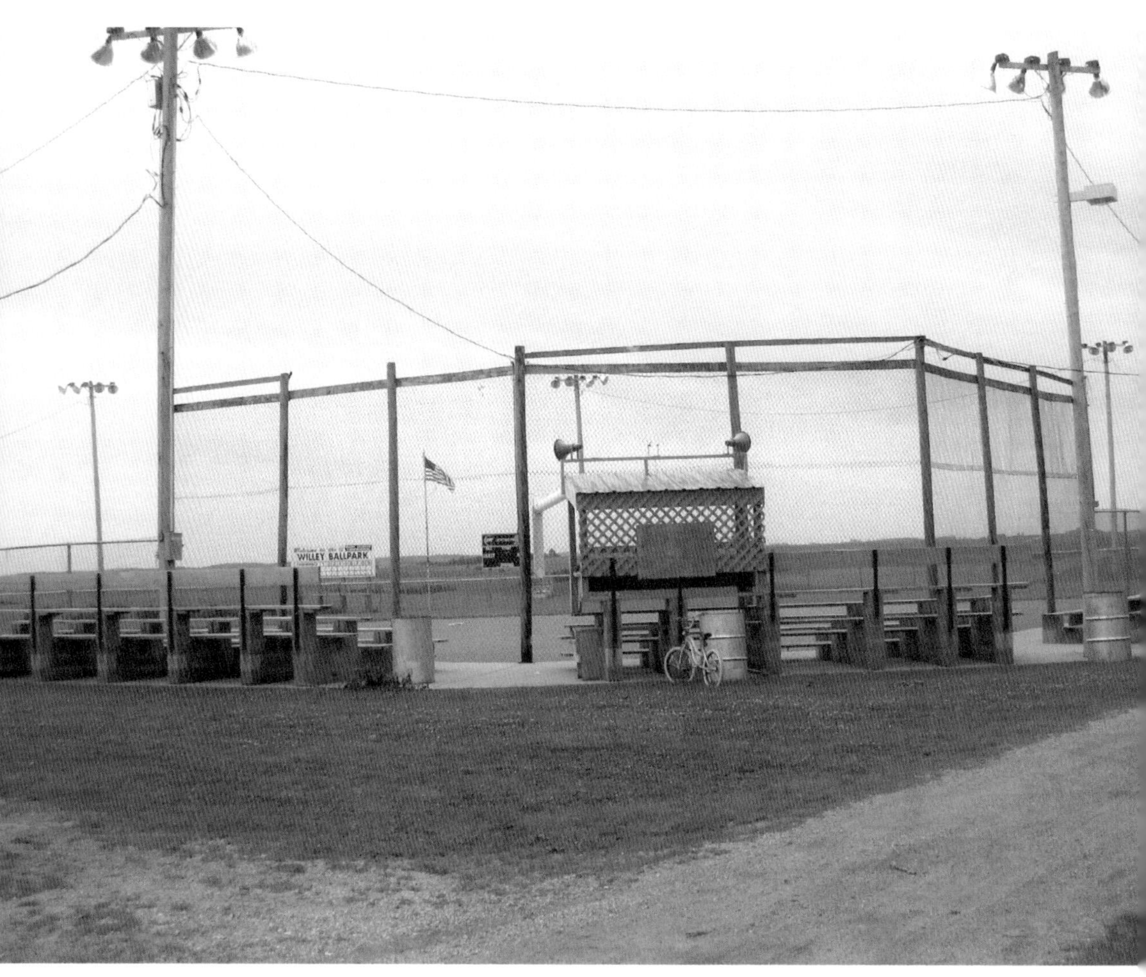

Baseball Park at Willey, 2010. Located in Carroll County, south of and bordering on Sac and Calhoun Counties, Willey's population consistently hovers around 100. Nonetheless, its baseball park, replete with grandstands and a concession stand, is meticulously maintained. Residents of the largely rural area still revere the sport.

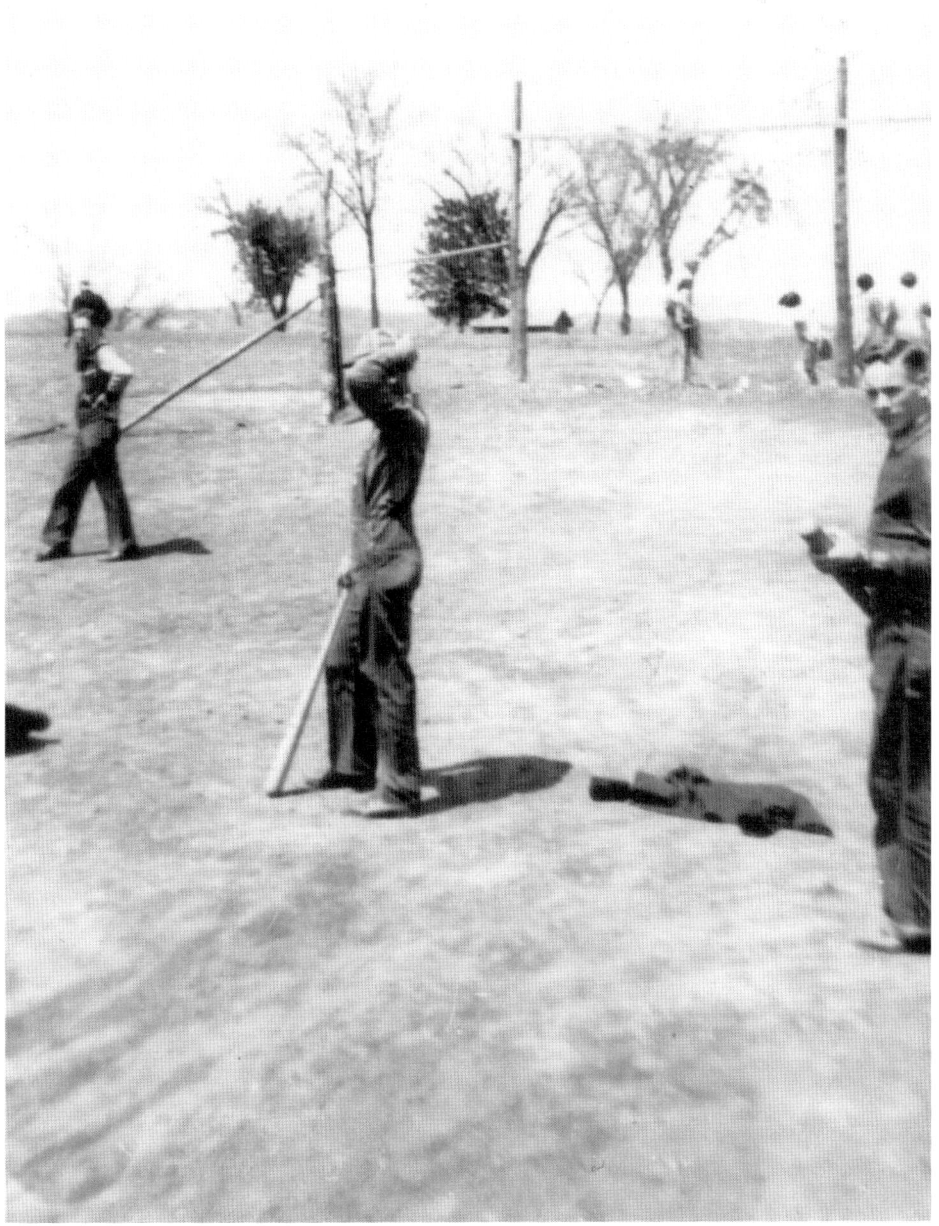

Boys at Play near Castana, 1936. This simple snapshot, most likely taken with a Kodak Brownie, was removed from an unknown family's album and sold on eBay. The location is near Castana, Monona County, which borders Woodbury County on the south. Such images convey a feel for the times, showing the universal allure of baseball.

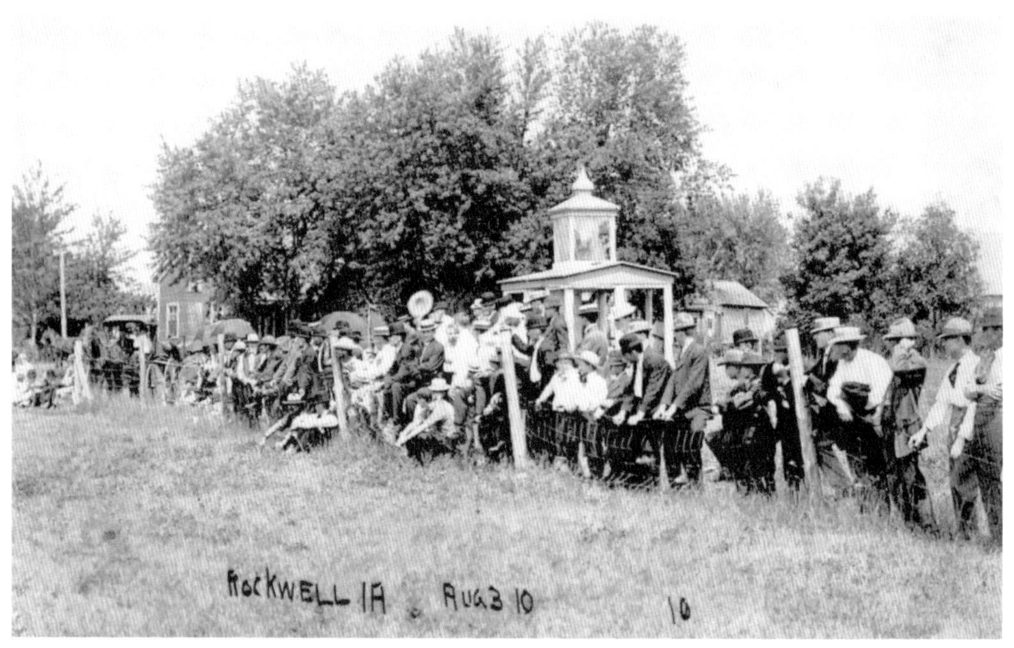

BASEBALL CROWD AT ROCKWELL, 1910. Not to be confused with Rockwell City in Calhoun County, Rockwell is located in Cerro Gordo County, two counties east of Kossuth. In 1910, the town's population was 700, considered large then. The ball game is obviously taking place in a country field, and the crowd on hand demonstrates the dress code of the day.

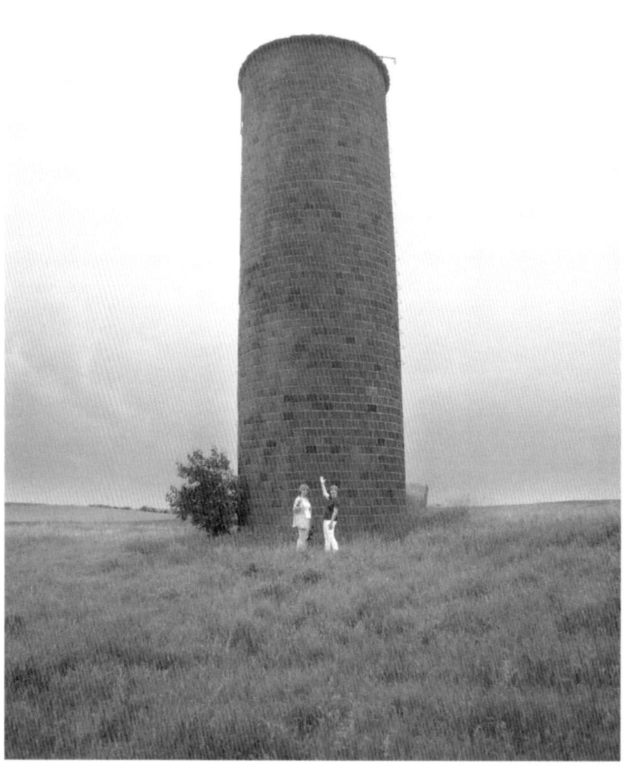

SILO NEAR CARROLL, 2010. Located near Carroll, the seat of Carroll County, this soaring grain silo is all that remains of a once-thriving homestead. The date of its construction is unknown, but it existed when the late parents of these two grown women first lived there. It was there long before their father listened to Cardinal baseball broadcasts on the radio. And baseball still survives.

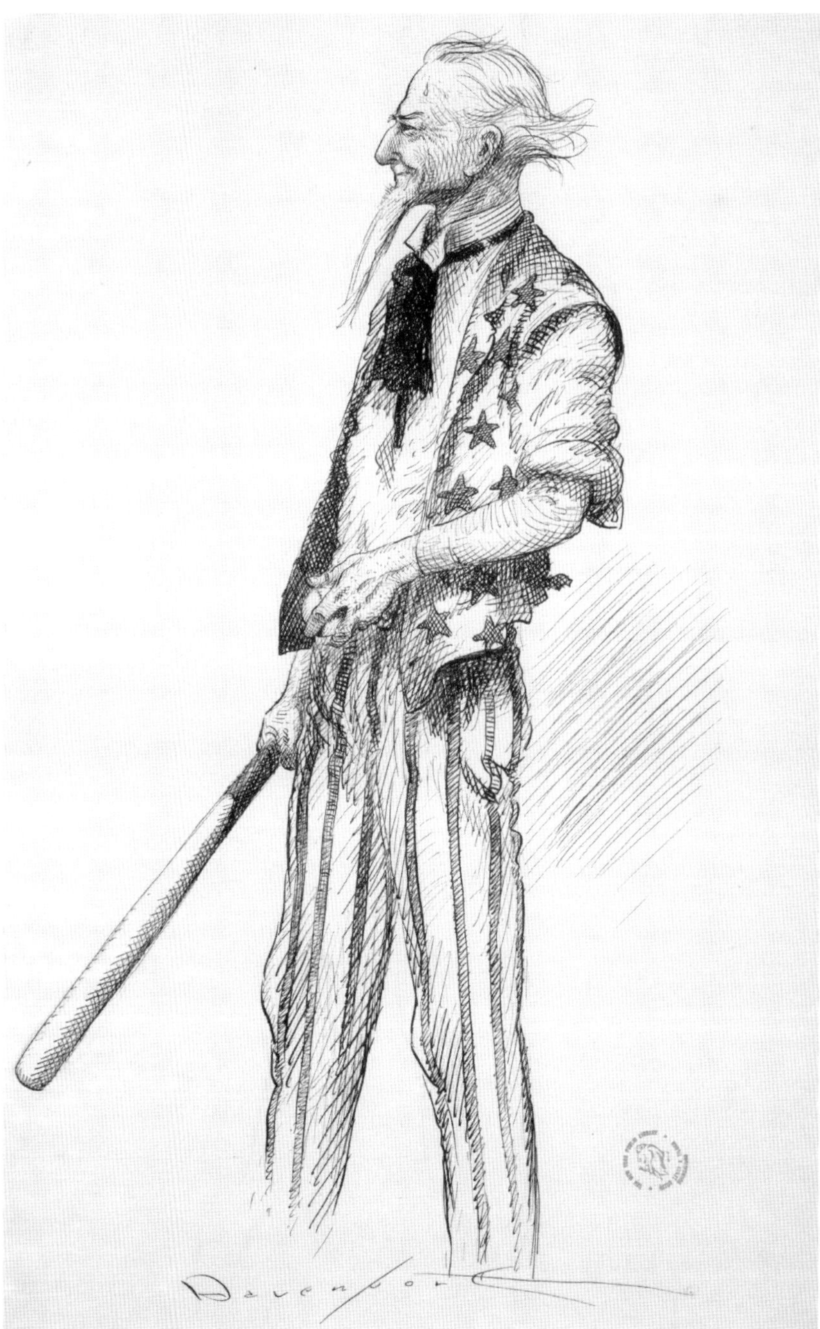

UNCLE SAM AT BAT. This vintage image housed at the New York City Public Library conveys a slightly different Uncle Sam. Rather than pointing and looking intently and directly at the viewer, he smiles and gazes toward the fences. A large drop of perspiration travels toward his brow. It reminds us that as Northwest Iowans, we are still Iowans, and we are all Americans. Bat and ball in hand, we look bravely beyond the horizon. (Courtesy of New York City Public Library digital collections.)